THE FOUR MARKS OF FATHERLY GREATNESS

DAILY DEVOTIONS FOR EVERY MAN

THE FOUR MARKS OF FATHERLY GREATNESS

DISCOVERING YOUR TRUE IDENTITY AND ULTIMATE DESTINY

DEVIN SCHADT

> IN A CULTURE WHERE THE FAMILY HAS BEEN DENIGRATED OVER TIME, IT IS OFTEN THE RESULT OF THE ABSENCE OF A FATHER WHO HAS SHIRKED HIS RESPONSIBILITY AS THE SPIRITUAL HEAD OF THE HOUSEHOLD SERIOUSLY. THE VOCATION OF THE FATHER IN THE FAMILY MUST BE RENEWED IF THE FAMILY IS TO ONCE AGAIN BECOME THE BASIC SOCIAL UNIT OF OUR SOCIETY. IN L | E | A | D, DEVIN SCHADT CLEARLY LAYS OUT THE PATH TO HELP MEN RECLAIM THEIR FATHERLY VOCATION BY CONVERTING THE PILLARS OF ST. JOSEPH'S SPIRITUALITY INTO THIS WONDERFUL, UPLIFTING DAILY DEVOTIONAL. ANY MAN WHO SEEKS TO UNDERSTAND WHO THEY ARE TRULY CALLED TO BE WILL FIND L | E | A | D INVALUABLE

—MOST REV. ROBERT D. GRUSS
DIOCESE OF RAPID CITY

L|E|A|D: The Four Marks of Fatherly Greatness
Copyright © 2018
The Fathers of Saint Joseph

With the exception of short excerpts used in article and critical reviews, no part of this work may be reproduced, transmitted, or stored in any form whatsoever, printed or electronic, without the prior written permission of the publisher.

Scripture passages are from the Douay Rheims Version, revised by Bishop Richard Challoner; Messrs John Murphy Co. of the Catholic Bible © 1749-1752; the Revised Standard Version Catholic Edition. Copyright © 1946, 1952, 1971, Division of Christian Education of the nation Council of the Churches of Christ in the United States of America. All rights reserved.

Stewardship: A Mission of Faith
11 BlackHawk Lane
Elizabethtown, PA 17022
StewardshipMission.org

Cover Design: Devin Schadt
Printed in the United States of America
ISBN: 978-1-732773-90-5

> THERE IS ONLY ONE ADVENTURER IN THE WORLD . . . THE FATHER OF A FAMILY. EVEN THE MOST DESPERATE ADVENTURERS ARE NOTHING COMPARED TO HIM. EVERYTHING IS AGAINST HIM. SAVAGELY ORGANIZED AGAINST HIM. EVERYTHING TURNS AND COMBINES AGAINST HIM . . . . EVERYTHING IS AGAINST THE FATHER OF A FAMILY, THE PATER FAMILIAS; AND CONSEQUENTLY AGAINST THE FAMILY. HE ALONE IS LITERALLY 'ENGAGED' IN THE WORLD, IN THE AGE. HE ALONE IS AN ADVENTURER. — CHARLES PÉGUY, FRENCH POET (1908)

To Scott,
As St. Joseph was granted a son—though not the fruit of his loins, but by means of spiritual adoption—who was and is greater, more virtuous and nobler than he; so I, through your marriage to my beautiful daughter, have been granted a son who is stronger, purer, and greater than myself. May you, my son, be like St. Joseph, a father on earth like the Father in heaven.

TABLE OF CONTENTS

INTRODUCTION: DISCOVERING YOUR PURPOSE: LIEIAID 17
STRUCTURE OF LIEIAID 19
HOW TO USE LIEIAID. 21

SECTION 1
ASSUMING YOUR LOCATION IN GOD'S PLAN

1. The Most Important Man 25
2. Does God Need You?. 27
3. What Will You Be Remembered For? 29
4. The Gaze We Desire 31
5. What Does God Really Desire? 33
6. The Most Difficult Job. 35
7. Where Are You?. 37
8. Is Your Role Any Different Than Your Wife's? 40
9. Are You Like God? 42
10. A Link Between Heaven and Earth 44
11. Discover Yourself by Giving Yourself Away 46
12. The Secret Path 48
13. Your Great Battle. 51
14. Understanding The Bully 54
15. The Sin of Loneliness. 57
16. The Devil's Six Darts. 60
17. The Paradox of Power 63
18. What Is Greatness? 65
19. Can a Father Be a Saint?. 67
20. How Does a Father Become A Saint?. 69
21. Fearing Exaltation. 71
22. Does God Desire to Exalt You? 73

23. The Final Battle 75
24. What Can One Man Do? 77
25. The Four Things That Every Successful Father Does 79

SECTION 2
LIVING YOUR VOCATION

PILLAR 1
LISTEN TO DISCERN YOUR MISSION

26. The First Mark of a Great Father 87
27. Picking Up Mixed Signals 90
28. Finding Your Way Home 92
29. Are You Showing Up for Battle? 94
30. Poop In the Brownie 96
31. The Word and the Wound 98
32. Do You Limit God? 100
33. Becoming a Reservoir of Grace 102
34. A Real Man Cave 104
35. Are You *With* Him? 106
36. Building a Real-Ationship 108
37. The 7 *R*'s of Prayer 110
38. Interior Life and Exterior Strength 113
39. Good Versus Greatest 115
40. The Kingdom of Noise 117
41. The Real Infusion 119
42. Prayer Demands Practice 121
43. Dealing with the Demon of Distraction 123
44. Silence Before Men 125
45. Building Upon Shifting Sand 128
46. Who Are You Following? 130
47. Silence That Speaks Loudly 132
48. The Secret Power of a Father 134
49. The Father in Secret 136
50. Secret Works Work 139

51. The Real Power Behind Prayer.......................... 142

PILLAR 2
EMBRACE YOUR ESSENCE

52. The Measure of a Man: His Relationship with Woman......... 147
53. Your Essence: Setting the Pace of Self-Giving Love............ 149
54. Do You Need Her?.. 151
55. The Mission of Marriage.................................. 153
56. Why Is It So Difficult?.................................... 155
57. Unveiling the Mystery.................................... 157
58. How a Dying Man Can Make His Marriage Beautiful......... 159
59. Where Are You From? Where Are You Going?............... 161
60. Moving from Day Six to Day Seven....................... 163
61. The Weight of Responsibility.............................. 165
62. Setting the Pace.. 167
63. Finding Yourself in Her................................... 169
64. Is She Worth Dying For?.................................. 171
65. Agony and Ecstasy....................................... 173
66. A Map for Marriage...................................... 176
67. A Key to a Successful Marriage............................ 179
68. God's Plan for Your Marriage.............................. 181
69. Do You Know What You Really Need?..................... 183
70. His and Her Four Complementary Needs................... 185
71. Are You Convinced of Her Beauty?........................ 187
72. Is Your Wife Still Beautiful? Her First Need (Cont.)........... 189
73. Wash Your Wife in the Word—A Nonnegotiable............. 191
74. How to Wash Your Wife In The Word...................... 193
75. What Makes You Strong?................................. 195
76. What Undermines Your Strength?......................... 198
77. What Undermines Your Strength?, Part 2.................. 200
78. What Gives Your Strength Power?......................... 202
79. The Motivation to Become Pure........................... 204
80. Your Second Need: Physical Intimacy...................... 206
81. How to Discuss "Sex" with Your Wife...................... 209

82. Pursuing Her 211
83. Responding to Rejection. 214
84. When She's Not Giving What You Need. 215
85. Beginning the Cycle of Healing and Restoration. 217
86. The Two Expressions of Lust 218
87. Defeat Lust in the Heart 220
88. Is There Something More?—His Third Need 222
89. Discovering Your Mission 224
90. Your Wife Is Not the Mission—Her Third Need 226
91. Your Fourth Need: Spiritual Authority. 228
92. Why Should She Respect You? Your Fourth Need (Cont.) 230
93. Does She Inspire You? Her Fourth Need. 232
94. How the Two Become One Spiritually. 234
95. How to Communicate with Your Wife, Part 1 236
96. How to Communicate with Your Wife, Part 2 238
97. The Greatest Scandal. 241
98. Initiating the Dance of Forgiveness. 243
99. You Can't Do It Yourself. 245
100. God Acting in the Sexual Act. 247
101. Are You Settling for Less?. 249
102. True or False Mercy. 251
103. Will You Set the World Ablaze?. 253
104. Treating Your Wife Like a Sister 255
105. Master of Her Own Mystery: Do You Have Any Say? 257
106. What If You Are Stuck?. 259
107. Does a "Real Man" Need a Mother?, Part 1. 260
108. Does a "Real Man" Need a Mother?, Part 2. 262
109. The Devil Inside. 264

PILLAR 3

ASSUME YOUR AUTHORITY

110. Strike the Shepherd. 269
111. Are You Prepared to Be Misunderstood? 271
112. The True Purpose of Authority 273

TABLE OF CONTENTS

113. Are You Really Working at the Office? 275
114. Who Do You Answer To? 277
115. The Risk of Responsibility 279
116. Unlocking God's Favor 281
117. Leading: An Expression of Loving. 283
118. Can You Surrender Your Glory? 285
119. Why Do Families Fail? 287
120. Do You Have to Be Perfect? 289
121. The Priestly Father. 291
122. Your Greatest Treasure 293
123. The Duties of a True Leader 295
124. A Most Insidious Enemy 297
125. Saving *From* and Saving *For*. 300
126. How to Overcome the Enemy of the World 302
127. Losing Your Talent 304
128. Your View of the Father Determines Your Fatherhood 306
129. Your Noble Role. 308
130. Learning from Joseph What Really Matters 310
131. A True Shepherd 312
132. Your Child's Six Enemies 314
133. Perversion of Sex: Enemy 1. 316
134. Peer Pressure: Enemy 2. 318
135. Protect to Inject: Peer Pressure, Part 2 320
136. Prestige and Popularity: Enemy 3 322
137. Pursuit of Pleasure: Enemy 4 324
138. Pervasive Media: Enemy 5 326
139. Pervasive Media, Part 2. 328
140. Pervasive Media, Part 3. 330
141. Poor Parenting: Enemy 6 332
142. Your Powerhouse. 334
143. Dominion Over Work—Or Does Work Dominate You? 336
144. The Divine Purpose of Work 338
145. The Enemies of Providing. 340
146. Is It Good Enough? 342
147. You Are Irreplaceable 344
148. Working for Respect 346

149. The Risk of Playing Catch-Up 348
150. Slave or Son?.. 350
151. The Sign of the Covenant 353
152. Why Are You Distracted?............................... 355
153. God's Supernatural Law of Glory 357
154. Eating to Glorify God.................................. 359
155. The Fundamental Lesson of Freedom 361
156. The Most Effective Teacher............................. 363
157. The Most Valuable Lesson 365
158. Teach What You Live; Live What You Teach 367

PILLAR 4
DISCOVER THE DISCIPLE

159. The Gaze of the Father 371
160. A Link Between Heaven and Earth 373
161. Show Us the Father 375
162. Biological and Spiritual Fatherhood 377
163. Receiving Your Child in Difficult Circumstances 379
164. Christ's Game Plan to Save Souls....................... 381
165. Learning from the Royal Official: Three Steps to Begin Restoring Your Relationship with Your Child 383
166. When God Is Silent.................................... 385
167. The Most Important Attribute of a Father 387
168. What Mercy Is and What It Isn't 389
169. The Target That We Are Shooting For.................. 391
170. The Two Conditions of Mercy 393
171. Magnetic Mercy, Part I................................. 395
172. Magnetic Mercy, Part 2................................. 397
173. Stretching Us 399
174. Becoming a Father on Earth Like the Father in Heaven 401
175. Identifying the Temple 403
176. The Prophetic Power of a Father's Words 405
177. Actually Seeing Your Child 407
178. Instilling Confidence in Your Child 409

179. Giving Your Child the Materials to Become a Temple. 411
180. Three Ways to Be the Living Face of God 413
181. Stop, Look, and Listen. 415
182. Training Your Child with Self-Giving Love 417
183. Working with Your Child. 418
184. Crafting the Cross of Self-Giving Love 420
185. Crafting and Conflict 421
186. The Biggest Man 423
187. One of the Most Difficult Things to Do. 425
188. Blessing Your Child to Become a Child of God 427
189. Giving Your Child the Ability to Thrive 429
190. Having Faith in the Power of the Blessing 430
191. Are You Worthy Enough to Bless Your Child?. 432
192. How to Bless Your Child. 433
193. The Prodigal Father. 435
194. Saving a Child, Saves a Father 437

CONCLUSION: A NEW BEGINNING 439

A FATHER'S EXAMEN

THE REASON FOR THIS EXAMEN 443
LISTEN TO DISCERN YOUR MISSION. 444
EMBRACE YOUR ESSENCE. 446
ASSUME YOUR AUTHORITY. 448
DISCOVER THE DISCIPLE 451

INTRODUCTION:
DISCOVERING YOUR PURPOSE: LIEIAID

We all want to be winners in life. Lord knows we sure do work hard enough at it. Still, when we look back on our life, at whatever age, we can see we've pretty much lost as much as we've won, and we are quite surprised to learn that what others have told us is true: we tend to learn more from our failures than our successes.

We sometimes wonder why that is and we often come to the conclusion that maybe it's because we want the wrong things—things that might not always be in our best longer-term interests. Maybe it's a particular job or home or contract or relationship, or even the gender of a child.

It's easy to get down on ourselves when this happens. And it's not all that much consolation to learn that this happens to pretty much all of us. The real challenge is trying to figure out the why of it.

Truth is, it most often has something to do with our core identity as men. Figuring out the who, what, and why of our existence is no small matter. Turns out it's not something we can do on the fly. Nor can we just kind of fall into it as we navigate our way through life. That's a sure-fire recipe for failure and it goes a long way to explaining why things are as they are today.

No, this core identity thing is something that forces us to sit and read and think and pray and discuss and discern. More than once. In fact, it can take awhile. But that's the way it's meant to be. If getting the who, what, and why of our existence right is truly the difference between living a largely successful life or a largely failed life, why shouldn't it take time—even a lot of time?

One of the fascinating things about entering this journey is what happens to us during it. We can't see it in ourselves; it is only seen by others, who say things to or about us we always wanted to hear but rarely do hear. In truth, what happens during the passage itself is something of a secret. While we are making time for the Lord and allowing him to guide us onto the path he created specifically for each of us, we are being formed to do what he is calling us to do. And it is in this doing of what we have been called to do that we come to a realization of the why we have been given life in this place and in this time.

Not much zigzagging through life happens after this. We can pretty much plot True North and set out on a different course and "make straight the way of the Lord." And while we have been told there are no shortcuts in life, an awful lot of wasted time can be spared by avoiding the potholes and ditches and simply staying on the path that's been charted for us.

Anything that can help us do that is quite rightly called a gift. You are holding one of those in your hands right now.

This book, an actual navigation chart, will help lead you to your destination, both temporal and eternal. When you finish it, you will not be in doubt as to your path to true greatness—that is to say, "fatherly greatness." It will speak to your heart, it will illuminate your mind, and it will forge your will to become the husband and father you have been called to be and are fully capable of being.

And in doing so, it will bring you a peace that transcends every other success you have had in life. Because it will be a peace born of purpose, your purpose.

When, not if, this happens for you, you will understand at the deepest level what winning in this life is truly all about.

— Brian J. Gail,
  Bestselling Catholic author of
  Fatherless, Motherless, and *Childless*

STRUCTURE OF L|E|A|D

You are holding in your hands the fruit of decades of thought, reflection, experience, and trial and error. This book is an attempt to distill the timeless wisdom and ageless example of St. Joseph's spirituality in an easily accessible, highly practical, daily devotional format for any man. More than a compilation of inspiring thoughts, it is a map for manhood, a systematic plan, a spiritual navigator to attain the glory that God promises to men through the Lord Jesus and His Gospel.

The Fathers of St. Joseph was founded on the premise of the necessity, vitality, and glory of the vocation of fatherhood, and to awaken men to that reality by transmitting the four pillars of St. Joseph's spirituality: to embrace silence, embrace woman, embrace charitable authority, and embrace the child. Men from around the world have discovered that the four pillars provide a true road map to real freedom and power in their lives.

L|E|A|D is a tremendous treasure; it converts the pillars of St. Joseph's spirituality into a daily devotional that enables men to discover the true path to fatherly glory.

L|E|A|D is segmented into two parts: Section 1: Assuming Your Location in God's Plan: Becoming the Custos (guardian and protector) and Section 2: Living Your Vocation to Greatness. Section 1 (Location) outlines your position in God's plan, and the necessity of you assuming your post as guardian of woman and the child. It explains why nearly everything depends upon you taking up this position.

Section 2 (Vocation) is segmented into the four ways we men are to live from our essential location in God's plan:

L—Listen to Discern Your Mission (Embrace Silence)
E—Embrace Your Essence (Embrace Woman)
A—Assume Your Authority (Embrace Charitable Authority)
D—Discover the Disciple (Embrace the Child).

L|E|A|D is compilation of succinct, authoritative, powerful, engaging reflections that express the call from the Father to fathers of our age to fulfill the heroic mission to be like St. Joseph, a father on earth like the Father in heaven.

L|E|A|D is a way of life for men and fathers that spans all ages. A program is temporary; a way of life is enduring, timeless, and sanctifying. Far from being a one and done product, L|E|A|D contains timeless wisdom that is worthy of revisiting again and again throughout one's life.

Just as the Dominicans, Benedictines, Franciscans, and Carmelites all have a particular spirituality, charism, and rule of life, so also the human father has a spirituality, a rule of life, a pattern for holiness that is founded upon the life and spirituality of St. Joseph. Today's father needs to know that he too has a specific charism, a spirituality and rule of life that if followed will aid him in becoming a man of glory. And just as each of those spiritualities played a major part in building the Church and claiming souls for Christ, we pray that St. Joseph's spirituality, summed up in the words "location" and "vocation," will also play its part in the conversion of the nations.

It is my prayer that you will join the worldwide movement of the Fathers of St. Joseph, whose aim is nothing less than the redemption, revitalization, and restoration of fatherhood, and answer the call to L|E|A|D.

We believe that society goes by way of the family, and the family goes by way of the father. If we want to change the world, we fathers must change.

HOW TO USE L|E|A|D

This book is to be approached in the manner that we approach life: one day at a time. Those who peer too far into the future suffer much angst, anxiety, and worry, while those who live in the past are riddled with guilt, depression, and a sense of failure. Both types of people fail to miss the adventure, joy, and hope of the present day. And so it is with this content. If you rush through the reflections contained in L|E|A|D you will, most likely run past the still, small, but powerful voice of God the Father. In addition to this, if you read these reflections and become plagued with guilt, wishing to change the past and despairing of the future, you will be misinterpreting the Father's call and mission for you. Remember, God's expertise is making crooked paths straight, wrongs into rights, sin and shame into grace and glory, the worst of sinners into the most glorious saints—and you are called to be one of them.

A house is not built in a day, but in stages, each literally building on the other. God desires to build you into His holy temple, in which He lives and from which His glory radiates. L|E|A|D has been created to give you the tools to trek the journey to authentic manhood—which culminates in spiritual fatherhood—methodically, intentionally, and with great purpose.

Each reflection is intended to be read, meditated upon, used as the basis of your morning conversation with God, and then reflected upon and applied during the remainder of the day. If you approach L|E|A|D in this manner you will begin to see your life, your family, your relationship with God, your marriage, your work and the world in an entirely new way. You will begin to have the keen ability to discern the difference between true divine freedom and slavery to selfishness, between God's voice and the devil's doubts, and you will discern your key role in God's epic plan.

At the end of each reflection is a segment titled "Take the L|E|A|D," which suggests how you might apply this content to your life. Rather than suggesting a practical application per each L|E|A|D reflection—which could easily cause spiritual burnout—L|E|A|D offers a single, focused, call to action that is repeated throughout a subsection (typically comprised of three to seven reflections). By approaching the content in this way, you will have more time to consider and understand the key principles offered in that particular series of reflections, while also applying and practicing those principles without proceeding too soon to a new practical application. "Repetition is the mother of learning" and by applying one Take the L|E|A|D call to action per subsection you will more effectively become a father on earth like the Father in heaven.

In addition to this, below the "Take the L|E|A|D" section (beginning with reflection 26), a page number is listed. The page referenced contains a "Father's Examen" comprised of several questions that sharpen your ability to understand what actions are needed to fulfill your vocational mission.

The Father's Examen is a powerful, easy-to-use tool. Individuals can use the Father's Examen at the end of their day as an examination of conscience. Those using L|E|A|D in small groups can use the Father's Examen that corresponds to that section as a means to initiate discussion after reading the reflection together. The seven questions contained in each of the Father's Examen will help the group focus, forge relationships and communion, and flourish as fathers in the image of the Father. Each "Take the L|E|A|D" section will point you to the appropriate examen.

By humbling yourself to engage and attempt to live the content in the book you have begun a life-altering journey that will enable you to L|E|A|D with confidence, courage, and clarity.

May God our Father grant you the grace to become like St. Joseph, a strong yet silent, humble yet strong father on earth like the Father in Heaven. I have been praying for you and will continue to pray for you daily.

— Devin Schadt, *cofounder of The Fathers of St. Joseph*

SECTION 1

ASSUMING YOUR LOCATION IN GOD'S PLAN

[Becoming the Custos]

GOD ASKS EACH OF US "WHERE ARE YOU?" THIS IS THE PERENNIAL QUESTION THAT HAUNTS THE DEEP SUBCONSCIOUS RECESSES OF MAN'S HEART. THE ANSWER TO THIS QUESTION DETERMINES EACH MAN'S LOCATION IN GOD'S PLAN OF SALVATION, HIS VOCATIONAL MISSION—THE VERY FOUNDATION OF THE SPIRITUALITY OF FATHERHOOD.

LEAD
THE FOUR MARKS OF FATHERLY GREATNESS

THE NECESSITY OF A FATHER

1. THE MOST IMPORTANT MAN

Have you ever considered who the world's most important man is? There are hosts of men who are marked by the character and attributes of power, influence, and popularity. Presidents of nations, popes, founders of megachurches, software developers, authors, philanthropists, investors, entrepreneurs, scientists, professors, professional athletes, actors, and inventors are commonly considered candidates who might qualify to meet this noble description. Though people in these positions rank high in authority and appear to have the ability to influence the masses, there is a man who is more important and more influential than all of these combined.

It is you, the human father.

Do you think this is an exaggeration? Consider that the majority of youth in prisons were raised in fatherless homes and that children from fatherless homes are far more likely to commit suicide or run away from home. Children who have a strained relationship with their father are far more susceptible to becoming addicted to drugs and alcohol, engage in premarital sexual activity, become divorced, deny belief in God, and have children out of wedlock.

You are indispensable. You have been endowed with the divine power to transmit grace and glory to your family and lead them to salvation. Fatherhood is like oxygen. Most people rarely set aside time to meditate upon the significance of oxygen, and yet without it mankind would perish. In a similar manner, the vitality, necessity and essential nature of fatherhood is rarely meditated upon, but nonetheless, without the human father the family crumbles. Your fatherhood, the manner in which you believe in its power, embrace it, and express it, significantly impacts your children's future—and not only your children's future, but the course of human history.

Though you may not be among the men of so-called greatness, taken from the pool of the wealthy, the influential, the powerful, and popular, though you may not be considered important to the world, you are the most powerful, influential, and important man in your children's world.

> **TAKE THE LEAD** You have embarked upon a journey that has the potential to alter the trajectory, and purpose of your life. From this point on, the way you understand your manhood and meaning will never be the same. With this new, potent understanding also comes tremendous responsibility. During these first six reflections, we will uncover the long-buried truth that you, the human father, are essential and vital to the restoration, redemption, and revitalization of the family, Church, and world. You may have the most challenging job in the world—to be a father on earth like the Father in heaven. God, the Church, and your family need you. It is up to you to take that first step toward reorienting your life toward this sublime purpose. Begin thanking God daily that He has created you with the mission to be a link between Him and your children.

SECTION 1: ASSUMING YOUR LOCATION IN GOD'S PLAN [BECOMING THE CUSTOS]

THE NECESSITY OF A FATHER

2. DOES GOD NEED YOU?

Consider that in one of the last prophecies uttered in the Old Testament, God transmitted the necessity and vitality of fatherhood through the prophet Malachi: "Behold I will send you Elijah before that great and terrible day . . . he will turn the hearts of fathers toward their children and the hearts of children toward their fathers lest I come and strike the land with a curse" (Mal 4:6). By means of these words, our heavenly Father disclosed His heart's desire, His purpose and intention: God desires to turn the hearts of fathers to their children for the purpose of compelling and convincing children to trustingly turn their hearts toward their fathers.

God our Father has endowed the human father with the potential to save mankind from self-implosion and nuclear disaster. If you turn your gaze, attention, and focus upon your child, your child will not only learn to trust in and love you, but also will begin to sense that the gaze of the Father is upon Him, and that His love is to be trusted. If your child knows that he is loved by his father on earth, your child will be certain that he is loved by his Father in heaven.

After recognizing that Mary, his wife, was pregnant without his cooperation, St. Joseph initially withdrew from his vocational path. Yet God relentlessly pursued Joseph, calling him and commanding him to heroically retrace his footsteps and become *Custos*, the defender and protector of not only Mary, but the Son of God within her. The message is clear: God the Father needed a human father to father God the Son, because God the Son needed a human father. In a certain, qualified sense, God has placed Himself in a position to need you to be a great father, because your children need the greatest Father. Society goes by way of the family and the family goes by way of the father; if we want to change the world, we fathers must change.

TAKE THE LEAD You have embarked upon a journey that has the potential to alter the trajectory, and purpose of your life. From this point on, the way you understand your manhood and meaning will never be the same. With this new, potent understanding also comes tremendous responsibility. During these first six reflections, we will uncover the long-buried truth that you, the human father, are essential and vital to the restoration, redemption, and revitalization of the family, Church, and world. You may have the most challenging job in the world—to be a father on earth like the Father in heaven. God, the Church, and your family need you. It is up to you to take that first step toward reorienting your life toward this sublime purpose. Begin thanking God daily that He has created you with the mission to be a link between Him and your children.

THE NECESSITY OF A FATHER

3. WHAT WILL YOU BE REMEMBERED FOR?

Have you ever trekked the grounds of a cemetery wondering if any of these people are remembered by those living on this earth today, and if they are remembered, for what precisely are they remembered? If you look closely at those gravestones you will notice that none of the chiseled words bear the titles of Engineer, Software Developer, Computer Programmer, Author, Newscaster, CEO, CFO, Mayor, Alderman, Entrepreneur, or Successful Investor, but rather, Father, Mother, Son, or Daughter. Your birth certificate has three names: your father's, your mother's, and yours. It bears your title, your identity: son. You came into this world as a son, but you will leave this world as a father. "As for the days of our life, they contain seventy years, or if due to strength, eighty years. Yet, their pride is but labor and sorrow; for soon it is gone and we fly away" (Ps 90:10).

You have such a brief time to live on this earth. How will you consume it, or how will it consume you? For what will you be remembered? Will you be remembered for what you did, or will you be remembered for something more fundamental—for who you are? What will be your legacy? What will be the epitaph permanently chiseled into the surface of your seemingly permanent gravestone? In the end, it is your family, or those considered to be family, who will bury you, and it will be those people who will remember you. The question is not *whether* they will remember, you but *how* will they remember you?

Doing proceeds from being, and being is fundamental to doing. Fatherhood is not as much something you do, but who you are. Fatherhood is not an occupation but a vocation. Fatherhood is an identity and a destiny. It is who you are and who you will become—like the Father. You are not defined by what you "do for a living" as much as for whom you are living. You are not defined as much by your occupation as by your vocation. At work, you will always be replaceable, but at home you are irreplaceable. Your work is transitional and passing; your fatherhood and its effect is eternal.

St. Joseph was a *tekton*, which is a Greek word that can mean master carpenter, one who works expertly with varying substrates, an engineer of sorts. Though Joseph was a master craftsman, he is not remembered for any work of craftsmanship, but rather for his heroic, valiant, resolute fatherly example and his unparalleled protection of and fidelity to his wife, Mary. St. Joseph is not remembered for building things, but for crafting his domestic church, his family. St. Joseph, though hidden, and apparently unknown in his day, is lauded and revered today as the greatest and most noble father of all time.

We don't love people as much for what they do as for who they are. So it is with your wife and children: they will not love us for our dedication to our occupation, but for our fidelity to our vocation.

For what will your children remember you? For what you produce, or for your person? For provided revenues, or a relationship you provided for? Will they remember you as a great failure or a great father? The word "Father" will be etched in your gravestone. Will you be worthy of such an honorable and noble title?

> **TAKE THE LEAD** You have embarked upon a journey that has the potential to alter the trajectory, and purpose of your life. From this point on, the way you understand your manhood and meaning will never be the same. With this new, potent understanding also comes tremendous responsibility. During these first six reflections, we will uncover the long-buried truth that you, the human father, are essential and vital to the restoration, redemption, and revitalization of the family, Church, and world. You may have the most challenging job in the world—to be a father on earth like the Father in heaven. God, the Church, and your family need you. It is up to you to take that first step toward reorienting your life toward this sublime purpose. Begin thanking God daily that He has created you with the mission to be a link between Him and your children.

SECTION 1: ASSUMING YOUR LOCATION IN GOD'S PLAN [BECOMING THE CUSTOS]

THE NECESSITY OF A FATHER

4. THE GAZE WE DESIRE

Have you ever met someone who avoids looking you in the eyes? He looks around you, but not into you? Have you ever struggled to make or retain eye contact with someone? Why do people avoid the gaze of another? The simple answer is that we are all afraid—afraid that the other may see something in us that we don't want them to see; or perhaps on a deeper level, we are fearful that they won't see something in us that is desirable.

Consider that all children from their earliest days, instinctively receive the loving gaze of others and gazes back at others. Children have no inhibition. They are not intimidated, or more importantly, they are not introspective; they simply peer out—and in—to others.

But somewhere along life's rocky path, a child begins to mistrust others and even begins to mistrust himself. He begins to spend more time looking in than out. He avoids the gaze of another because he wants to avoid being rejected by the other. One of the reasons many of us stop gazing into others is because sometimes, early in our lives, the most important people stopped gazing into us.

Every single human being has the authentic desire to be desired, delighted in, chosen, affirmed, and loved. Children look for validation, affirmation, and approval. Children crave their father's approval, they want his eyes to rest on them with delight because his gaze transmits and communicates something transcendent. Deep down, we all long for our father's gaze because we desire the Father's gaze. We desire our father's approval because we desire to be approved by the Father. We desire to be a chosen son because we want God to choose us as His son—not just any son, but a chosen son in whom He delights.

But if our daughters don't receive our gaze of love and affection, they will seek for that gaze of love and affirmation in a disordered manner from boys who are incapable of loving them truly. If our sons don't have our gaze of approval, they will seek approval from those of whom we don't approve. If our children do not have our gaze of love, attention, and delight, it will be gravely difficult for them to trust and believe that they have the Father's gaze.

> **TAKE THE LEAD** You have embarked upon a journey that has the potential to alter the trajectory, and purpose of your life. From this point on, the way you understand your manhood and meaning will never be the same. With this new, potent understanding also comes tremendous responsibility. During these first six reflections, we will uncover the long-buried truth that you, the human father, are essential and vital to the restoration, redemption, and revitalization of the family, Church, and world. You may have the most challenging job in the world—to be a father on earth like the Father in heaven. God, the Church, and your family need you. It is up to you to take that first step toward reorienting your life toward this sublime purpose. Begin thanking God daily that He has created you with the mission to be a link between Him and your children.

SECTION 1: ASSUMING YOUR LOCATION IN GOD'S PLAN [BECOMING THE CUSTOS]

THE NECESSITY OF A FATHER

5. WHAT DOES GOD REALLY DESIRE?

Have you ever wondered why God created us? What is the purpose of our existence? What does He want from you? What is the desire of His "heart"?

By means of one of the last prophecies in the Old Testament, God transmitted His message of the necessity of the human father's gaze: "Behold, I will send you Elijah the prophet before the great and terrible day of the Lord comes. And He will turn the hearts of fathers to their children and the hearts of children to their fathers, lest I come strike the land with a curse" (Mal 4:5–6).

By means of these words, the Father disclosed His heart's desire, his purpose and intention: God desires to turn the hearts of fathers to their children in order that the hearts of children will turn to their fathers. Why? Because if human fathers turn their gaze, their attention, and their focus upon their children, their children will not only see their father's love, but begin to feel the loving gaze of their heavenly Father.

Even St. Joseph himself lost sight of the twelve-year-old Jesus momentarily, leaving Him behind in Jerusalem, as he and Mary began their trek home after the feast of the Passover. However, after realizing that his gaze upon Jesus was disrupted, he did everything within his fatherly power, seeking anxiously for his son, until his eyes finally rested upon Him in the temple.

You and I may lose sight of our children and forget that they desire and yearn for our gaze of love and approval. Let us, however, be like Joseph and relentlessly seek their face and gaze into their eyes with the Father's look of love. If we continue to do so, they will one day have the confidence to break free from self-absorbed introspection, and rather than looking in, will look out into others, giving them the gaze of Christ's love. This is the intention, will, and desire of God: to share Himself, His glory, His eternal love with you and your child.

TAKE THE LEAD You have embarked upon a journey that has the potential to alter the trajectory, and purpose of your life. From this point on, the way you understand your manhood and meaning will never be the same. With this new, potent understanding also comes tremendous responsibility. During these first six reflections, we will uncover the long-buried truth that you, the human father, are essential and vital to the restoration, redemption, and revitalization of the family, Church, and world. You may have the most challenging job in the world—to be a father on earth like the Father in heaven. God, the Church, and your family need you. It is up to you to take that first step toward reorienting your life toward this sublime purpose. Begin thanking God daily that He has created you with the mission to be a link between Him and your children.

SECTION 1: ASSUMING YOUR LOCATION IN GOD'S PLAN [BECOMING THE CUSTOS]

THE NECESSITY OF A FATHER

6. THE MOST DIFFICULT JOB

Often, when a person is given a role, a job, or a duty that someone else—who has skill, talent, and great capability—previously had, someone will inevitably say to them, "You have some big shoes to fill." You and I have experienced such moments in our own lives, when we have been asked to "step up" and be the man that others depend on. Presidents, quarterbacks, professors, owners of companies and the like have experienced the challenge of replacing someone of greatness to whom people will compare and rate them.

It is difficult enough to be compared to another human being, but it's another thing entirely to be compared to the perfect, all-knowing, all-loving, all-giving, all-powerful God. And yet, Jesus audaciously challenges us and even desires us to make this comparison: "If you then, who are evil, know how to give good gifts to your children, how much more will your Father who is in heaven give good things to those who ask him" (Mt 7:11).

Our Lord invites you to meditate upon the fact that there is a *connection in the comparison*: by comparing your fatherhood with God's fatherhood you and your children will discover God's fatherly goodness and be forever connected to Him. Great fathers connect the world to the greatest Father. But to become great fathers it is imperative that we understand what a father is, what his essence is, what constitutes his identity. The human father has perhaps one of the most challenging jobs in the world—he is divinely ordained to be an icon, a grace-transmitting symbol of God the Father. As Pope St. John Paul II said, the human father is called to relive and reveal the very fatherhood of God (see FC 25). Those are some infinite shoes to fill!

You are called to be a link between your children and God the Father. You are called to be the voice of the Father that your child cannot hear, the face of the Father that your child cannot see, the touch of the Father that your child cannot feel. The human father is the visible icon of the heavenly Father. This is not mere wishful thinking or pious idealism; it is the divine plan. Sacred Scripture and St. Paul the Apostle attest to this truth: "For this cause I bow my knees to the Father of our Lord Jesus Christ, of whom all paternity in heaven and earth is named" (Eph 3:14). This indicates that you as a human father are named and claimed in the image of the eternal Father. You are called to be a father on earth like the Father in heaven, to ensure that your children, who are on earth, can hear, see, and touch the Father in heaven—through you.

Remember, there exists a connection in the comparison, you are invited by Jesus to connect your limited desire for your children to receive good things with the heavenly Father's unlimited, eternal, desire for our good. In other words, if we fathers want good things for our children, then God wants the best for His children. This is why your iconic fatherhood is not only important, but essential to God's plan.

By meditating on the love we have for our own children and comparing it to the heavenly Father's love for us, we make the discovery—the connection—that God profoundly loves, chooses, desires, and delights in us. When we begin to understand, believe, and receive the love of the Father, then we can give to our children the love we have been given.

> **TAKE THE LEAD** You have embarked upon a journey that has the potential to alter the trajectory, and purpose of your life. From this point on, the way you understand your manhood and meaning will never be the same. With this new, potent understanding also comes tremendous responsibility. During these first six reflections, we will uncover the long-buried truth that you, the human father, are essential and vital to the restoration, redemption, and revitalization of the family, Church, and world. You may have the most challenging job in the world—to be a father on earth like the Father in heaven. God, the Church, and your family need you. It is up to you to take that first step toward reorienting your life toward this sublime purpose. Begin thanking God daily that He has created you with the mission to be a link between Him and your children.

SECTION 1: ASSUMING YOUR LOCATION IN GOD'S PLAN [BECOMING THE CUSTOS]

YOUR LOCATION IN GOD'S PLAN

7. WHERE ARE YOU?

Have you ever heard someone say that the key to having a successful business is location, location, location? Or that one of the keys to success is being in the right place at the right time? And so it is with the vocation of fatherhood. The success of your vocation depends upon your spiritual location.

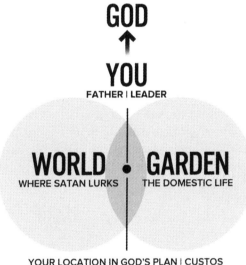

"Where are you?" were the first words spoken by God after the original man's fall from grace. This haunting question thundered and crashed upon Adam's convicted soul. The Father proposed this question not to obtain an answer for Himself—as if He didn't know Adam's physical location—but to help man obtain the answer to the riddle of himself; to help you and me understand our vital role in God's epic plan. God was not concerned with Adam's geographical position, but rather with his theological position, that is, his relationship to God and to his bride.

What is your location in the context of God's plan of salvation? How does your location affect your vocation? The answer to the divine question "Where are you?" is the key to understanding and unlocking the power of your masculinity and fatherhood, and will help you understand why you are essential to God's plan, to your wife, and to your children.

Adam was "created by God from the slime of the earth," in the unknown, in the wild—outside of the garden of paradise. Then "The Lord God took the man and put him in the garden of Eden to till it and keep it," commanding him not to eat of the tree of knowledge of good and evil.

Notice that the man is created in the undomesticated, undiscovered, uncharted world; yet God removed him from that unknown wilderness and placed him in the garden.

The word "garden" in ancient Hebrew literature was often used as a symbol to describe the mystery of woman. Adam's position was not exclusively in the wild, in a world of adventure—nor was his location to be reduced to living in the garden, that is, to being completely domesticated. Adam was called by God to stand on the horizon between the uncharted, outer world and the interior, domesticated world of the garden and to integrate these two worlds in his being.

It was Adam's duty and honor to protect and defend the garden of woman, his bride, from Satan, who was lurking in the wild.

Yet he failed.

Adam allowed the evil one to slither his way into the garden and manipulate Eve, convincing her to succumb to sin, to distrust the Father.

Like Adam, you are called to be the guardian of your garden, ensuring that the evils of the world not contaminate your wife and children—ensuring that they trust in the Father. This is the incredible and demanding vocation of fatherhood—your fatherhood.

Assume your location and begin to live your vocation so that when God asks "Where are you?" you may respond, "Here I am Lord. I am ready to do your will."

TAKE THE LEAD There is a real tendency among men, who after realizing their noble position in God's plan, to succumb to the temptation of condemning themselves for their failure to stand in the breach between the hostile world and his family. You and I are only culpable to the level that we had this prior understanding, which few these days have. Yes, we have failed. And perhaps we are plagued with guilt. Guilt is only good if it leads to repentance—turning away from selfishness and toward God. Consider confessing your sins to a priest, and if needed, make a general confession of your entire life. Surrender your guilt to God, ask Him for forgiveness, and receive grace to reassume your post as guardian of the garden.

YOUR LOCATION IN GOD'S PLAN

8. IS YOUR ROLE ANY DIFFERENT THAN YOUR WIFE'S?

Is your theological position any different than your wife's? Recall that Adam was divinely ordained to stand in the breech between the unknown, uncharted, undiscovered world and the garden—the domestic life. Adam's mission was to integrate these two worlds, while protecting the one—the world of his family.

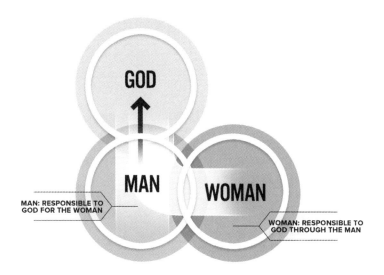

You and I have the same calling: to be the guardian who stands guard at the gate of the garden, on the horizon between the competitive and hostile world and our family, to ensure that the evils of the world not contaminate them.

Adam was given the command to till and keep the garden. The Hebrew words for "till" and "keep" are *abad*, that is, to cherish, and *shamar*, which means to protect. Like Adam, you and I are fundamentally charged to protect woman and the child—at all cost. This is your responsibility and mission.

SECTION 1: ASSUMING YOUR LOCATION IN GOD'S PLAN [BECOMING THE CUSTOS]

Notice that after the fall, God did not address Eve, the one who sinned first, but rather Adam—the one who was given the command first. God questioned Adam because it was his responsibility to cherish, protect, and defend his bride. It is important that we men understand that Eve did not even exist when God gave Adam the command to till and keep the garden. The point is that you and I are responsible to God *for the woman*, and woman is responsible to God *through the man*. In a certain, qualified sense, your wife receives God's protection and power through you.

St. Joseph, a type of Adam, commanded by God to take his wife into his home, obediently refused to "expose Mary to shame." St. Joseph "shamared" Mary's garden from the shame of the serpent, and because of this the fruit of her womb not only survived but lived to die for the salvation of mankind.

Like Joseph, it is your duty as man, father, husband, and leader to transmit the love, protection, and teachings of God to your wife and children; to stand on the horizon between the outer hostile world and your domestic church to ensure that the evil serpent doesn't enter your home. This is your unique, divinely ordained role.

TAKE THE LEAD There is a real tendency among men, who after realizing their noble position in God's plan, to succumb to the temptation of condemning themselves for their failure to stand in the breach between the hostile world and his family. You and I are only culpable to the level that we had this prior understanding, which few these days have. Yes, we have failed. And perhaps we are plagued with guilt. Guilt is only good if it leads to repentance—turning away from selfishness and toward God. Consider confessing your sins to a priest, and if needed, make a general confession of your entire life. Surrender your guilt to God, ask Him for forgiveness, and receive grace to reassume your post as guardian of the garden.

YOUR LOCATION IN GOD'S PLAN

9. ARE YOU LIKE GOD?

Have you ever sensed that you are called to something more, to accomplish something, or to be someone great? Have you ever thought that you have an essential mission that, if fulfilled, will greatly impact humanity? The authentic version of that desire and call to greatness is divinely inspired. It is God's voice calling you to be like Him.

But wasn't that the sin of our first parents? Weren't they deceived into believing the lie that by eating of the tree of knowledge of good and evil that they would become like God?

Their sin was not *desiring to be like God*, but rather *believing that God did not desire them to be like Him*; and therefore, rather than trusting in, waiting for, and receiving the gift of divinity from God, they grasped for it, believing that God would not give it.

What does God say about this? God, through His word, tells us that "[w]e shall be like Him, for we shall see Him as He is" (1 Jn 3:2). Jesus prayed that "The glory which Thou [Father] hast given me I have given to them, that they may be one as we are one" (Jn 17:22). God desires that you become like Him. He desires to share his divine nature, power and glory with you. But what is this glory? What is this oneness that Jesus speaks of?

God is a Trinity of Persons: three distinct Persons who are so completely self-giving that they are in substance (essence) one. Oneness, or unity, springs from the self-giving, the mutual self-sacrifice, between two people. A husband and wife become one like God when giving themselves to one another. The pinnacle expression of this oneness is the marital embrace. The Father, the principal source of the Trinity, loves the Word, and the Word loves the Father, and the love that proceeds from them is the Holy Spirit. In a similar way, God creates the family to be like the Trinity's exchange of love—an exchange of persons. A husband and wife give themselves to one another, particularly in the one-flesh union, and that union produces a third, a child.

SECTION 1: ASSUMING YOUR LOCATION IN GOD'S PLAN [BECOMING THE CUSTOS]

What God does in eternity (total self-giving love) He desires to reproduce in our humanity. God desires His Trinity to animate your family. Just as the Trinity cannot exist without the Father, the human family will struggle to thrive in love without the human father. St. Joseph's fatherhood was not ancillary, or simply ordained to avoid the scandal of the Virgin's pregnancy, but rather was essential to God's plan of making the Holy Family the primary example of the Trinity's self-giving love.

Like St. Joseph, God has entrusted you with the challenging yet noble task of initiating and sustaining the self-giving glory of God in your family. If you respond to His call, you and your family—by divine design—will become like God.

> **TAKE THE LEAD** There is a real tendency among men, who after realizing their noble position in God's plan, to succumb to the temptation of condemning themselves for their failure to stand in the breach between the hostile world and his family. You and I are only culpable to the level that we had this prior understanding, which few these days have. Yes, we have failed. And perhaps we are plagued with guilt. Guilt is only good if it leads to repentance—turning away from selfishness and toward God. Consider confessing your sins to a priest, and if needed, make a general confession of your entire life. Surrender your guilt to God, ask Him for forgiveness, and receive grace to reassume your post as guardian of the garden.

YOUR LOCATION IN GOD'S PLAN

10. A LINK BETWEEN HEAVEN AND EARTH

How do children encounter the unknowable, invisible, distant God? What on earth transmits the face of the Father that they cannot see, the voice of the Father that they cannot hear, the touch of the Father that they cannot feel?

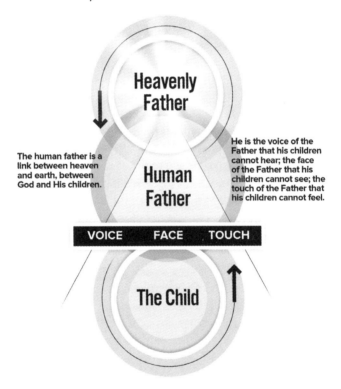

You, my fellow father, have been created by the heavenly Father to relive and reveal God the Father's love to your child. Your mission is to assist God in the great mission of reproducing the love of the Trinity in your family by means of transmitting the generosity, sacrificial love, authority, and power of God the Father to your family.

SECTION 1: ASSUMING YOUR LOCATION IN GOD'S PLAN [BECOMING THE CUSTOS]

The author of Ephesians testifies to this truth: "I bow my knees to the Father of our Lord Jesus Christ from Whom all fatherhood derives its name" (Eph 3:14).

You have been created, named, and claimed by God the Father as a father for the purpose of expressing His fatherhood to this fallen, broken world. Indeed, if you don't accomplish this great mission, who will?

The principal and source of the Trinity is the unbegotten Begetter, the Father of the Begotten One, the Word—Jesus. As fatherhood is expressed in the divine Godhead and in St. Joseph's family, you are to express fatherhood in your family. Your fatherhood is the initiating, human, "source" that transmits God's life of grace to your family. Without you initiating self-sacrificial love, your family will struggle if not fail to be animated by God's self-giving love.

You are a link between heaven and earth, between God and man, between the Father and His (your) children. Your greatest mission is to become like God, a human father who becomes the very presence of God the Father's love.

> **TAKE THE LEAD** There is a real tendency among men, who after realizing their noble position in God's plan, to succumb to the temptation of condemning themselves for their failure to stand in the breach between the hostile world and his family. You and I are only culpable to the level that we had this prior understanding, which few these days have. Yes, we have failed. And perhaps we are plagued with guilt. Guilt is only good if it leads to repentance—turning away from selfishness and toward God. Consider confessing your sins to a priest, and if needed, make a general confession of your entire life. Surrender your guilt to God, ask Him for forgiveness, and receive grace to reassume your post as guardian of the garden.

YOUR IDENTIFICATION, DESTINATION,
AND GLORIFICATION DISCOVERED IN YOUR VOCATION

11. DISCOVER YOURSELF BY GIVING YOURSELF AWAY

If your identity leads and determines your destiny; if becoming who you really are—who God has created you and destined you to be—will inspire you to set the world ablaze, it seems that one of man's most important goals is to discover who he truly is. To discover who we really are, to discover who God has designed and destined us to be, can be one of life's greatest challenges.

Often as children, we were asked, "What are you going to do when you grow up?" Will you be a lawyer, a doctor, a fireman, a policeman, the president? Most likely no one ever asked you, "Who are you going to be?" But this is the real question. When we meet people for the first time, we often ask them "What do you do?" But the question that ought to be asked is "Who are you?" We are all searching for our true self, our true person, but how do we discover this God-given identity?

The paradoxical secret to discovering yourself is obtained by giving yourself away. "Man can only discover himself by means of being a sincere gift" (GS 24). Or as Jesus said, "He who loses his life will gain it." In other words, your identity is not about what you have, but rather what you give. And in giving you receive your identity and the seed of your destiny. There exist many people who have accumulated great wealth and are little more than black holes of selfishness, imploding upon themselves and sucking the very life from the people around them. Some of the saddest, most miserable people are those who are attached to their possessions. The truth is that the more you give yourself authentically to another, the more you will be confirmed by others in your gift of self, and when you are confirmed for your giftedness, you discover more of who you are: your talents, abilities, and mission.

TAKE THE LEAD Over the next several reflections you will discover the true path to glory and the insidious enemy who is determined to drive you from that path. The key

SECTION 1: ASSUMING YOUR LOCATION IN GOD'S PLAN [BECOMING THE CUSTOS]

to overcoming the enemy and remaining on the path to glory is to become who God has created and destined you to be—truly. This is the moment to make an honest assessment of who you have become. Discern what "masks" you wear to obtain what you desire; the false persona of pretending to be more than you are for fear of being less than others. Realize that this pseudo self appears to be profitable, but in reality, leads you further and further from your destiny, which is glory. Over the next several sessions ask God to strip away the false self and uncover your real self, which is nothing less than a manifestation and revelation of the Father's glory.

YOUR IDENTIFICATION, DESTINATION,
AND GLORIFICATION DISCOVERED IN YOUR VOCATION

12. THE SECRET PATH

God has created a secret path between earth and heaven, between God and man, between our nascent identity and our ultimate destiny. If you follow this secret path you will become a man of greatness. This secret path is the context in which God has ordained for you to continually and perpetually give yourself away and thus discover who you are, your mission, and your ultimate destiny. The secret path is your fatherly vocation. Your identification is discovered by means of your vocation, which leads to your destination, which is your glorification—deification, that is, to be a partaker in the divine nature (2 Pet 1:4). Your vocation is your path to glory, to greatness. If you are a husband and father, then this is your path to glory and no other path will be given.

God the Word is always speaking for the purpose of leading us to Him. From the moment of your conception, throughout your human life, the Word whispers His voice into your being. The context in which we hear the Word is in and amidst our fatherly vocation. Remember that the word "vocation" is derived from the Latin word *vox,* which means voice. It is in and through your fatherly vocation that you will receive the voice of God, which will continually reveal more of your mission.

St. Joseph, amidst his fatherly vocation, in self-donation to Mary and Jesus, embraced celibacy for the Kingdom, left his home in Nazareth, on the night of the Savior's birth he was shunned by his own in Bethlehem, and worked his trade in the foreign land of Egypt to ensure that the Holy Family would not only survive but thrive. Joseph discovered, amidst his fatherly vocation, that he was an essential part of God's plan to redeem the world. In and through the mission of Joseph's fatherhood, he discovered his identity, and in fulfilling his vocation he achieved his God-ordained destiny.

You and I have a choice: to withdraw ourselves from the secret path that leads toward greatness, or to remain steadfast on the vocational path of fatherhood. If you "[w]alk worthy of the *vocation* in which you are called" (Eph 4:1) you will, like Joseph, become a father of glory.

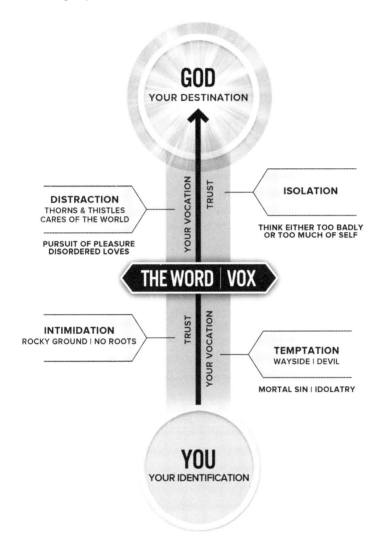

TAKE THE LEAD Over the next several reflections you will discover the true path to glory and the insidious enemy who is determined to drive you from that path. The key to overcoming the enemy and remaining on the path to glory is to become who God has created and destined you to be—truly. This is the moment to make an honest assessment of who you have become. Discern what "masks" you wear to obtain what you desire; the false persona of pretending to be more than you are for fear of being less than others. Realize that this pseudo self appears to be profitable, but in reality, leads you further and further from your destiny, which is glory. Over the next several sessions ask God to strip away the false self and uncover your real self, which is nothing less than a manifestation and revelation of the Father's glory.

SECTION 1: ASSUMING YOUR LOCATION IN GOD'S PLAN [BECOMING THE CUSTOS]

YOUR IDENTIFICATION, DESTINATION,
AND GLORIFICATION DISCOVERED IN YOUR VOCATION

13. YOUR GREAT BATTLE

Have you ever wondered why, when making a purchase, we are often influenced to buy a product that has a particular logo on it? Often people attempt to affiliate themselves with, and derive value from, a brand. We attempt to find our identity in something that we believe will grant us value and meaning—although the attempt always falls short. We are all searching for the true self and identity that God has created and destined us to be. But often we look for identity in logos rather than the Logos.

Why do so many men experience a midlife crisis? They wake-up to the reality that they are not who they desire to be and therefore believe that they need to do something to determine or discover their own identity. This may be the deepest, most fundamental challenge for every man: to know who he *really* is.

If you doubt that discovering, embracing, and living from one's God-given identity is one of man's greatest battles, consider Jesus Christ, who after His baptism was promptly led by the Holy Spirit into the desert to be tempted by the evil one. What was the core content of our Lord's temptation? "*If you are* the Son of God, turn these stones into bread. *If you are* the Son of God, throw yourself off the parapet of the temple. *If you are* the Son of God, worship me and I will give you the nations."

The evil one is questioning Jesus' identity. "Who are you *really*, Jesus? What is your identity?" It is as if the evil one is saying, "Prove yourself." If Jesus fell prey to the temptation to prove that He is the Son of God, He would have betrayed His very identity, because God doesn't have to prove anything—He is simply God. Thus, by overcoming the temptation to prove His identity, Jesus proves that He is God the Son—the one who overcomes all temptation.

This narrative of Jesus' battle to retain and proclaim His identity is threaded throughout the short story of Jesus' earthly life, culminating at the foot of the cross, where the Pharisees, priests, and elders goad Jesus: "If you are the Son of God come down from that cross." Like the devil, they are saying essentially, "Prove your identity. Show us who you really are."

In fact, during Jesus' Passion, He is questioned three times regarding His identity. First in the garden, the cohort, led by Judas the betrayer, ask, "Which one of you is Jesus the Nazarene?" Jesus responded, "I AM." Jesus, in the face of immanent death, while confronting great opposition and intimidation, witnessed and testified to His human identity: I am fully man—I am Jesus of Nazareth. Again, Caiaphas, the Jewish high priest, interrogated Jesus, asking Him, "Are you the Son of the Living God?" To which Jesus responded, "I AM." Jesus confessed His divine identity, that He is fully God, God the Son—fully divine. And again, Pilate asked Jesus,"Are you a king?" Jesus responded, "It is you who say I AM. My kingdom is not of this world." Jesus admits His sovereign identity as king and lord of mankind. In the face of great intimidation, Jesus did not deny His identity as fully man, fully God, and Lord and King of all. Jesus did not acquiesce, but rather stood his ground, battled, and courageously persevered to confess and maintain the truth of His identity.

Like his son, Jesus, St. Joseph was tempted regarding his vocational identity and mission. Joseph was called to be the husband of Mary, and therefore the father of her child. It was here, amidst the context of his fatherly vocational path, that Joseph experienced the tremendous temptation to reject his identity. Your marriage will have trials and tests. Your fatherhood will be blasted by challenges and crises. As with Jesus and Joseph, the evil one will work tirelessly, using the forces and powers of this world to intimidate you; to tempt you to hide, diminish, or altogether reject your personal, marital, and fatherly identity. This will be one of your greatest battles: to remain true to the person and father that God our Father has created and destined you to be.

> **TAKE THE LEAD** Over the next several reflections you will discover the true path to glory and the insidious enemy who is determined to drive you from that path. The key to overcoming the enemy and remaining on the path to glory is to become who God has

created and destined you to be—truly. This is the moment to make an honest assessment of who you have become. Discern what "masks" you wear to obtain what you desire; the false persona of pretending to be more than you are for fear of being less than others. Realize that this pseudo self appears to be profitable, but in reality, leads you further and further from your destiny, which is glory. Over the next several sessions ask God to strip away the false self and uncover your real self, which is nothing less than a manifestation and revelation of the Father's glory.

YOUR IDENTIFICATION, DESTINATION,
AND GLORIFICATION DISCOVERED IN YOUR VOCATION

14. UNDERSTANDING THE BULLY

Your fatherly vocation is the path by which you are to travel from this earth to heaven. It is through your vocation that you will hear the *Vox*, the Word that helps you discover your true identity and thus attain your destiny.

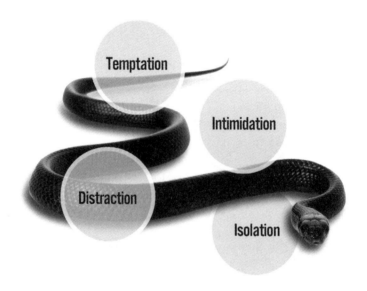

The hellish bully, the evil one, stands amidst this path, tirelessly attempting to intimidate you and drive you from it. He will do nearly anything to keep you from hearing the voice of God, because he knows that if you cannot hear the orders from your divine captain you certainly cannot fulfill them. Indeed, if you cannot hear the Word regarding your identity, you cannot lead your family to their destiny.

The evil one knows that you are called to be a manifestation, a revelation of God's fatherly glory. If the devil drives you from your vocation, the many people to whom you would have revealed God's glory may never encounter Him and be eternally lost. And so would the others that they would have touched down through the decades and centuries.

The evil one's strategy can be described as having four aspects or stages: temptation, intimidation, distraction, and isolation (see diagram on page 49). The first stage is temptation. If the evil one cannot tempt you or keep you in mortal or ongoing venial sin, he will use intimidation to drive you from your vocational path. If he cannot intimidate you, he will use the tactic of distraction; and if he cannot distract you from your vocation, he will lure you into isolation.

The essence of this truth is disclosed by Jesus in the Parable of the Sower and the Seed. Jesus interprets the birds that steal the seed sowed on the wayside as the devil who robs us of the seed of the Word, the voice of God, which speaks of our identity, mission, and destiny. The evil one robs us of the seed before it can take root by means of temptation. When a man is bound by such temptations he cannot hear the Word nor is he truly capable of transmitting it to his wife and children.

If the devil cannot lead you into temptation, he will try to intimidate you. Jesus said that the seed that fell on rocky soil and was scorched by the sun because it had no roots symbolizes those who initially believe, but when they are persecuted or experience suffering because of their belief in Jesus, lose heart and fall away. If the evil one cannot tempt us or intimidate us, he will distract us. Jesus said the seed that began to spring up was choked by thorns and thistles, which symbolize the pursuit of pleasures and riches, and the cares of the world. The evil one derives great pleasure in giving us something good for the purpose of keeping us from that which is greatest. Money, entertainment, relaxation, hobbies, and pleasure are all good, but if they rob your attention from God, your wife, and children, they become an obstacle to the success of your vocation.

If he cannot lure us with temptation, intimidation, or distraction, the devil will use the tactic of isolation. Isolation occurs when we separate ourselves from people because we don't believe them to be as holy as we are. By doing this we separate ourselves from God. Hence the name "Pharisee" actually means *separated one*. Isolation also occurs when we separate ourselves from God because we don't believe that we are holy enough, and consequently we separate ourselves from His people.

Consider St. Joseph. When he discovered Mary pregnant without his cooperation, he initially withdrew from his vocational path and decided to *separate* himself from Mary. The evil one intimidated and tempted Joseph to believe that he was not worthy of Mary—or God within her—attempting to drive him into isolation. Joseph, rather than isolating himself from God, placed himself in prayerful silent solitude *with God*. It was in the silent solitude that Joseph received the *Vox*, the Word, the voice that communicated his identity and mission: "Joseph son of David [this is his identity: he is a son of David and therefore a son of God], do not fear to take Mary your wife, for that which is conceived in her is of the Holy Spirit [this is his vocation: to be a husband to the Mother of God and a father to the Son of God]."

Remain strong like Joseph. Do not give the devil permission to drive you from your vocational path. By following St. Joseph's heroic example and relying upon his intercession, you can overcome temptation, intimidation, distraction, and isolation and become a great father who by means of discovering your identification in your vocation will lead your family to their destination, which is their glorification—their deification.

> **TAKE THE LEAD** Over the next several reflections you will discover the true path to glory and the insidious enemy who is determined to drive you from that path. The key to overcoming the enemy and remaining on the path to glory is to become who God has created and destined you to be—truly. This is the moment to make an honest assessment of who you have become. Discern what "masks" you wear to obtain what you desire; the false persona of pretending to be more than you are for fear of being less than others. Realize that this pseudo self appears to be profitable, but in reality, leads you further and further from your destiny, which is glory. Over the next several sessions ask God to strip away the false self and uncover your real self, which is nothing less than a manifestation and revelation of the Father's glory.

SECTION 1: ASSUMING YOUR LOCATION IN GOD'S PLAN [BECOMING THE CUSTOS]

YOUR IDENTIFICATION, DESTINATION,
AND GLORIFICATION DISCOVERED IN YOUR VOCATION

15. THE SIN OF LONELINESS

The ultimate goal for your family is to experience heaven on earth today that they may experience heaven in the eternal day. You, as father and leader of your family, by your self-donation, carve the path through the thicket and thorns of this world to heaven. This is precisely why the enemy's intention is to isolate you in the "sin of loneliness." Isolation is hell. Isolation is the polar opposite of communion, union, and self-giving love. It is easier to avoid communion with others, live in isolation, and suffer loneliness, rather than to suffer to overcome loneliness and isolation for the purpose of living in communion with others.

Jesus, speaking of this dynamic, said, "Unless a grain of wheat falls to the ground and dies it remains alone"(Jn 12:24). In other words, if you don't give yourself away, you will, in the end, die a lonely, isolated unloving and unlovable man. To the level that you give is the measure that will be given to you. To the degree that you give love is the level that you will be given love.

But notice that the cost of communion is death to your selfish self. One of the most persistent, relentless, perpetual sufferings that you will experience is the battle to overcome the temptation to remain alone with your hobbies, projects, work, and vain ambitions, rather than surrender your vain ambitions for the purpose of intentionally participating in your wife's and children's lives.

Karol Wojtyla, in his play *The Radiation of Fatherhood*, speaking of Adam said, "He stepped once on the frontier between fatherhood and loneliness." Which raises the question: What is this frontier between fatherhood, communion, and loneliness? Later Wojtyla wrote: "Loneliness opposes love. On the borderline of loneliness, *love must become suffering*." And if suffering is to be redeemed, it must become sacrifice.

If you desire to magnetically attract your family to yourself and ultimately to God, it is imperative that you move from the world of isolation and loneliness, across the threshold and frontier of suffering, intentionally offering those sufferings as a sacrifice in union with Christ to God, for the purpose of entering the world of fatherhood—a world of harmony, communion, and familial love.

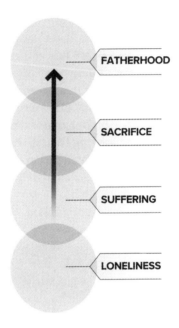

Those men who choose to be selfish, who choose not to sacrifice for their family by being present to them, will, in the end, be alone. But if you transform your sufferings into a sacrifice unto God, you will be surrounded by love. Your fatherhood is the antidote to loneliness. Indeed, "[u]nless a grain of wheat falls to the ground and dies, it remains alone; but if it dies it bears much fruit." Indeed, this is how a father unites his family—in dying to himself his family bears the fruit of communion.

It was St. Joseph who burst free from the world of isolation and loneliness, courageously stepped out on the frontier of fatherly suffering, transformed his sufferings into a sacrifice to God the Father for God His Son, and by doing so, his fatherhood bore the greatest fruit—Jesus the Savior of the world.

SECTION 1: ASSUMING YOUR LOCATION IN GOD'S PLAN [BECOMING THE CUSTOS]

And so it will be with you. By overcoming the sin of loneliness and offering yourself to your family, your fatherhood will bear great fruit—fruit that will endure.

TAKE THE LEAD Over the next several reflections you will discover the true path to glory and the insidious enemy who is determined to drive you from that path. The key to overcoming the enemy and remaining on the path to glory is to become who God has created and destined you to be—truly. This is the moment to make an honest assessment of who you have become. Discern what "masks" you wear to obtain what you desire; the false persona of pretending to be more than you are for fear of being less than others. Realize that this pseudo self appears to be profitable, but in reality, leads you further and further from your destiny, which is glory. Over the next several sessions ask God to strip away the false self and uncover your real self, which is nothing less than a manifestation and revelation of the Father's glory.

YOUR IDENTIFICATION, DESTINATION,
AND GLORIFICATION DISCOVERED IN YOUR VOCATION

16. THE DEVIL'S SIX DARTS

Your fatherly vocation has been divinely designed to enable you to be lifted up (your crucifixion), and by your sacrificial love draw those around you to Christ and His love (your glorification). Your exaltation demands nothing less than a resolute and enduring faith in God. Faith is more than assenting intellectually to a belief or truth. In its deepest essence, faith is trust in another person, ultimately trust in God, and the truth of His identity. Original sin attempts to abolish from our hearts trust in the Father's love ("Original sin then attempts to abolish fatherhood"—St. John Paul II).

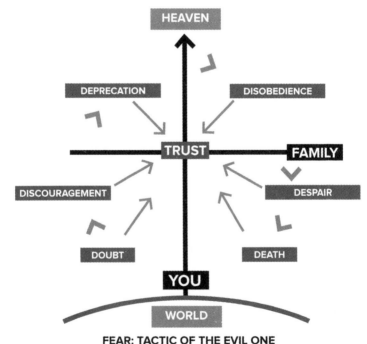

FEAR: TACTIC OF THE EVIL ONE

SECTION 1: ASSUMING YOUR LOCATION IN GOD'S PLAN [BECOMING THE CUSTOS]

For this reason, it is vital that "In all things take up the shield of faith, which you may be able to quench all the fiery darts of the most wicked one" (Eph 6). Again, faith is trust in God, *your* Father, and such trust deflects and extinguishes the fiery darts of the devil and affords you the confidence and freedom to become who you are intended to be: a manifestation and revelation of God's glory.

The evil one assails us with six darts for the purpose of preventing us from being lifted up in sacrificial glory. Theses six darts are: doubt, discouragement, deprecation, disobedience, despair, and ultimately death.

The dart of doubt instills a mistrust of God and lures us into believing that God is neglecting us; that He is distant; that He is against us; that He will not bless us as He blesses others; and that He is the source of our angst, trials, and sufferings.

When we doubt God and His fatherhood we become discouraged; we lose the courage and will to sacrifice, to battle and suffer for something transcendent and greater—such as the salvation of your wife and children—than temporary, illusive fleshly appetites and comforts. After the disease of discouragement lodges itself into our souls we will be tempted to self-deprecate, that is, to think less of ourselves rather than thinking of ourselves less. Self-deprecation manifests itself in behaviors like self-pity; measuring and comparing ourselves to others; saying things to ourselves about ourselves that are not echoing the voice of God. Such self-pity can often convince us to lift ourselves from our desperation by attempting to do something that grants us temporary self-worth. This action is usually expressed in an act of disobedience that is contrary to God's will, such as using women to make us feel more like a man, grasping for more because we feel like we are less, pretending to be someone else because we resent the person we are.

Eventually we wake from our dazed stupor of disobedience and become dejected due to the new awareness of our sins. It is during this moment that the evil one turns on us, rubs our noses in our sinful poop, and attempts to convince us that our sins are unforgivable, for the purpose of leading us into despair. Such despair convinces us to avoid turning to God and instead remain in the depravity of ongoing continual sin. Such despair ultimately leads to the death of the soul.

"Let no man, when he is tempted, say that he is tempted by God. For God is not a tempter of evils, and he tempteth no man; But every man is tempted by his own concupiscence, being drawn away and allured. Then when concupiscence hath conceived, it bringeth forth sin. But sin, when it is completed, begetteth death." (Jas 1:13–16). In other words, the foundation of every sin is mistrust in God's fatherhood instilled by the fiery dart of doubt, which leads to erroneous, misleading desires. But "Blessed is the man who endures trial, for when he stood the test he will receive the crown of life which God has promised to those who love him" (Jas 1:12).

St. Joseph, after discovering his wife, Mary, pregnant without his cooperation, was assailed by the fiery dart of doubt, which initially caused him to withdraw from his fatherly vocation. However, Joseph turned to God, changed his course, and reconciled himself to God and Mary. We also will do well to learn from Joseph how to overcome the dart of doubt and turn in trust to God our Father in time of trial.

> **TAKE THE LEAD** Over the next several reflections you will discover the true path to glory and the insidious enemy who is determined to drive you from that path. The key to overcoming the enemy and remaining on the path to glory is to become who God has created and destined you to be—truly. This is the moment to make an honest assessment of who you have become. Discern what "masks" you wear to obtain what you desire; the false persona of pretending to be more than you are for fear of being less than others. Realize that this pseudo self appears to be profitable, but in reality, leads you further and further from your destiny, which is glory. Over the next several sessions ask God to strip away the false self and uncover your real self, which is nothing less than a manifestation and revelation of the Father's glory.

THE CALL TO FATHERLY GREATNESS

17. THE PARADOX OF POWER

We, as men, desire not only to appear strong, but to be truly powerful. Men attempt to achieve this in a variety of ways. At the bottom of most disordered motives for power is the authentic desire to influence others. Comedians desire to have the power to influence their audience to laugh; actors desire to have the power to entertain and influence their audience to react emotionally. Those with power are influential, and the influential have power. The psalmist, knowing that God was the greatest source of influence in his life, prayed, "O God, you are my God, I seek thee, my soul thirsts for thee; my flesh faints for thee, as in a dry and weary land where no water is. So, I have looked upon you in the sanctuary beholding your glory and power."

Perhaps you desire to be strong and powerful, yet realize, all too well, your weaknesses and deficiencies, and your need for the One Who is more powerful than you to strengthen you.

Perhaps you have longed for God to influence you, guide you, inspire and empower you. Where do you look to see His power and glory for the purpose of being influenced and empowered by Him? The psalmist says that we are to look in the sanctuary of the temple. You and I have been in countless Catholic churches, gazing upon numerous sanctuaries, but have we ever seen God's glory and power? What do we see? A little Host, an apparent piece of bread. How could that be the glory and power that we are seeking? Jesus throughout the centuries has chosen to be little, silent, and hidden. Little, in that He appears to be as small as a piece of bread. Silent, in that his voice is not audibly recognized. Hidden, in that under the species of bread and wine is His body, blood, soul, and divinity. This little, silent, hidden presence is so powerful and influential that over the course of centuries billions of human beings have approached Him, received Him, and in receiving Him, received eternal life.

Like Son, like father. Not one word of the silent, humble father St. Joseph was recorded in Sacred Scripture. His fatherhood was obscure, hidden and virtually unknown to the world. Rather than Joseph being a giant figure in salvation history, he is perhaps considered by some, as insignificant or unimportant to the divine plan. Yet Joseph's silence speaks profoundly of the vital nature of fatherhood. His littleness reflects the greatness of God the Father, and his hiddenness reveals the Father who is in secret. To be little, silent, and hidden is to be vulnerable, welcoming, and attractive. Jesus in the Eucharist is not intimidating but approachable. Joseph's secret fatherhood invites us to approach the Father. This is the paradox of power. A father who uses his power to dominate loses what he has dominion over, but a father who embraces the little, silent, hidden attributes of fatherhood wields a magnetic love over his family that invites and inspires response.

TAKE THE LEAD Every man desires exaltation, glory, greatness. However, few understand the true meaning behind these words. Those who live for the world's definition of glory have by now stopped reading this book. To be glorified is not for the fainthearted. It does not mean that somehow a man muscles up and plays the strongman, the individual who steals the show. The true hero realizes that to be lifted up in glory demands that he lower himself to serve his wife and children. During these sessions, become aware of the needs of your family, and determine ways to serve them.

THE CALL TO FATHERLY GREATNESS

18. WHAT IS GREATNESS?

What is greatness? Is it possible that greatness is actually discovered in littleness? What does it mean to be little, silent, and hidden? It simply means not to be full of self, arrogant, prideful, and self-serving. It simply means to sacrifice in a hidden, secret manner for your family's sake. Many, many fathers look to gain the respect of men to assure them that they have influence and power. However, if we look to men for power and strength, we will disqualify ourselves from receiving the ultimate strength of God. The psalmist says, "It is better to take refuge in God than in men. It is better to trust in God than to trust in princes." Trust in God—not in men—unlocks within us a real, divine power that is liberating.

In our pursuit of the respect of men, we demonstrate that rather than influencing and gaining men's respect, we are conditioned and influenced by men's respect.

Human respect is shifting sand upon which no father should build his house. As one confessor said, "Do not become a street lamp only for your house to go dark." Too often men chase after money, promotions, lauds at work, and acclaim among the people, only to allow the light of Christ to be extinguished in their very own homes. You and I don't need the glory that men can give; for the glory of God has been granted to us in the secret, hidden vocation of fatherhood.

From the earliest age, our children believe us to be the biggest man in their lives; and the greatest lesson they learn is when the biggest man in their lives overcomes vain ambitions and disordered self-serving and instead humbles himself in donation to, and love of, his family. This is your strength and power to influence not only your family; by means of your family you will influence the world.

As our Lord said, "What is hidden will be revealed; what is secret will be made manifest." When we believe this truth, we refrain from being dependent on being noticed and lauded by men, but rather experience the freedom of knowing that when we secretly glorify God, God will glorify us.

God, though infinitely great, was attracted by our littleness, and because of this became small, so that we—learning to be little like Him—would truly participate in His greatness. St. Joseph's little, secret, hidden fatherhood was not revealed by him, but by His Son. So it is with you. Your little, silent, hidden vocation of fatherhood will summon your children to greatness. Yes, your hidden strength and power will be revealed in the end—in your children.

> **TAKE THE LEAD** Every man desires exaltation, glory, greatness. However, few understand the true meaning behind these words. Those who live for the world's definition of glory have by now stopped reading this book. To be glorified is not for the fainthearted. It does not mean that somehow a man muscles up and plays the strongman, the individual who steals the show. The true hero realizes that to be lifted up in glory demands that he lower himself to serve his wife and children. During these sessions, become aware of the needs of your family, and determine ways to serve them.

SECTION 1: ASSUMING YOUR LOCATION IN GOD'S PLAN [BECOMING THE CUSTOS]

THE CALL TO FATHERLY GREATNESS

19. CAN A FATHER BE A SAINT?

The short answer is: yes, a father can be a saint. We know that it is possible, but is it probable? Sometimes we fathers have received an idea that we've not so much been taught as much as caught: that sainthood is for the monks, priests, nuns, religious, scholars, and theologians. Somewhere along the way we've come to believe that marriage, sex, occupations, and children are compromises with the world that have disqualified us from achieving great sanctity. Although many married saints have been canonized, and though there are saints who were also fathers, they are few in comparison to those who lived a celibate life; and among these fatherly saints, even fewer are lauded precisely for their fatherhood. This lack of recognition of the human father initially appears to indicate a great deficiency in fatherhood as a means of pursuing holiness. While it's true that "[h]e who is married is concerned about the things of the world, how he may please his wife, and he is divided" (1 Cor 7:33), the same apostle also said, "Let every man remain in the calling [vocation] in which he was called. If you cannot be free"—that is, not married—"make use of it [marriage] rather" (1 Cor 7:20).

Though marriage and fatherhood appear to be a deficiency or weakness in our pursuit of sainthood, we are called to "make use" of this apparently "weak" vocation for the purpose of achieving this worthy and attainable goal. God assures us, "My grace is sufficient for you, for strength is made perfect in weakness" (2 Cor 12:9). And with St. Paul we can respond, "Gladly therefore I will glory in my infirmities [the vocation of fatherhood] that the strength of God dwell in me.... For when I am weak, then I am strong." By embracing the apparent weakness of fatherhood—that is, it is a vocation that is less effective in making us saints—you will be allowing God to demonstrate His strength in you. He will use your fatherhood as a means to transform not only you, but your wife and your children, into saints.

TAKE THE LEAD Every man desires exaltation, glory, greatness. However, few understand the true meaning behind these words. Those who live for the world's definition of glory have by now stopped reading this book. To be glorified is not for the fainthearted. It does not mean that somehow a man muscles up and plays the strongman, the individual who steals the show. The true hero realizes that to be lifted up in glory demands that he lower himself to serve his wife and children. During these sessions, become aware of the needs of your family, and determine ways to serve them.

SECTION 1: ASSUMING YOUR LOCATION IN GOD'S PLAN [BECOMING THE CUSTOS]

THE CALL TO FATHERLY GREATNESS

20. HOW DOES A FATHER BECOME A SAINT?

Jesus reveals the secrets to becoming a saintly father in two particular verses: "Whoever humbles himself as this little child, he is greatest in the kingdom of heaven. And whoever receives one such child for my sake, receives Me" and "He who receives Me, receives not only Me but the one who sent me." The two foundational actions needed for you to be a saintly father are first, to become a father who becomes a little child by being dependent upon God the Father—precisely in expressing your need to God that He help you provide, protect, teach, and love your family. This childlike trust is the essence of sonship. To be a great father we must first become great sons—little children who trust God their Father. Second, by receiving your child as Christ, you receive Christ in your child and enable your child to receive Christ.

The rewards, which Jesus promises to you for your accomplishing these two fatherly actions, are among the greatest: "Whoever therefore humbles himself as this little child, he is the *greatest* in the kingdom of the heaven." And again, "whoever receives one such child for My sake, *receives Me*." By humbling yourself in these two ways, you will become the greatest in the Kingdom. Despite your "infirmities . . . the strength of God dwell[s] in you."

The two most notable, lauded and glorified saints were both husband and wife, father and mother—Joseph and Mary. By choosing two humble, human, parents as His own, God is proclaiming that your marriage, your fatherhood, the raising of your children, is an essential, proper, and vital path to personal holiness.

Can you be a saint? Yes. By receiving your child as Christ, you will become a father in Christ. By raising your child as Christ, you will become dependent upon God the Father and will become a child in Christ. By becoming a father, little and humble, you will be among the greatest in the kingdom, inheriting God Himself.

TAKE THE LEAD Every man desires exaltation, glory, greatness. However, few understand the true meaning behind these words. Those who live for the world's definition of glory have by now stopped reading this book. To be glorified is not for the fainthearted. It does not mean that somehow a man muscles up and plays the strongman, the individual who steals the show. The true hero realizes that to be lifted up in glory demands that he lower himself to serve his wife and children. During these sessions, become aware of the needs of your family, and determine ways to serve them.

SECTION 1: ASSUMING YOUR LOCATION IN GOD'S PLAN [BECOMING THE CUSTOS]

THE CALL TO FATHERLY GREATNESS

21. FEARING EXALTATION

St. Paul commands us to "Lead a life worthy of the calling you received" (Eph 4:1). The Latin word used in this passage for "life" is actually *vocatione*, meaning "vocation." This indicates that there is a profound connection between your life and your vocation. In fact, your life is discovered in and through your fatherly vocation. If you withdraw or flee from this path, you flee from life itself. The evil one is keenly aware of this and will relentlessly assail you with fear for the purpose of moving you from this path.

On the surface fear appears to be prudence. It encourages us to avoid risk and to play it safe. Prudential fear is good, but not fear that convinces us to avoid short–term suffering and thus lose the long–term gain. Fear is always at odds with the truth. Fear binds us in spiritual paralysis, barring us from achieving and receiving God's glory. God himself says, "My just man liveth by faith; but if he withdraws himself, he shall not please my soul" (Heb 10:38). When we make decisions based on fear and doubt, rather than trust in God, we deflect His blessing. Again, "[w]ithout faith it is impossible to please God" (Heb 11:4).

Truth is never based on fear but always on trust. If fear is driving your decisions, then you are most likely not walking in truth or trust in God. Christ says, "The truth shall set you free" (Jn 8:32). Free from what? Free from slavery to sin and slavery to the devil's intimidation. The key to overcoming fear is to "[p]ut on the mind of Christ;" to know the truth concerning God's mission for us as fathers.

Truth inculcates trust in God. You and I will encounter our greatest sufferings in our attempt to overcome fear. Jesus' agony in the garden, His sweating of blood, testifies to the intensity of the battle to overcome the fear imposed by the evil one and to trust in God and His plan.

The world continuously instills fears of not having enough financial security, of not belonging, of not obtaining the heights of pleasure, of not being comfortable. The world goads us with the fear of "not having enough," which compels us to desire for "more than we need." By acting in this way we become increasingly attached to the world, selfishly hoarding gifts for fear that we could lose them.

By overcoming attachment to sexual intimacy and committing himself to a celibate marriage; by overcoming attachment to homes and lands in Nazareth and Bethlehem; by overcoming attachment to material riches for the purpose of making room for the riches contained in the poverty of Christ, St. Joseph overcame his fear of inadequacy and insecurity. Joseph trusted the Lord, and because of this God has exalted him as head of the Holy Family, patron of the Church, and exemplar of all fathers.

God also desires to exalt you, but it will demand you overcome your fears and become the father that God has created and destined you to be.

TAKE THE LEAD Every man desires exaltation, glory, greatness. However, few understand the true meaning behind these words. Those who live for the world's definition of glory have by now stopped reading this book. To be glorified is not for the fainthearted. It does not mean that somehow a man muscles up and plays the strongman, the individual who steals the show. The true hero realizes that to be lifted up in glory demands that he lower himself to serve his wife and children. During these sessions, become aware of the needs of your family, and determine ways to serve them.

SECTION 1: ASSUMING YOUR LOCATION IN GOD'S PLAN [BECOMING THE CUSTOS]

THE CALL TO FATHERLY GREATNESS

22. DOES GOD DESIRE TO EXALT YOU?

Have you ever considered that it is God's will and intention to exalt you? Yes, God desires to exalt you. God demonstrated this in Christ who said, "When the Son of man is lifted up, He will draw all men to Himself." The Greek word for "lifted up," *hypsoō*—used by Jesus on three occasions (John 3, 8, 12)—can be interpreted as being lifted up from the earth—as in being crucified; or being lifted up in exaltation. The fact that Jesus uses the word interchangeably indicates that He equates His Crucifixion with His exaltation.

The lesson that Christ is teaching demands a radical mind shift: our exaltation will only occur if we are lifted up, *hypsoō*, from slavishly being chained to comforts and disordered attachments. God desires to lift you up from the world for the purpose of making of you a holy spectacle who will magnetically draw your family, friends, and even your enemies to Christ's love. There exists a direct correlation between the level of your sacrificial love and the level of your exaltation. Therefore you must fight to overcome fear by having the mind of Christ; to know, believe, and reaffirm the truth that God desires to *hypsoō* you, to exalt you.

The Father eternally loves us and desires to exalt us as He glorified St. Joseph and as He ultimately exalted Jesus the son of Joseph. Notice that in order for Jesus to be lifted up—*hypsoō*—He became very, very small. And frankly, isn't that what we are afraid of?—being unnoticed, unimportant, little, silent, and hidden. This is the enduring example Jesus gives us—not only by becoming a babe in the womb of Mary, but also by being present in the Eucharist, where He is truly little: little enough to enter into you. He is truly silent: He quietly listens to you without saying a word. He is truly hidden: He is often unnoticed even as He is elevated on our altars.

The key to Jesus' glory, the secret to becoming a great father like St. Joseph, the way to become a man of glory, is a great paradox: the lower you go, the more God will *hypsoō* you—lift you up—and in the end exalt you.

TAKE THE LEAD Every man desires exaltation, glory, greatness. However, few understand the true meaning behind these words. Those who live for the world's definition of glory have by now stopped reading this book. To be glorified is not for the fainthearted. It does not mean that somehow a man muscles up and plays the strongman, the individual who steals the show. The true hero realizes that to be lifted up in glory demands that he lower himself to serve his wife and children. During these sessions, become aware of the needs of your family, and determine ways to serve them.

SECTION 1: ASSUMING YOUR LOCATION IN GOD'S PLAN [BECOMING THE CUSTOS]

WHERE YOU ARE NOW

23. THE FINAL BATTLE

Sister Lucia, who witnessed the apparitions of Our Lady of Fatima, said, "The final confrontation between our Lord and Satan will be over family and marriage." It was Lucia, who on May 13, 1917, at age ten, saw a vision of a great Lady who pointed to the sky saying, "I have come from Heaven. I have come to ask you to come here for six months on the thirteenth day of the month at this hour." During the Lady's fifth apparition, she said, "In October . . . St. Joseph will appear with the Child Jesus to bless the world." She also promised that during the sixth apparition in October she would perform a miracle for all to see.

On October 13, the three children, along with approximately seventy thousand pilgrims, gathered at the Cova da Iria outside the village of Fatima, Portugal, amidst heavy rainfall that drenched the onlookers and made the ground a muddy mess. During the apparition, which lasted ten minutes, the sun began to spin wildly, zigzagging across the sky, and then proceeded to dart down upon the crowd. The onlookers were so terrified that many of them screamed with alarm, "We are going to be killed!" Others began confessing their sins aloud, begging for God's mercy. Simultaneously, the three visionaries were in an ecstatic vision, wherein Our Lady revealed St. Joseph and the Child Jesus blessing the world. It was precisely at this moment of the blessing of Jesus and Joseph that the sun ceased its radical descent and returned to its proper place in the sky. The secular newspapers attested to the miraculous nature of the event. After the apparition was over, the muddy field and the pilgrims' clothing, which had been soaked, were now completely dry.

It appears that Our Lady revealed the manner in which the world would avoid degeneration, disaster, and war. What is the remedy? The message of Our Lady of Fatima is: "In the end, my Immaculate Heart will triumph." How will Our Lady's Immaculate Heart triumph? Our Lady is directing us to the solution: "Go to Joseph, what he says to you, do" (Gen 41:55). When fathers turn their attention to St. Joseph, and His relationship with Mary, his wife, and Jesus, his son, they will learn what it means to be fathers who beget spiritual life in the people around them. Mary is saying, in a sense, "I'm not enough. The world needs Joseph as well, because the world needs fathers like Joseph."

Recall the words of God, "And he shall turn the hearts of fathers to the children and the hearts of children to their fathers; lest I come and smite the earth with a curse." God is giving us the key to avoiding nuclear disaster; the solution for world peace; the key to saving souls from permanent anguish and loneliness: Fathers, turn your hearts, souls, and minds toward the filial relationship of Joseph and Jesus, and Joseph and Mary, and learn from him and embody his example of what it means to assume your charitable authority to lead by embracing the woman and the child.

The conversion of the world, the renewal of the Church, the restoration of marriage and the family will occur when men like you, who are both husband and father, turn to the just man Joseph and learn how to embody God the Father's love and how to transmit this gaze of love to their children.

St. Joseph blessing the world in union with Jesus demonstrates his patriarchal, fatherly right to bless, and that this right to bless is confirmed by the Son of God. This means that you also, like Joseph, are ordained by God, as father and priest of your family, to bless and transmit God's favor to your wife and children. Blessed Isidore of St. Joseph said, "The victory bell will sound in the Church when the faithful recognize the sanctity of St. Joseph." How will the faithful recognize the sanctity of St. Joseph? When you and I begin to embody his timeless wisdom and ageless example.

> **TAKE THE LEAD** The word authority sounds negative, antiquated, and domineering. Yet, authority and leadership are two sides of the same coin. To lead one must have authority; and to use authority one must lead. If we reject authority, we reject leadership. If society lacks true leaders, society lacks truth. St. Joseph is the quintessential father-leader who exercised his authority humbly yet powerfully over the Holy Family. Over the next several reflections, entrust your office of authority to St. Joseph, pray to him daily asking him to empower you with the ability to "write the story of God's glory" in the lives of your wife and children.

SECTION 1: ASSUMING YOUR LOCATION IN GOD'S PLAN [BECOMING THE CUSTOS]

WHERE YOU ARE NOW

24. WHAT CAN ONE MAN DO?

Have you ever heard someone say in reaction to the current cultural crises, international wars, poverty and famine, dismal moral standards, the degeneration of marriage and the family, or other significant challenges, "What can one man do?" That question brings to mind the account of the Old Testament patriarch Joseph, the favorite son of Jacob, whose brothers grew exceedingly jealous, selling him to a group of nomadic gum traders, who in turn sold him as a slave to the Egyptians.

While in Egypt, in prison, Joseph was summoned to interpret Pharaoh's dream, which he did accurately. Pharaoh's dream foretold that the world would benefit from seven years of bountiful, fruitful harvest, which would be followed by seven years of famine.

Because of Joseph's ability to interpret Pharaoh's dream, Pharaoh granted Joseph authority over all of Egypt, and made him master of his household, second only to Pharaoh himself. During the seven years of plenty, Joseph had his people gather grain and retain the harvest in Egyptian storehouses for the purpose of preparing for the foretold famine. When the famine struck the land, the inhabitants of the Middle Eastern world turned to Egypt and its Pharaoh, who directed the people to "[g]o to Joseph; what he says to you do." It was from Joseph that the people obtained grain for the purpose of making bread for themselves and their families, and thus were spared from starvation.

God, through one man, saved the world.

Today, much like during the epoch of the Old Testament Joseph, son of Jacob, there exists a famine—the famine of fatherhood. Wives and children, our Church and parish communities, are starving for authentic leadership. To whom should we turn to obtain spiritual food, that is, the spiritual leadership that will feed our families? As Jesus put it: "'Who then is the faithful and wise servant, whom his master has set *over his household*, to *give them their food* at the proper time? Blessed is that servant whom his master when he comes will find so doing. Truly I say to you, he will set him *over all his possessions.*"

The New Testament Joseph, son of Jacob, is the just man, the faithful servant who was placed by God over the Master's—that is, Jesus' household. Truly, it was Joseph's duty and responsibility as head of the Holy Family to give Mary and Jesus "bread at the proper time," to protect, feed, and teach them. Joseph brought the grain of Jesus into his storehouse in Nazareth, raising Him to be the sacrificial bread that feeds and saves our spiritually starving world.

What can one man do? By embracing his identity as husband of the Mother of God and father of the Son of God, Joseph became the savior of the Savior; the teacher of the Teacher; the master of the Master; the king of the King of kings; one who fed bread to the Bread of Life and from this Bread we all receive life. One man, with God, can change the world. Joseph's fatherly identity led him to his ultimate destiny. Joseph's fatherhood leads us also to God's fatherhood.

And what about you? Do you believe that you, one man, can change the world? With God all things are possible. If you allow Joseph to be "Master of your household," by means of His intercession and by following His persevering example you can become a true man, faithful husband, fearless father, and heroic leader who changes the course of history by leading your family to their destiny.

Just as St. Joseph was placed over his household as head and leader, so also you have been called to be over your household as protector, provider, teacher, and leader. "Go to Joseph, and what he says [by his example], you do."

> **TAKE THE LEAD** The word authority sounds negative, antiquated, and domineering. Yet, authority and leadership are two sides of the same coin. To lead one must have authority; and to use authority one must lead. If we reject authority, we reject leadership. If society lacks true leaders, society lacks truth. St. Joseph is the quintessential father-leader who exercised his authority humbly yet powerfully over the Holy Family. Over the next several reflections, entrust your office of authority to St. Joseph, pray to him daily asking him to empower you with the ability to "write the story of God's glory" in the lives of your wife and children.

SECTION 1: ASSUMING YOUR LOCATION IN GOD'S PLAN [BECOMING THE CUSTOS]

WHERE YOU ARE NOW

25. THE FOUR THINGS THAT EVERY SUCCESSFUL FATHER DOES

Some of the most secure and strong things in our world have four points of contact with the ground. Consider that animals usually have four legs; automobiles rest on four tires; building foundations usually consist of four walls; tables and chairs have four legs; even the New Testament has four Gospels. And so it is with every great father. If you are to become the man, husband, father, and leader that God has created and destined you to be, your fatherhood should consist of the four pillars that constitute St. Joseph's spirituality: first, *learn to listen* to the voice of God by embracing the silence; second, *embrace your essence*, which is to set the pace of self–giving love by defeating lust in the heart and remaining yoked to your wife by bearing her burdens as your own; third, *assume your authority* to lead by loving and love by leading; and fourth, *discover the disciple* in your child by embracing your child as Christ so that your child will embrace Christ. Before we examine each of these individually and in depth, it is imperative that we understand our charitable authority.

If there is none to lead, none will follow. If you do not lead your family from evil, evil will lead your family. In fact, Jesus said, "Strike the shepherd and the sheep of the flock will scatter." If you, the shepherd, are struck down by evil, your family will most likely be scattered.

St. Augustine, during one of his famous homilies, addressed the fathers in his audience, saying, "Fulfill my office in your home." He was speaking of his office of bishop. "Bishop" actually means supervisor. "Supervisor" is comprised of the words *super*, which means above, and *visor*, which is related to the word "vision." In other words, you as a father are called to have and transmit a vision of God's glory, of heaven—the goal of our faith—to your wife and children.

God's glory is His essence, and His essence is eternal self–giving love. Recall that God is three divine persons who are essentially one in self-giving love. From this communion of persons is an explosion of life, love, bliss, ecstasy, joy, creativity, power, and vitality that spills over in the act of creating creation, flooding it with His love. In the Trinity, the Father is the principal, the initiator, that sets in motion God's love for the human family. As the Father is the principal in the Trinity, you are the principal of your family, who sets in motion the glory of God's self-giving love. Your family is called to be a vessel of life and love that spills over into this fallen world, offering hope that there is something greater than selfishness and sin.

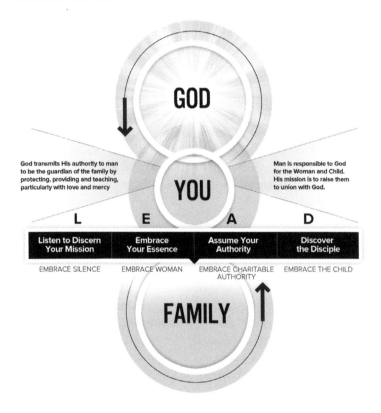

SECTION 1: ASSUMING YOUR LOCATION IN GOD'S PLAN [BECOMING THE CUSTOS]

As bishop and shepherd (pastor) of your family, you are called to use your charitable authority to communicate this incredible vision of self-giving love to your family. The Latin word for authority is *auctoritas*, and is derived from the root word *auctor*, which means "author." Charity simply means love. God has given you the noble honor and responsibility to write the story of God's glory in your family's life—the story of God's self-giving love. To effectively write this story you will need to exercise your charitable authority by protecting, providing for, and teaching by your example and your word.

Consider that Joseph was called to be "head of the Holy Family" (see Litany of St. Joseph) by being the husband of Mary, full of grace, and the father of Jesus, full of grace and truth. Joseph was divinely ordained to lead two sinless individuals despite his being the least perfect member of his family. Joseph's example helps us to understand that God does not call the qualified, but rather He qualifies the called. God has called and appointed you to be the bishop, pastor, and author—even if you may believe yourself to be the least qualified member of your family—to initiate the dynamic of self-giving love in your family. By doing so, the vision you communicate, which will be nothing less than the "super vision" of God's glory, will be reflected and relived in your family.

TAKE THE LEAD The word authority sounds negative, antiquated, and domineering. Yet, authority and leadership are two sides of the same coin. To lead one must have authority; and to use authority one must lead. If we reject authority, we reject leadership. If society lacks true leaders, society lacks truth. St. Joseph is the quintessential father-leader who exercised his authority humbly yet powerfully over the Holy Family. Over the next several reflections, entrust your office of authority to St. Joseph, pray to him daily asking him to empower you with the ability to "write the story of God's glory" in the lives of your wife and children.

SECTION 2

LIVING YOUR VOCATION

[The Four Pillars]

TODAY'S FATHER NEEDS TO KNOW THAT HE TOO HAS A SPECIFIC CHARISM, A SPIRITUALITY AND RULE OF LIFE THAT IF FOLLOWED WILL AID HIM IN BECOMING A MAN OF GLORY. ST. JOSEPH'S SPIRITUALITY, SUMMED UP IN THE WORDS "LOCATION" AND "VOCATION," WILL PLAY ITS PART IN THE CONVERSION OF THE NATIONS.

PILLAR 1

LISTEN TO DISCERN YOUR MISSION

[Embracing Silence]

GOD ASKS EACH OF US "WHERE ARE YOU?" THIS IS THE PERENNIAL QUESTION THAT HAUNTS THE DEEP SUBCONSCIOUS RECESSES OF MAN'S HEART. THE ANSWER TO THIS QUESTION DETERMINES EACH MAN'S LOCATION IN GOD'S PLAN OF SALVATION, HIS VOCATIONAL MISSION—THE VERY FOUNDATION OF THE SPIRITUALITY OF FATHERHOOD.

PILLAR 1: LISTENING TO DISCERN YOUR MISSION [EMBRACING SILENCE]

SILENCE IN YOURSELF

26. THE FIRST MARK OF A GREAT FATHER

Have you ever wondered, "What can I do to be a better man? How can I become a father who leaves a legacy? What is the secret to becoming the man that God has created me to be?" Often men who have been doing the "Church thing" for years become discouraged because they see little spiritual growth or positive character progress shaping their lives. We can fall into the trap of believing that by going to Sunday Mass, listening to Christian music, being on Church committees, or praying an Our Father, Hail Mary, and Glory Be, that we are fulfilling our Christian duty—and because of this, our life should be more blessed than it is.

Of course, Holy Mass, acts of charity, serving Christ's Church, and praying are essential to becoming a great man. But why, even after doing all these things, do we struggle to improve spiritually?

One of the most fundamental reasons that we stall spiritually is that we succumb to the temptation to focus on the letter of the law while we neglect the spirit of love. We can easily fulfill exterior duties while neglecting the interior soul.

Sometimes we pray but don't listen. We may pray "God give me this," or "God grant me that," but when was the last time we prayed "God give me You?" When we exclusively pray to obtain things, we are, in a sense, fulfilling the letter of the law—yes, we are praying. Yet when we pray to obtain God Himself, we are fulfilling the spirit of the law, since the very purpose of prayer is to be with God.

It's been said that we have two ears and one mouth, therefore we ought to listen twice as much as we talk. And when in the presence of someone more intelligent and knowledgeable, we definitely should listen more than speak. These statements apply to our relationship with God. Rather than fulfilling the law of prayer by only reciting prayers or requests, we ought to fulfill the love of prayer by listening to God.

Archbishop Fulton Sheen said, "Those who would become wise must become silent. A mirror is silent, yet it reflects forests, sunsets, flowers, and faces. Great ascetic souls, given to years of meditation, have taken on a radiance and beauty which are beyond the outlines of the face. They seem to reflect, like the mirror on the outside, the Christ they bear within. Silence alone gives them inner sanctuary in which solitude is born. A place where the soul stands naked before God."

If you and I desire to reflect the power, goodness, strength, and generosity of the Father, it is imperative that we dedicate ourselves to simply being in the presence of God, waiting on Him to give Himself to us. Ask yourself: When was the last time I spent fifteen minutes with God in silence? Your answer reveals how much you desire and believe in God's power afforded by prayer.

Prayer is much like being in the sun. If you simply expose yourself to the sun, your skin will eventually tan and those around will know that you've spent time in the sun. When we spend time with the Son of God, others cannot help but notice that we are becoming a reflection of His glory.

PILLAR 1: LISTENING TO DISCERN YOUR MISSION [EMBRACING SILENCE]

The first mark of a great father is being a man dedicated to remaining in the silence before God with the purpose of reflecting his Fatherhood in our own.

> **TAKE THE LEAD** One of the greatest challenges for men is to carve space into their oversaturated schedule and make time for God. And that is one of the main reasons why so many men are highly ineffective in changing the world for the better, living a fulfilled life, and winning souls for God. Over the next several reflections, simply commit yourself to carving out that sacred time each day for God. Hint: Make your meeting with God the same time every day.*

* See Examen *Silence in Self* on page 444

SILENCE IN YOURSELF

27. PICKING UP MIXED SIGNALS

You and I are like soldiers on the battlefield who have the difficult task of deciphering the real message—the divine message of our mission—being transmitted among the many mixed signals. Whose voice, whose message are we receiving—our divine commander's, or our enemy's? It is imperative that we become capable of sifting through the messages and discerning the *Vox* of the divine commander.

To receive God's message and carry it out, it is essential that we embrace periods of silence throughout the day for the purpose of intentionally listening to God and discerning His voice in our hearts. Carving out time for silence and embracing silence is becoming exceedingly difficult for modern man. The enemy is bent on keeping you from the silence. Consider the constant assault on our beings. Whether we are at the grocery store, or a restaurant, gas station, or in our car, music, television, and smartphones bombard us and invade us with countless messages, robbing us of our ability to hear and discern God's voice.

The enemy tempts us to turn on the radio when we are in the car, to have the television continually running in the background, to check and send emails and texts, all in order to fill us with something other than God. The evil one is satisfied with giving us "good things" as long as those good things keep us from the "greatest thing"—communion with God. The evil one is bent on keeping our minds occupied, racing, concerned; he lures us to be busy to distract us from hearing the *Vox* of God that will reveal God's mission, vision, and plan for your life. As Thomas Merton said, "The biggest disease in North America is busyness."

You and I have a choice. We can listen to the voice of the devil, which has saturated most of today's technological mediums, and become like him: a weak, selfish, restless, anxious, manipulative, uncontrolled user; or we can regularly enter silence before God, and become like Him, reflecting His power, beauty, strength, mercy, and wisdom.

PILLAR 1: LISTENING TO DISCERN YOUR MISSION [EMBRACING SILENCE]

Perhaps you are thinking: What do I do while I am in silence? Scripture notes that St. Joseph turned aside and considered the matter of Mary's pregnancy. In other words, he entered the silence and presented himself to the Lord. This is Joseph's first step to his call to fatherly greatness. Joseph simply stopped what he was doing and placed himself in God's presence and *remained there*. He didn't bombard God with a host of requests or a litany of empty words. He trustingly waited on the Lord, believing that God would direct his life. And God did.

St. John Vianney noticed that a peasant farmer would silently sit in his church each morning for an extended time. The Curé of Ars asked him what he was doing and the peasant responded, "I don't say anything to God, I just sit and look at Him and He looks at me." This is our first step to fatherly greatness: to be courageous enough to simply stop, look at Him, and listen, and believe that He will speak and direct our lives to glory.

> **TAKE THE LEAD** One of the greatest challenges for men is to carve space into their oversaturated schedule and make time for God. And that is one of the main reasons why so many men are highly ineffective in changing the world for the better, living a fulfilled life, and winning souls for God. Over the next several reflections, simply commit yourself to carving out that sacred time each day for God. Hint: Make your meeting with God the same time every day.*

---

* See Examen *Silence in Self* on page 444

SILENCE IN YOURSELF

28. FINDING YOUR WAY HOME

Salmon are defined as being anadromous, that is, they are fish that swim upstream. Annually, thousands upon thousands of salmon, after living in the ocean, reaching full maturity, and accumulating full body mass, migrate upstream to return to their place of origin. The human person, like a salmon, is programmed by God to swim upward to return to his origin.

God creates everything by the power of His Word. God created the universe, the solar systems, seas, stars, the human person—his mind, his heart—by means of His Word. Through His Word, God thought, willed, and spoke you into existence for a particular purpose: to be an expression, a manifestation, a revelation of His glory to those around you, while also achieving your destiny: full communion and eternal union with God.

But before God sealed you for delivery into this world, He whispered His Word, His Voice, into you. This divine Word is sealed within us. It is hardwired, programmed into us. This Word is your origin and your destiny. As mentioned previously, the Latin word from which we derive the word vocation is *vox,* which means "voice." It is this *Vox* of God, this call, that defines your vocation, your identity, your existence, and your call to greatness. This *Vox* may haunt you, but it will never leave you. This voice within will chase after you, while calling you to chase after it.

The Word whispers in your soul. It speaks of your mission, your call to glory. The *Vox* is subtle, gentle, soft, and easily crowded out by the clamoring of the world and its responsibilities, allurements, unneeded needs, and incessant demands and concerns. The Word of God, as powerful as it is, doesn't bang against us, force itself upon us, or barge into our personal freedom (see 1 Kings 19:11–13). The Word, which is outside of us, is always speaking to us from within us—if only we would stop, turn toward Him, and listen. From the moment of your conception and throughout your life to this very day, the Word continues to whisper His voice into your soul. The primary context in which you will hear the Word is in and amidst your vocation.

It is this voice, this vocation that calls you to run upward to return to your origin. Unfortunately, by doing so, like the salmon, which become easy prey during their migration, so also do we land squarely in the evil one's crosshairs. It is precisely in the midst of our vocational path that the evil one stands, poised and ready to intimidate us, always striving to instill doubts and feelings of inadequacy and insecurity within us. The devil's desire is that you flee, withdraw, neglect, resent, or altogether reject your vocation—because if you do, you will have great difficulty hearing the *Vox*, and fail to fulfill your mission of achieving your identity, which ultimately leads you and your family to their destiny.

> **TAKE THE LEAD** One of the greatest challenges for men is to carve space into their oversaturated schedule and make time for God. And that is one of the main reasons why so many men are highly ineffective in changing the world for the better, living a fulfilled life, and winning souls for God. Over the next several reflections, simply commit yourself to carving out that sacred time each day for God. Hint: Make your meeting with God the same time every day.*

* See Examen *Silence in Self* on page 444

THE BATTLE TO TRUST THE FATHER

29. ARE YOU SHOWING UP FOR BATTLE?

The evil one is waging war on our families, our wives, our children in hopes of robbing from them eternal salvation, and the battleground is our prayer life. Most men, however, rarely show up for battle and consequently lose the fight even before it begins.

The human father is the man who can lead the charge in winning the war. Unfortunately, many fathers are not aware of the primary battlefield.

Consider that only one third of devoted Catholic men pray daily, and for most of them their prayer consists of a rapidly recited "Bless us, O Lord, and these thy gifts." Again, most of us are not showing up for battle.

Prayer is a battle because it demands trust—trust that God will be present, that God will speak and infuse Himself—His power to overcome the world—into our souls. Yet the normal condition for God to make Himself present to us is that we are willing to be present to God. The essence of a true son is his trust in the Father, and to become great fathers we must first become great sons who trust in the greatest Father. This trust is expressed by faithfulness to consistent prayer.

Why is this important? Because "[w]ithout faith, it is impossible to please God" (Heb 11:4). Faith, that is, trust in God, is the foundation of our relationship with Him. Faith unfetters our soul, affording us the possibility to receive his grace and power. Without such trust, we are simply working alone—without God; and as Christ tells us, "Without Me, you can do nothing."

St. Joseph was truly a son of the Father, for he continually trusted in God as proved by his repeated turning to God in prayer. Joseph's trust in God enabled him to become a trusting son of the Father who became capable of being a father to the Son of God. St. Joseph's trust in the Father allowed him to hear God's message through an angel, which led him to his origin and destiny. So it will be with us, if we follow his example and become determined to present ourselves to the God who desires to present Himself to us.

TAKE THE LEAD The fundamental component of any relationship is trust. Without trust there exists no relationship. Over the next several reflections we will be examining the essence of sonship, which is trust in God the Father. Begin to identity those aspects of your life that cause you fear, anxiety, depression, anger, and frustration. You will discover that at the bottom of each of these sentiments is a lack of trust in God. Throughout your day, when you encounter these doubts, turn to the Father and say, "Abba, I trust in you. You can do all things, even in me, a sinner."*

* See Examen *Silence in Self* on page 444

THE BATTLE TO TRUST THE FATHER

30. POOP IN THE BROWNIE

Have you heard someone describe an attractive idea that contains mostly truth, but a little untruth, as having a "little poop in the brownie"? "Oh, the brownies are soooo good, even if there is a little poop in them." Nobody likes poop in their brownies, and no one likes being duped into believing an attractive truth, only to discover later that it is a lie.

Often we are tempted to believe that God is absent, uncaring, or even desires that we be miserable. This temptation can become particularly strong after we sin, fall from grace, and damage our relationship with God and His Son. This guilt tends to haunt us and secretly accuse us. In fact, at a very subconscious level, we may believe that because of our sins, God is not really for us, and that He doesn't want us to succeed, or be happy, or experience pleasure, or that He wants to make our lives miserable.

But when we are feeling like this, we can be thankful and trust that God the Father sacrificed His Son so that we don't have to experience His disfavor. Right?

Wrong.

This is the attractive "truth" that we have not been taught as much as we have caught. This is a big, fat, demonic lie. This is the poop in the brownie. We may not have been taught the idea that God the Father sacrificed His Son, but we have caught this idea, and it has slithered its way into the deep subconscious of our souls. Perhaps the reason so many men believe that God is against them is because they believe that God killed His own Son, and if He is willing to kill His own Son, what is stopping Him from destroying us?

God the Father, however, did not kill His own Son. We did. Our sins cost Him His life. God's intention is to heal our woundedness, and He accomplishes this by becoming the most wounded—the crucified Son, whose love we can trust. It was not God who killed the Son, but rather the evil one, through man, who killed the Son. God the Son freely offered Himself to God the Father on behalf of men, so that men would be empowered by His grace to freely offer themselves to God the Father.

Why does this matter? The truth regarding God the Father's character sets us fathers free to live in His image. When a father begins to have confidence and trust in the Father, God's power begins to animate his life.

When you believe that God is not against you, but relentlessly for you, that confidence cannot help but to inspire you to reflect His benevolence to your own children.

> **TAKE THE LEAD** The fundamental component of any relationship is trust. Without trust there exists no relationship. Over the next several reflections we will be examining the essence of sonship, which is trust in God the Father. Begin to identity those aspects of your life that cause you fear, anxiety, depression, anger, and frustration. You will discover that at the bottom of each of these sentiments is a lack of trust in God. Throughout your day, when you encounter these doubts, turn to the Father and say, "Abba, I trust in you. You can do all things, even in me, a sinner."*

* See Examen *Silence in Self* on page 444

THE BATTLE TO TRUST THE FATHER

31. THE WORD AND THE WOUND

Do you feel as though God is against you becoming successful or attaining glory? In the beginning, God gave our first parents dominion over and access to all things, with the exception of the fruit of the tree of knowledge of good and evil. From this we learn that God the Father is generous and wills for us to have all that He has.

But in order to give us the choice to freely receive His divine generosity, He gave us an option: to love God as He loves us, or to love ourselves above God. Without this freedom to choose love, God would be coercing us into loving Him. But God does not force us to do anything, just as He did not force His Son to offer His life. God simply gives us the freedom to choose to love.

But we voted, and we lost the election. We chose selfishness instead of selflessness. We chose slavery to sin instead of freedom to love; we chose to make ourselves god rather than allow God to make us like Him. The serpent tempted the woman saying, "You will not die. For God knows that when you eat of it your eyes will be opened, and you will be like God, knowing good and evil" (Gen 3:4–5).

It was in that moment that Satan cut deep into the heart of the human person, inflicting the ever-haunting father wound. Satan attempts to convince us, as he did our first parents, that God doesn't want us to succeed. As Pope St. John Paul II said, "Original sin, then, attempts to abolish fatherhood." When we believe that God is set on undermining our desire to be glorified, we fall prey to the evil one's deception that God is against us. Ironically, St. Paul tells us, "For this purpose [God] also called you by our preaching *to gain the glory of our Lord Jesus Christ*" (2 Thess 2:14, emphasis added). God's intention and desire is to share His glory with us. It is the evil one who plants within our wounded hearts the seed of the lie that God is against us.

This is the real, original father wound. This is precisely the satanic agenda. Interestingly, it is God's agenda that we "shall be like Him" (1 John 3:2).

To defeat the evil one we must strive to overcome the father wound and the doubt and discouragement that it causes. We need the Word to heal the wound. The primary and best way to hear the Word and heal the wound is to embrace silence and train ourselves, like St. Joseph, to hear the *Vox*. Ironically, more trust is given to the one who trusts God enough to enter the silence.

> **TAKE THE LEAD** The fundamental component of any relationship is trust. Without trust there exists no relationship. Over the next several reflections we will be examining the essence of sonship, which is trust in God the Father. Begin to identity those aspects of your life that cause you fear, anxiety, depression, anger, and frustration. You will discover that at the bottom of each of these sentiments is a lack of trust in God. Throughout your day, when you encounter these doubts, turn to the Father and say, "Abba, I trust in you. You can do all things, even in me, a sinner."*

* See Examen *Silence in Self* on page 444

THE BATTLE TO TRUST THE FATHER

32. DO YOU LIMIT GOD?

If you could have any spiritual gift—besides love—what would it be? As great as the spiritual gifts are, without peace, none of them can be enjoyed truly. It is no coincidence that after Jesus' Resurrection, His first statement to His disciples was not "Money be with you," "Success be with you," "Love be with you," but rather, "Peace be with you."

It is very common for people who, from the world's perspective, have "everything," to be anxious, worried, and filled with unrest. Why do these people lack peace?

Peace demonstrates that despite the anxieties and afflictions that batter and assail a man, he remains confident in God, and the person God has created him to be. As Mother Teresa said, "The fruit of silence is prayer, the fruit of prayer is faith, the fruit of faith is love, the fruit of love is service, the fruit of service is peace." Notice that peace begins with silence in prayer.

The enemy will assault you, distract you, overwhelm you with an urgency to be doing something, anything—even good things—with the purpose of keeping you from prayer. Neglecting or avoiding prayer, in the long run, robs you of peace. As Pope Francis said, "The most frequent lament of Christians is 'I should pray more . . . I would like to, but often lack the time.'" Does this sound familiar? We easily forget that when we resist entering the silence and listening to God we are actually resisting a life of peace.

By not entering the silence and intentionally listening for God's direction, we will struggle to become confident, resilient, unshakable men who are capable of transmitting peace to our families. If you are not praying and entering silence consistently, you are spinning your wheels spiritually. Our Lord promised, "Seek ye first, the kingdom of God and all these things will be granted to you besides" (Mt 6:33) If you enter silence, seek God in prayer, and apply yourself to listening to Him, all things will be granted to you.

Often, however, we limit God, and doubt that He will grant "all" things to us. We tend to restrain God's generosity by not trusting in

Him; and we—knowingly or unknowingly—express this distrust by neglecting to be silent before Him, attentively gazing upon and listening to Him.

This gaze of "loving attention" (St. Teresa of Avila) will afford you one of the greatest gifts that God can bestow: peace. What is this gaze of loving attention? This is the key to the success of the mystics' and contemplatives' prayer lives: They believe that God is present before them, and in them; and they spend a large portion of their prayer time gazing (spiritually) attentively upon that holy presence.

Perplexed by his wife's virginal pregnancy, St. Joseph entered the silence and presented his dilemma to God. Notice that Scripture states that the angel appeared to Joseph in a dream, and after he awoke he did all that the angel had commanded him (see Matt 1). The point is that Joseph's trust in God the Father was so profound that he became capable of resting in God, and therefore was at peace. It was in that state of peace and trust that he received divine guidance regarding his vocation. It appears that even amidst what was a difficult situation, Joseph was able to "rest in peace."

So it will be with you and me. If we trust God the Father enough to enter the silence before Him, the waves of life's anxieties and stressors will wash away, and we will arise with a renewed confidence in God that will make us fathers of peace.

> **TAKE THE LEAD** The fundamental component of any relationship is trust. Without trust there exists no relationship. Over the next several reflections we will be examining the essence of sonship, which is trust in God the Father. Begin to identity those aspects of your life that cause you fear, anxiety, depression, anger, and frustration. You will discover that at the bottom of each of these sentiments is a lack of trust in God. Throughout your day, when you encounter these doubts, turn to the Father and say, "Abba, I trust in you. You can do all things, even in me, a sinner."*

* See Examen *Silence in Self* on page 444

THE BATTLE TO TRUST THE FATHER

33. BECOMING A RESERVOIR OF GRACE

A husband cannot give to his wife and his children what he does not possess. We cannot transmit Christ's presence if we neglect to be in the presence of Christ; for in Christ's presence we discern Christ present within us and in those around us. God always desires to give us His presence, but to "make room" for that generous gift, it is essential that we carve out time and space to listen attentively to the Word of the Father.

To know who we are—to know God's mission, vision, and plan for our lives—we must know God. To know God, we must speak His language, and to paraphrase St. John of the Cross, God's first language is silence.

It is in the silence that God speaks and without sound that His voice is heard. As the psalmist says of God, "Sacrifice and offering you do not desire; but you have given me an open ear" (Ps 40:6). This message is confirmed by the fact that Christ's public ministry began and ended with miracles pertaining to the act of listening. At the wedding of Cana, where Christ performed His first miracle by transforming water into wine, Mary told the servants, "Do whatever He tells you" (John 2:5). God the Father, on numerous occasions in the Gospel accounts, commands us: "Listen to Him." Can there be any doubt that one of the most important things we can ever do is to listen to God?

The last miracle of Christ's public ministry occurred after Peter cut off the ear of Malchus, the high priest's slave. Jesus restored Malchus's ear. The message is clear: God desires to restore our spiritual hearing.

To open ourselves to Christ's ability to restore our hearing it is important to use several basic strategies: First, plan your day around God rather than God around your day. If God is the most important "thing" in your life, He deserves pride of place. Second, establish sacred meeting times with God throughout your day. Most people eat at least three times a day. Your soul has priority

PILLAR 1: LISTENING TO DISCERN YOUR MISSION [EMBRACING SILENCE]

over your belly; therefore, you ought to pray three times a day—if not more. Third, don't worry about what you will do or say when you pray. Simply begin by being present.

St. Joseph's prayer is characterized by his profound silence. Words are not always necessary. The key to becoming a person who has true, lasting spiritual impact on others is to consistently show up for prayer.

To paraphrase Jean-Baptiste Chautard: too often we act as channels of grace rather than reservoirs. A channel transmits water and then afterward is empty. A reservoir is constantly full of water, while continually overflowing with water. If you are not constantly connected to the source of Living Water, you will become a channel that eventually runs dry and has nothing left to give to your family. However, if you remain connected to the source of Living Water by means of prayer and listening in prayer, you will become a reservoir of unshakable peace and grace for your family.

> **TAKE THE LEAD** The fundamental component of any relationship is trust. Without trust there exists no relationship. Over the next several reflections we will be examining the essence of sonship, which is trust in God the Father. Begin to identity those aspects of your life that cause you fear, anxiety, depression, anger, and frustration. You will discover that at the bottom of each of these sentiments is a lack of trust in God. Throughout your day, when you encounter these doubts, turn to the Father and say, "Abba, I trust in you. You can do all things, even in me, a sinner."*

* See Examen *Silence in Self* on page 444

ESSENTIALS FOR PRAYING

34. A REAL MAN CAVE

Threaded throughout the history of mankind is the lived experience, the unspoken law, of men having their own "sacred space." Woodworking sheds, garages, basements, and the modern so-called man cave have all contributed to providing men with a place of solitude and respite.

These sacred spaces have witnessed hours upon hours of craftsmanship, the rebuilding of car engines and oil changes, the drinking of whiskey, and the smoking of fine—and not-so-fine—cigars. And as glorious as these things are, few of them have been marked and claimed as a space dedicated wholly and exclusively to God.

The verse "Their idols are made of wood, the work of their hands" (see Ps 115:4) speaks to the fact that sometimes we men can value the "work of our hands" more than the God who made our hands work.

Many men have desired to commit themselves to carving out time and silence for the interior life, but have been wanting for a space in which they can meet their God. And consequently, a man attempts to pray in his office amid piles of paperwork, or in his living room among the unfolded clean laundry and playing children, but repeatedly leaves his prayer, defeated by distractions.

During Israel's wanderings in the desert, Moses erected what was called a tent of meeting outside the Israelite camp, where individuals could go for the purpose of seeking consultation with God. From this account we learn several things: First, Moses erected a place dedicated *specifically* to meeting with God. Second, this place of meeting was *outside* the camp, that is, it was away from the place where the Israelites' daily activities occurred. Third, it was in this tent that God met with Moses and others, offering them consolation and guidance.

To be successful fathers, we need to hear the voice of the Father, and to do this, we need to establish our own tent of meeting—a place of prayer outside the camp of daily life. In other words, we ought to find or create a space dedicated exclusively to God—away from electronic devices, the projects, the paperwork, and life's daily messes—and set aside time to meet with God in this space.

Your place of meeting could be your attic, an empty room, perhaps the bathroom (usually people will leave us alone while we are in there), or the adoration chapel, or the church down the street. But it should be close and accessible.

Without a dedicated place of prayer outside the camp of everyday life, you will struggle to make time for prayer. If, however, you have a place dedicated for prayer, it will become a place of pilgrimage—a place to which we set out to pray. Sometimes we need to "go there" to find God "in here"—in our hearts.

By separating the sacred space from life's daily clutter, you will remove many of life's distractions and become more capable of entering into and embracing silence, listening, and discerning the voice of God.

> **TAKE THE LEAD** The Bible can be intimidating. It contains accounts that seem unrelatable, let alone understandable. Yet God spent all human history preparing this gift from which we can benefit today. The Word of God is alive and can truly change our lives for the better. Jesus himself says, "Learn from Me." You and I can take that command literally by selecting one of the Gospels and using it as the basis of our fifteen-minute meeting with God. But this takes trust—trust that He will speak to you, and trust that what He will ask of you is worthy of you.*

* See Examen *Silence in Self* on page 444

ESSENTIALS FOR PRAYING

35. ARE YOU *WITH* HIM?

In the account of Joseph's annunciation, when the angel commanded Joseph to return to his wife, Mary, and take Jesus as his own son, the evangelist notes: "They shall call His name Emmanuel which is interpreted 'God with us'" (Mt 1:23). We have heard these words so often that we can become numb to the power of their meaning. God is with us. God is truly with you and me. God accomplished this "being with us" by sending His Son; and by becoming a son of a human father, God is now the *God with fathers*. The question for us is: "Are we with Him?" The Father is with us, but are we with the Father?

St. Joseph, when faced with the reality that his wife had conceived of the Holy Spirit, recognized his deficiency, his inadequacy, his inability to measure up to the holiness of "God with us" in Mary. Joseph, animated by a holy fear of God, was humble enough to understand that he was not truly worthy of the mystery occurring in Mary. Can we not relate to Joseph's sentiments? We are not as holy as we ought to be. We are deficient. We continually miss the mark of self-giving love.

Yet Joseph, despite his deficiencies, trusted that "[w]ith God all things are possible," and that he, by God's grace, could express the Father's love to Jesus. So it is with you. Despite your deficiencies, fears, failures, miserable attempts to love, the terrible things you've said and done, the challenge to show your children the Father's love is worthy of you, and more importantly, can be accomplished in you, if you—like Joseph—are determined to be with God the Father who is with fathers in prayer. St. Joseph continually sought the Kingdom of God first, and because of this the Kingdom "lived within him," and he became capable of showing Jesus the Father. Because of his faithfulness to prayer, he received divine commands, and because of his obedience to these commands, he was "placed over his Master's house," and had "charge of all his possessions;" meaning that Joseph was granted the responsibility and authority to lead Jesus and Mary to their glory.

PILLAR 1: LISTENING TO DISCERN YOUR MISSION [EMBRACING SILENCE]

How can we be like Joseph? How do we "be with God"—the God who is with us? The answer is very simple, but for most, difficult to do: establish a prayer schedule and abide by it. It sounds incredibly simple, but how many men actually apply this principle to their lives? A prayer schedule demonstrates to yourself and to God that God is not an afterthought, but rather the essential centerpiece of your life. Without a prayer schedule, your meeting times with God will be pushed aside continually for what appears to be more pressing. But remember, "Seek ye first the Kingdom of God, and all these things will be granted to you besides." In other words, in God you will be satisfied; because you will be with the God who is within you, who alone can satisfy.

TAKE THE LEAD The Bible can be intimidating. It contains accounts that seem unrelatable, let alone understandable. Yet God spent all human history preparing this gift from which we can benefit today. The Word of God is alive and can truly change our lives for the better. Jesus himself says, "Learn from Me." You and I can take that command literally by selecting one of the Gospels and using it as the basis of our fifteen-minute meeting with God. But this takes trust—trust that He will speak to you, and trust that what He will ask of you is worthy of you.*

* See Examen *Silence in Self* on page 444

ESSENTIALS FOR PRAYING

36. BUILDING A REAL-ATIONSHIP

For those who realize the vital importance of prayer and who have committed themselves to establishing a prayer schedule, the question inevitably rises in their hearts: How do I pray?

For most of us, prayer is a monologue, a series of requests, recitations, or even complaints. We often tell God our plans, our problems, our pains, our petitions. After two to three minutes of expressing these concerns we bow our head, make the sign of the cross, and proceed with a sense of minor accomplishment that we can check the task of prayer off our to-do list. Yet if we have any sensitivity to the Holy Spirit, we cannot help but to notice a disquiet in our soul, a nagging feeling of dissatisfaction. This feeling of dissatisfaction can dupe us, leading us to believe that prayer is the problem and the cause of our unfulfillment. But if we probe more deeply, we begin to understand that the problem is not prayer, but rather, how we pray.

The Father certainly desires us to share our plans, problems, pains, and petitions, but He wants more—He wants our hearts. Imagine if your child only shared with you his problems, petitions, and pains. How would you feel? Perhaps a bit used? We want more for, and from, our children. We desire to have a relationship with them—a "real-ationship." God our Father wants to have a real relationship with us. A relationship consists of two persons relating, communicating, giving, and being with the other. When a relationship grows, strengthens, and becomes intimate, it is inevitable that the two persons become one, sharing the other's qualities, dreams, character, and virtues. Prayer affords us the opportunity to relate to God and share in His qualities, to such a degree that we embody His characteristics and become capable of showing our family the Father. Prayer is the foundation of our relationship with God—and our family.

PILLAR 1: LISTENING TO DISCERN YOUR MISSION [EMBRACING SILENCE]

TAKE THE LEAD The Bible can be intimidating. It contains accounts that seem unrelatable, let alone understandable. Yet God spent all human history preparing this gift from which we can benefit today. The Word of God is alive and can truly change our lives for the better. Jesus himself says, "Learn from Me." You and I can take that command literally by selecting one of the Gospels and using it as the basis of our fifteen-minute meeting with God. But this takes trust—trust that He will speak to you, and trust that what He will ask of you is worthy of you.*

* See Examen *Silence in Self* on page 444

ESSENTIALS FOR PRAYING

37. THE 7 *R*'S OF PRAYER

There is a way to transform our prayer from a monologue to a dialogue; from a relationship to a "real-ationship;" from being filled with words to making us capable of discerning and receiving the true Word. This way is the seven Rs of prayer. The seven Rs is an outline for prayer that if used daily will open you to God who will transform you into a father of glory.

The steps to effective prayer are, first, *recognize* God's presence *in you*. Often we begin prayer, launching into what we want to say,

PILLAR 1: LISTENING TO DISCERN YOUR MISSION [EMBRACING SILENCE]

directing our thoughts to the God who seems to be somewhere "out there." Pause and greet God who lives within you. This can be done by making the sign of the cross devoutly and slowly, bowing your head, or simply saying, "Hello, God, I'm here. Hello, God, you are here." But most importantly, we ought to pause for a moment of silence reverently acknowledging that we are humbly placing ourselves in the presence of God who has placed His presence within us.

Second, every conversation has a context, a topic for discussion. It is no different with our relationship with God. Considering this, the second R of prayer is *read*. It is important to read God's Word, particularly the Gospel, which contextualizes our prayer. We read until something strikes us, or a phrase connects with us. Perhaps we reread the same passage a couple of times. Third, after you have identified a phrase or a word that God is using to speak to you, *reflect* on that word or phrase. Meditate and consider what God is trying to communicate to you through His word.

Fourth, after reflecting, we *respond* to God. We do this by discussing our dreams, aspirations, desires, struggles, plans for the day, our sins, fears, and anxieties—we simply tell Him all about it. During this time we ask for His help and guidance, and for Him to grant success to the work of our hands (see Psalm 90). The fifth R is *rest*. After you have recognized God's presence, read His Word, reflected on the phrase that resonates with you, and responded to His Word, then it is time to rest in Him. Simply remain in His presence silently for several minutes. This, perhaps, is the most essential aspect of prayer. During this time of rest God infuses His very presence and life into us.

Sixth, after you have rested in God, then make a *resolution* in the form of a request: God please help me do this today. The seventh R is to *remember* your resolution throughout the day, returning to the divine guidance that you received during prayer.

By humbly entering the silence daily and listening in this manner, you can be certain that God will transform your life. You will become a father of purpose, peace, power, and passion, who is capable of transmitting God's love and mercy to his family.

TAKE THE LEAD The Bible can be intimidating. It contains accounts that seem unrelatable, let alone understandable. Yet God spent all human history preparing this gift from which we can benefit today. The Word of God is alive and can truly change our lives for the better. Jesus himself says, "Learn from Me." You and I can take that command literally by selecting one of the Gospels and using it as the basis of our fifteen-minute meeting with God. But this takes trust—trust that He will speak to you, and trust that what He will ask of you is worthy of you.*

* See Examen *Silence in Self* on page 444

PILLAR 1: LISTENING TO DISCERN YOUR MISSION [EMBRACING SILENCE]

ESSENTIALS FOR PRAYING

38. INTERIOR LIFE AND EXTERIOR STRENGTH

Sometimes it can be difficult to assess ourselves and determine the bad and the good, the failures and successes, our sins and our gifts, what hinders or helps us. In addition to God's Word, we may need something that will help launch us into conversation with God, a springboard that will allow us to dive into the mystery of God, while also understanding the mystery that we are.

In the Sermon on the Mount, Our Lord Jesus alluded to a simple, effective, three-step way for fathers to pray: "Or what man of you, if his son asks him for bread, will give him a stone? Or if he asks for a fish, will give him a serpent? If you then, who are evil, know how to give good gifts to your children, how much more will your Father who is in heaven give good things to those who ask him!" (Mt 7:9–11).

First, notice that Jesus invites each of us to come to our place of prayer with something—namely ourselves, and our fatherly experiences. We are to bring our experiences as a father to prayer, present them to the Father, and meditate upon them, attempting to discover within them what God desires to disclose to us by means of those experiences.

Second, by meditating upon these experiences, we begin to compare our sentiments for our children to God the Father's eternal love for us. When Jesus asks, "What man of you, if his son asks him for bread, will give him a stone . . . ," He is inviting us fathers to compare our human fatherhood to God's fatherhood. We who are "evil" want good gifts for our children, yet how much more does the Father care for us and our children, wanting what is truly the best for us? Our personal fatherly experiences—which reveal our love, hopes, and desires for our children—if meditated upon, afford us a window into the Father's love for us and our children.

Which leads us to the third step: we realize by means of the comparison that God loves us personally and desires infinitely more for us than we can "hope for or imagine" (see Eph 3). It is this realization that affords us the ability to understand and believe that we are beloved sons of God.

Your interior life gives your exterior life form. Your private prayers will manifest publicly the presence of the Father who lives within you. A father who prays privately will eventually lead his family in prayer. As Fr. Peyton said often, "A family that prays together stays together."

It is certain that St. Joseph on numerous occasions meditated upon his love for his son, Jesus, and in doing so came to the conclusion that as great as his human love is for his son, infinitely more does the Father love him, and Jesus. By meditating upon his own fatherhood, Joseph understood his own dependence upon God; and being dependent upon the Father, he became a most trusting beloved son of God.

When your child is sick, loses the championship game, wins the scholarship, struggles to have friendships, fights addictions, or simply gives you affection, consider your feelings and then consider how God loves you infinitely more. This is the secret to becoming a father who loves like his heavenly Father.

> **TAKE THE LEAD** The Bible can be intimidating. It contains accounts that seem unrelatable, let alone understandable. Yet God spent all human history preparing this gift from which we can benefit today. The Word of God is alive and can truly change our lives for the better. Jesus himself says, "Learn from Me." You and I can take that command literally by selecting one of the Gospels and using it as the basis of our fifteen-minute meeting with God. But this takes trust—trust that He will speak to you, and trust that what He will ask of you is worthy of you.*

---

* See Examen *Silence in Self* on page 444

PILLAR 1: LISTENING TO DISCERN YOUR MISSION [EMBRACING SILENCE]

OVERCOMING THE CHALLENGES OF SILENCE

39. GOOD VERSUS GREATEST

During the Middle Ages, cities were often surrounded and protected by thick, towering stone walls of defense. The wall that surrounded the city had gates that allowed pilgrims and inhabitants to enter. In times of war the enemy battered against these gates, intent on weakening and breaking the bars that braced them. If those bars broke or collapsed under the immense pressure, the enemy could enter the breach, penetrate the city, and from the inside overrun it, create havoc, and ultimately claim it as its own.

The enemy, the devil, has one goal: to overthrow your internal city, your soul, by invading and penetrating your walls of defense. He can only rule you if he gets inside of you, and he can only invade your being if you relinquish your wall of defense, which is your relationship with God—your prayer life. It is little wonder why so many men are "sifted like wheat," influenced and overthrown by evil: they have surrendered their wall of defense, their prayer life.

Carving out time for silence and setting aside periods of silence for the purpose of listening to God is becoming increasingly difficult for modern man. The enemy is bent on keeping us from silence and from discerning the voice of God. Consider the constant stimuli that batters against the gates of our soul. At the gas station, the restaurant, the grocery store, in the car, and at home, music, television, video streaming, ringtones, and text alerts bombard us with countless messages, many of which rob us of our ability to hear and discern God's voice—*Vox*.

The enemy pulls out all the stops for the purpose of keeping you from hearing and listening to the *Vox*. The enemy tempts us to turn on the radio when we're in the car, to have the television constantly running in the background, to check or send emails and texts in order to stay connected, to be up to date regarding the latest news—all with the diabolical purpose of filling us with something other than God.

The evil one is satisfied with filling us with "good things" as long as these good things keep us from the "greatest thing"—communion with God. His purpose and intention is straightforward: he desires to keep you occupied, keep your mind racing, prompt and compel you to busyness for the purpose of distracting you from hearing the *Vox* of God, which will reveal God's mission, vision, and plan for your life.

> **TAKE THE LEAD** It is easy to set oneself to the task of praying and realize afterward that the majority of time was spent mulling over distractions. The evil one will then tempt you to believe that prayer is unattainable, or a waste of time. Yet, God wants you—all of you—including your distractions. The next time you pray and become distracted (and you will), try not to suppress the distraction, but rather lift it up to the Lord and ask Him to breathe His guidance and life into the situation. *

* See Examen *Silence in Self* on page 444

PILLAR 1: LISTENING TO DISCERN YOUR MISSION [EMBRACING SILENCE]

OVERCOMING THE CHALLENGES OF SILENCE

40. THE KINGDOM OF NOISE

Adolf Hitler, relating how he despised those who embrace silent contemplation, said, "Only the man who acts becomes conscious of the real world. Men misuse their intelligence. It is not the seat of a special dignity of mankind, but merely an instrument in the struggle for life. Man is here to act. Only as a being in action does he fulfill his natural vocation. Contemplative natures, retrospective like all intellectuals, are dead persons who miss the meaning of life . . . only deeds and perpetual activity give meaning to life . . . . All passivity, all inertia, on the other hand is senseless, inimical to life. From this proceeds the divine right of destroying all who are inert" (from Hermann Rauschning, *The Voice of Destruction*).

Hitler, an obvious pawn of Satan, realized that his greatest threat is the man who enters the silence and prays. In his cleverly insightful *The Screwtape Letters*, C.S. Lewis discloses the evil one's agenda. Screwtape, an archdemon, writes a letter to his demon nephew, Wormwood. In the letter he says, "Music and silence—how I detest them both! How thankful we should be that ever since our Father [the devil] entered Hell . . . no square inch of infernal space and no moment of infernal time has been surrendered to either of these abominable forces, but all has been occupied by Noise—Noise, the grand dynamism, the audible expression of all that is exultant, ruthless, and virile . . . . We will make the whole universe a noise in the end. We have already made great strides in this direction as regards the Earth" (*The Screwtape Letters*, C.S. Lewis).

Modern music, videos, movies, and programming have the incredible power to inspire, and yet overwhelm our mind, manipulate our thoughts, and bully us into meditating upon things that will undermine if not altogether thwart our ability to love truly. The human brain is more active when a person sleeps than when he watches television. One of the most powerful and effective ways to fast is to detach oneself from the kingdom of noise, because it makes room in our souls for God.

The most fundamental step in becoming a man of greatness is manning your defense wall against the kingdom of noise. Perhaps you could shut off the television several nights a week. Perhaps you discontinue your subscription to particular bloggers and news sites. Perhaps you deny yourself texting and emailing during family time. By giving God these sacrifices, He will in turn fill that space with Himself. God will never be outdone in generosity. As Fr. Ronald Rolheiser notes, "In my long experience, every extraordinary person I have ever known has had one secret in common: they prayed privately."

> **TAKE THE LEAD** It is easy to set oneself to the task of praying and realize afterward that the majority of time was spent mulling over distractions. The evil one will then tempt you to believe that prayer is unattainable, or a waste of time. Yet, God wants you—all of you—including your distractions. The next time you pray and become distracted (and you will), try not to suppress the distraction, but rather lift it up to the Lord and ask Him to breathe His guidance and life into the situation.*

* See Examen *Silence in Self* on page 444

PILLAR 1: LISTENING TO DISCERN YOUR MISSION [EMBRACING SILENCE]

OVERCOMING THE CHALLENGES OF SILENCE

41. THE REAL INFUSION

If you had in your possession a winning lottery ticket worth $500 million, would you have it framed, tuck it away in a drawer, or use it as a bookmark? Of course not. Yet God has given us the greatest power on earth: prayer, silence, and His presence, which enable us to do great things for Him and his Kingdom.

Unfortunately, prayer is often treated like the lottery ticket lost in a drawer: unused. Our interior life gives our exterior life form. Who we are on the inside determines who we become on the outside. To give God you must have God. To infuse others with God you must be infused by God. When a person receives a blood transfusion, knowledge of what a blood transfusion is, how it works, or even what it accomplishes is not necessary for the transfusion to be effective. Only one thing is required: that the patient shows up, sits still, and allows the physician to perform the transfusion.

Prayer is much like a blood transfusion. You are not required to understand God, how He is working, what He is accomplishing in you. Only one thing is required: that you are present and wait on His presence. He will do the rest—he will infuse you with Himself, removing the old boy and replacing it with the God-man.

Keep in mind that the soul gives form to the body—it is not the other way around. It is not necessary that during prayer you hear God's audible voice, but rather that your soul receives the infusion of His Word.

The infusion of God's presence that occurs during prayer is the winning lottery ticket; it is of inestimable value. If you persevere in practicing the presence of God, waiting in the silence, allowing the God-infusion to occur, after years you will notice that your belief in God and who He has created you to be is unshakable. This unshakable confidence is the mark of a true son of God.

TAKE THE LEAD It is easy to set oneself to the task of praying and realize afterward that the majority of time was spent mulling over distractions. The evil one will then tempt you to believe that prayer is unattainable, or a waste of time. Yet, God wants you—all of you—including your distractions. The next time you pray and become distracted (and you will), try not to suppress the distraction, but rather lift it up to the Lord and ask Him to breathe His guidance and life into the situation.*

* See Examen *Silence in Self* on page 444

PILLAR 1: LISTENING TO DISCERN YOUR MISSION [EMBRACING SILENCE]

OVERCOMING THE CHALLENGES OF SILENCE

42. PRAYER DEMANDS PRACTICE

Silence and prayer and silence in prayer may pose one of the greatest challenges to the human father. The Father invites all fathers to enter His silence that they may become like Him, and image His fatherhood to this broken world. But many, if not most, men decline God's invitations to prayer and silence because deep down they don't trust Him—they don't really believe that He will speak to them or infuse them with His divine power. By entering silence and prayer you demonstrate that you are a true son of God who trusts his divine Father.

Many men believe that they know the will of God, but most don't ask Him what His will is. Others ask, but neglect to pause and listen. Yet without the divine compass received in silence, we quickly become lost, blind leaders who lead blind followers into error—particularly the error of busyness.

Prayer demands practice. It's not something we can master or become an expert at by praying only when we need something, are experiencing difficulty, or once a week or haphazardly. Prayer is nothing less than friendship with God, and good friends spend time—a lot of time—together. A world-renowned violinist, who was retired and up in age, was asked why he continues to practice playing his violin daily. He responded: "If I stop practicing for one day, I notice; two days, my friends notice; and any more than that, the world notices." If you don't have a consistent daily prayer life, your wife, children, and the world will notice that you are not connected to God. However, if you trust God enough to entrust the first-fruits of your time to Him daily, He will entrust you with greater responsibilities.

> **TAKE THE LEAD** It is easy to set oneself to the task of praying and realize afterward that the majority of time was spent mulling over distractions. The evil one will then tempt you to believe that prayer is unattainable, or a waste of time. Yet, God wants you—all of

you—including your distractions. The next time you pray and become distracted (and you will), try not to suppress the distraction, but rather lift it up to the Lord and ask Him to breathe His guidance and life into the situation.*

* See Examen *Silence in Self* on page 444

OVERCOMING THE CHALLENGES OF SILENCE

43. DEALING WITH THE DEMON OF DISTRACTION

For most of us the real reason we postpone or neglect prayer is because our minds are distracted, and these distractions create an anxiety that compels us to act rather than wait on God. We sense that prayer is a waste of time—time that could be spent on doing things "that matter." Dealing with the circus of distractions can be daunting. How should we deal with distractions during prayer?

One thing that we should not do is attempt to bury or suppress the distraction. C.S. Lewis's' Screwtape advises his nephew, demon Wormwood, as to how he should deal with a soul he is trying to damn: "You seem to be doing very little good at present. The use of his 'love' [girlfriend] to distract his mind from the Enemy [God] is, of course, obvious, but you reveal what poor use you are making of it when you say the whole question of distraction and the wandering mind has become one of the chief subjects of his prayers. That means you have largely failed. When this, or any other distraction, crosses his mind you ought to encourage him to thrust it away by sheer will power and to try to continue to normal prayer as if nothing had happened: once he accepts the distraction as his present problem and lays *that* before the Enemy [God] and makes it the main theme of his prayers and his endeavors, then, so far from doing good, you have done harm. Anything, even a sin, which has the total effect of moving him close up to the Enemy makes against us in the long run" (C.S. Lewis, *The Screwtape Letters*).

We ought to deal with distractions and temptations during prayer much like a surfer deals with a wave: ride it. Use its energy to raise you up to God; present the temptation and distraction as the basis of your conversation with Him. By doing this, the temptation can become a means to salvation. As St. Bernard of Clairvaux said, "However great the temptation, if we know how to use the weapon of prayer well we shall come off as conquerors at last, for prayer is more powerful than all devils."

Do not allow the fear of distraction to keep you from spending time with God. Rather, allow your distraction to lead you to the ultimate attraction. By doing so, God will breathe peace, solace, and solutions into your many struggles and sufferings.

> **TAKE THE LEAD** It is easy to set oneself to the task of praying and realize afterward that the majority of time was spent mulling over distractions. The evil one will then tempt you to believe that prayer is unattainable, or a waste of time. Yet, God wants you—all of you—including your distractions. The next time you pray and become distracted (and you will), try not to suppress the distraction, but rather lift it up to the Lord and ask Him to breathe His guidance and life into the situation. *

* See Examen *Silence in Self* on page 444

SILENCE BEFORE MEN

44. SILENCE BEFORE MEN

The evil one, if he cannot lure and entice you to surrender to deliberate sin, will often tempt you to choose something good over that which is great: to receive honor and glory from men rather than honoring and glorifying the God of men; to perform the works of God to be noticed, rather than to be known by the God of works.

Nearly all men interiorly suffer from insecurities, inferiority complexes, or perhaps a lack of confidence in a particular area. Such feelings of inadequacy are rooted in a man's lack of belief and trust that he is a chosen son of the Father; that the Father has a specific, unique, plan for him. Often when a man, a father, lacks trust in God and doubts the Father's love for him, he will succumb to the temptation to seek affirmation from human beings in disordered ways, to attempt to make himself noticed that he may be lauded, affirmed, and honored. This is especially prevalent among fathers who have begun to believe that their fatherhood is ineffective, powerless, and is having little impact on their children; or among a father who doesn't receive instant, or consistent, affirmation from his wife and children.

Herein lies the battle. It is during such times of doubt that you and I are called to exercise trust that the Father sees us, chooses us, and has a specific plan for us. Many a good church man has neglected his vocation, his family, and his children for the purpose of doing "greater things" at the local parish level, with the hidden motive to be noticed by men—only to fail at home. As one confessor said, "Do not become a street lamp only for your house to go dark." Often we believe that we are doing God's will and "letting our light shine" by attending Bible studies, parish council meetings, small groups, and other good and noble initiatives, while our families receive the leftovers and their light is extinguished. If we are not leading our families in prayer, we shouldn't lead a prayer group. If we're not teaching our children from Scripture, we shouldn't profess and teach God's word at a Bible study. What we do publicly ought to be an outgrowth of what we do in our domestic church.

A Dominican priest once said, "You will become a saint by means of your vocation as a father—not outside of it." St. Francis of Assisi said, "Blessed is the servant who esteems himself no better when he is praised and exalted by people than when he is considered worthless, simple and despicable, for what a man is before God, that he is and nothing more." In other words: strive to be a great father for God, and do not concern yourself with being noticed by men.

By asking God for *the desire* to be little, silent, and hidden, we become capable of receiving the grace of being released from the tension and temptations of being noticed by men. Consider that St. Joseph was a most hidden father. Not a single word of Joseph's was recorded in Sacred Scripture. Joseph was virtually unnoticed by the men of his age, yet God has spoken through his silence and has revealed his greatness by means of his hiddenness; and today God has exalted Joseph as the most revered father of all time. Truly "[w]hat is hidden will one day be revealed" (Lk 8:17).

PILLAR 1: LISTENING TO DISCERN YOUR MISSION [EMBRACING SILENCE]

Seek not to glorify yourself, for that is not your duty but God's. Glorify God, and by glorifying God, He cannot help but glorify you. This is a supernatural principle: God cannot be outdone in generosity. The more you glorify Him, the more He will glorify Himself in you. By silencing ourselves before men, we allow God to speak powerfully through our hidden example. "A man who eats too much honey does himself no good; similarly, the man who seeks his own glorification will be crushed by that same renown" (St. Bernard).

> **TAKE THE LEAD** Building your life on human respect is a certain way to fail and become miserable. Over the next several reflections, make every effort to identify behaviors that undermine your ability to experience the freedom to be who you truly are. Be honest with yourself and God. Ask God to impart His courage and boldness into your soul, that you may be given the freedom to do everything for the praise of God alone.*

* See Examen *Silence Before Men* on page 444

SILENCE BEFORE MEN

45. BUILDING UPON SHIFTING SAND

To be a great father you must first become a great son; and to be a great son, it is imperative that you learn to trust in the Father. At the heart of the battle to trust God is the challenge to be receptive to His divine will, believing that His favor and blessing is and will be upon you—without resorting to the temptation to earn His favor.

Most men don't view themselves as "earners," that is, a person who believes that "doing good" is the way to win the Father's love. It is all too easy to subconsciously believe that "If I do good, God will love me *more*. If I do *great* things, I will receive God's favor and approval." Often, but not always, this behavior is an outgrowth and consequence of a wound that was inflicted upon us during our childhood.

Men who didn't receive the approval, interest, blessing, and favor from their human father can be more easily tempted to obtain validation, honor, accolades, and affirmation from human beings. And if such a man does not have a rich interior life, entering the silence consistently, he will have very little defense against this temptation.

The enemy appeals to our woundedness, our lack of trust in the Father, and works tirelessly to lure us into the trap of being noticed by others rather than to be known by God. The evil one attempts to convince us to be exteriorly active, seen by others, deriving value from what others think of us rather than what God knows of us. This is a diabolical trap. Human respect is shifting sand upon which no man should build his house—his domestic church. By living for human respect, a man tends to shift his behavior and shape his personality in order to maintain his following, keep his fans, and grow his number of friends. When others disagree with the man bound by human respect, if others are chosen over him, or if he is not included in their circles, he will adapt his personality, his behaviors, and his appearance for the purpose of pleasing them and winning them over again. However, the more a man alters his character and adapts his personality for the purpose of earning the respect and approval of others, he moves further from his true identity. If he continues on this path, his false identity will be incapable of leading him toward his destiny, and thus incapable of leading his family toward their destiny.

When we live for the respect of men, we make the mistake of identifying ourselves by *what we do*, rather than *who we are*. When we do not become the person that God created us to be, not only do we lose, but our families lose. They lose the presence and glory of God, the very unique presence that God desires us to transmit to them by means of our fatherhood. We are not called to be shaped by the world's expectations, but rather, we are to become who God has created and destined us to be: a father on earth like the Father in heaven. Then we will set the world ablaze.

> **TAKE THE LEAD** Building your life on human respect is a certain way to fail and become miserable. Over the next several reflections, make every effort to identify behaviors that undermine your ability to experience the freedom to be who you truly are. Be honest with yourself and God. Ask God to impart His courage and boldness into your soul, that you may be given the freedom to do everything for the praise of God alone.*

* See Examen *Silence Before Men* on page 444

SILENCE BEFORE MEN

46. WHO ARE YOU FOLLOWING?

Do you consider yourself to be a follower of Jesus? Many of us believe, with little doubt, that we are among those faithful disciples of our Lord. But how can we be certain that we are following His lead? What if we are following our own leadership?

The disorder of living for the approval of men always begins when a man neglects the interior life. The level to which a man protects his interior life is the level to which he will protect his children and wife. When a father neglects meeting with God regularly, his understanding of God and His fatherhood becomes distorted. Rather than aligning his fatherhood to the fatherhood of God, he attempts to make God in his own image and redefine God's fatherhood in a way that demands little of him. When our image of God becomes distorted, we can no longer see ourselves as God sees us, and therefore our understanding of ourselves either becomes too inflated or too negative.

If I think too highly of myself, I look to men to confirm my self-evaluation; or if I consider myself too lowly, I will be tempted to turn to men to deliver me from my insecurity. Consequently I begin to use my work, my service in the public sphere, or my charitable contributions at church as a way to become noticed and affirmed by men. Even if I fulfill the purpose of accomplishing something good, my motives are flawed. "God does not judge by appearances but by the heart" (1 Sam 16:7). Our families also can intuit the difference between a father who is motivated by his family, and a man who is motivated at the expense of his family.

As St. John of the Cross said, "Let the men eaten up with activity and who imagine they are able to shake the world with their preaching and outward works, stop and reflect a moment. It will not be difficult for them to understand that they would be much more useful to the Church and pleasing to the Lord, not to mention the good example they would give those around them, if they devoted more time to prayer and to the exercises of the interior life.

PILLAR 1: LISTENING TO DISCERN YOUR MISSION [EMBRACING SILENCE]

Under these conditions, by one single work of theirs they would do far more good and with much less trouble, than they do by a thousand others on which they exhaust their lives."

If we are not praying, we are not listening to God, and if we are not listening to God, we are not really following Him, but rather following ourselves, as though we are God.

TAKE THE LEAD Building your life on human respect is a certain way to fail and become miserable. Over the next several reflections, make every effort to identify behaviors that undermine your ability to experience the freedom to be who you truly are. Be honest with yourself and God. Ask God to impart His courage and boldness into your soul, that you may be given the freedom to do everything for the praise of God alone.*

* See Examen *Silence Before Men* on page 444

SILENCE BEFORE MEN

47. SILENCE THAT SPEAKS LOUDLY

Why do we admire Peter Parker, Captain America, Frodo Baggins or any modest man of deep interior strength? Perhaps we admire these characters because of their secrecy. They don't strut around flaunting their power. They don't boast about their conquests or share with the world their latest successful endeavor. Quite the contrary: they veil their power. Or to use an expression of Jesus': they do not cast their pearls before swine. Do we cast our power before the pigs of this world for the purpose of obtaining temporary and fleeting validation?

Consider that Jesus, the very Word of God, God the Son, did not arrive on our planet in a celestial cosmic electrical storm, or upon a fire-wheeled chariot, shooting lightning bolts from His divine eyeballs. Rather, His eternal creative power was veiled by His becoming a little, helpless infant who was dependent upon a very young, simple virgin and her husband. In fact, the glorious event of Christ's Resurrection occurred in the silent, shadowed, dark, early Sunday morning hours. The most incredible, life-changing, soul-transforming event—a dead man definitively defeating sin and overcoming bodily death—was so sacred that it was accomplished in secret.

Life's most sacred and meaningful events are intended to occur in secret. Human beings are conceived in secret, men's sins are confessed to a priest in secret, and authentic fatherhood is accomplished in secret. It is that sacred.

Perhaps this is one of the reasons Jesus' silent years of living in Nazareth under the patronage of St. Joseph are veiled—because of their sacred character. There is, however, an even more fundamental reason why our fatherhood should be accomplished in secret: because that is how the heavenly Father lives His fatherhood. His works are described as "glorious, hidden and secret" (Eccles 11:4). You and I are called to be Like St. Joseph, an icon of the heavenly Father, a secret, hidden power that effectively transmits God's fatherly mercy, love, and power to this world.

TAKE THE LEAD Building your life on human respect is a certain way to fail and become miserable. Over the next several reflections, make every effort to identify behaviors that undermine your ability to experience the freedom to be who you truly are. Be honest with yourself and God. Ask God to impart His courage and boldness into your soul, that you may be given the freedom to do everything for the praise of God alone.*

* See Examen *Silence Before Men* on page 444

SILENCE BEFORE GOD

48. THE SECRET POWER OF A FATHER

Have you ever wondered why the idea of the modest, unassuming character that veils a resilient, hidden hero is so appealing and admirable? Spider-Man, Superman, Batman, or Bill Bixby all had this quality of hidden strength. Perhaps that is why J. R. R. Tolkien's hobbits Frodo and Sam are such magnetically attractive characters. Though small, modest, and apparently powerless, they carry an interior strength, and in Frodo's case, he carries the very power that will determine the fate of Middle Earth—the Ring of Power.

Authentic fathers, whether we like it or not, are like hobbits: we appear to be common folk, discreet, modest, regular, run-of-the mill guys, but like Frodo we have a power and richness within us that determines the destiny of the world.

Recall that when Herod sought to murder the Christ Child, Joseph, who was directed by an angel, escaped in the darkness of night, fleeing to the foreign land of Egypt, and by doing so, he saved his family. Herod is a symbol of Satan, who incessantly attempts to destroy the

PILLAR 1: LISTENING TO DISCERN YOUR MISSION [EMBRACING SILENCE]

child, the woman, and the family. Joseph is a symbol of all fathers, who are called to save their family by means of the "dark night"—the secret hidden life of fatherhood—in the midst of this world of exile.

Unfortunately, many men inadvertently make the mistake of going "out there," with the subconscious motivation to derive value from being needed by the local community, rather than going "in there," to their domestic church, serving their family for the purpose of leading them to God. Often we are duped into believing that to be a true disciple of Christ we must go out there and evangelize the nations. But Christ often calls certain select individuals for such missions, while others He summons to return home and evangelize and build their domestic church for the purpose of preparing their children to be God's saints.

Consider that the man of Geresene who Christ delivered from the demon Legion, begged Jesus that he might remain with Him. But Jesus "[d]id not allow him, but said to him 'Go home to thy relatives, and tell them all the Lord has done for thee, and how he has had mercy on thee'" (Mk 5:18–19).

This man's mission, and every father's duty, is to "go home," "in there" to his family, and in the secret, hidden vocation of fatherhood share with his wife and children "all the Lord has done for [us] and how he has had mercy on [us]." Our family's salvation depends upon this secret sacrifice. You and I become silent before God by offering ourselves to God in silence. It is this silent fatherly sacrifice that saves the world.

> **TAKE THE LEAD** Those who work in the government's Secret Service consistently embark on and accomplish missions of which the world is unaware; yet these hidden undertakings are effective in shaping the world. God has created you, the human father, to enter His "Secret Service" and undertake the mission to secretly win the world for Christ. Over the next several reflections, make a point to accept the sufferings that come your way without grumbling or boasting, but rather offering them to God on behalf of the conversion of fathers and their families.*

* See Examen *Silence Before God* on page 445

SILENCE BEFORE GOD

49. THE FATHER IN SECRET

The idea of being a man, a father of hidden sacrifice, seems contrary to our nature. Even Christ Himself said, "You are the light of the world. A city set on a mountain cannot be hidden. Neither do men light a lamp and put it under the measure, but upon a lamp stand, so as to give light to all in the house. Even so let your light shine before men, in order that they may see your good works and give glory to your Father in heaven." It seems that Jesus is commanding us to do just the opposite of being little, silent, and hidden. It appears that our Lord is asking us to "show off" our light.

Let's examine our Lord's words. Jesus says that we are the light of the world. Just as the light of the earth is the sun, which affords life, warmth, growth, and vision; so also God calls us to be among those who are to bring supernatural life, spiritual growth, eternal vision, and the warmth of self-sacrificial love to this world. However, notice that it is not our light, but the supernatural light of the Son that enlightens us. The light is not my own, but rather Christ sharing His light with me, that it may shine through me. Jesus is commanding us not to be ashamed of the "Son light" that is within us. Just as the sun naturally shines, so also we effortlessly let Christ shine through us. When we allow the Son to shine through us we give light to all in our house—our family—and eventually the world.

Often men misunderstand Jesus and instead of "allowing" Jesus' power, humility, love, and compassion to shine through them, they place their own works, accomplishments, successes, talents, and gifts on the lamp stand for the purpose of bringing more attention to themselves than to God. They spend themselves to *make* their light shine, rather than *letting* the meek, humble power of Christ shine through them.

Our Lord revealed how fathers are to imitate God the Father: "But when you give alms, do not let your left hand know what your right hand is doing, so that your alms may be given in secret;

PILLAR 1: LISTENING TO DISCERN YOUR MISSION [EMBRACING SILENCE]

and your Father Who sees in secret, will reward you" (Mt 6:3-4). "But when you pray, go into your room and shut the door and pray to your Father in secret; and your Father who sees in secret will reward you" (Mt 6:6). "But when you fast anoint your head and wash your face, that your fasting may not be seen by men but by your Father *who is in secret;* and your Father who sees in secret will reward you" (Mt 6:17-18).

Jesus' words indicate that all of a father's actions should be motivated by the desire to perform these works for God alone—who sees in secret—rather than for the glory and praise of men. For if we do our works to be noticed by men, we are like the Pharisees who "[h]ave already received their reward"—meaning that we lose all the graces and supernatural benefits that God desires to grant to us, trading them for the crusty, hard bread, the soggy cereal, the wet, musty towel of men's affections.

But there is something else that our Lord reveals, something that is often overlooked. The reason for a father's secrecy is to imitate and *participate* with the "Father who is in secret." God the Father lives in secret, moves in secret, and blesses in secret—for He *is* in secret. In other words, the Father's secret to His glory is the secret to every human father's success, and the secret is secrecy itself.

Fatherhood is little, silent, and hidden. Your fatherhood changes the world silently. Your fatherhood is like the stud behind the drywall. You can't see it, but it holds up the drywall, the frame of the wall, the structure of the house. Fatherhood, your fatherhood, silently, secretly, holds up the structure of the family, the Church, and the world. This means that you are a stud.

St. Joseph was a most hidden father. In fact, as we have seen, Scripture does not record a single word spoken by him. Yet, Joseph's silent, hidden, humble example testifies that God can accomplish great things through you and me if we perform our good deeds for, and offer our sufferings to, God, rather than for the purpose and motivation of being noticed and acclaimed by men.

TAKE THE LEAD Those who work in the government's Secret Service consistently embark on and accomplish missions of which the world is unaware; yet these hidden undertakings are effective in shaping the world. God has created you, the human father, to enter His "Secret Service" and undertake the mission to secretly win the world for Christ. Over the next several reflections, make a point to accept the sufferings that come your way without grumbling or boasting, but rather offering them to God on behalf of the conversion of fathers and their families.*

* See Examen *Silence Before God* on page 445

SILENCE BEFORE GOD

50. SECRET WORKS WORK

How can works performed secretly make any real, lasting impact? No one, at least on a grand scale, will see your good works, and therefore no one will be aware of them, and consequently no one will be inspired by them. Right? It does appear that way, but let's examine how secret works work.

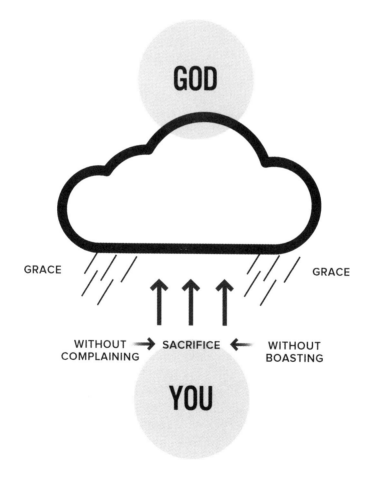

Clouds are known to contain hundreds of thousands of gallons of water. It is as though a lake is floating overhead. These tremendously large water sources are hidden, yet exist in plain sight. In order for clouds to develop, the dew from the fields, the moisture from the rivers, seas, and oceans, the mist contained in the air—all imperceptible to the human eye—rise into the atmosphere and, over time, collect and eventually become clouds. These masses of moisture gather into larger cloud formations, eventually becoming so heavy that they release rain upon the earth—rain that brings forth bountiful harvests.

Your works, as a father, are like the mist in the air and the moisture from the seas, which if offered consistently—without boasting or complaining, and with the intention of glorifying God—will be gathered by God, who eventually by His divine command orders that they shower graces upon humanity.

For example, at the wedding of Cana, Jesus commanded the servants, who represent each of us, to take six stone jars, used for the Jewish rites of purification, and fill them with water. The servants, without grumbling or complaining, filled those six extraordinarily heavy clay vessels—each holding twenty to thirty gallons of water—to the brim. That's a lot of water and a lot of work. Regardless of their superior efforts, the water was just that—water.

However, when they offered to Jesus the water that they had gathered—without boasting or complaining—He blessed their offering, transforming it into wine, which is a symbol of grace. This is how secret works work. Notice that even Christ's participation in performing the miracle was hidden from the chief steward of the feast: "After he had tasted the water after it had become wine, *not knowing from where it came . . .*"

Our fatherly efforts and works, regardless of how grand and effective they may appear, are merely dirty, murky water. Why? The first reason is that our works are almost always alloyed with our imperfect motives and a touch of pride. The second reason is that you and I cannot transform our works into grace—only God can truly transform the inner person of another.

Your task and mine as fathers is to gather the water; that is, we work in secret for the salvation of our family and friends by offering to God our humble works. By doing this, we provide God with the "matter" that can be transformed into wine, that is grace for others. You can only provide water and not wine, but God will provide the wine if you provide the water.

> **TAKE THE LEAD** Those who work in the government's Secret Service consistently embark on and accomplish missions of which the world is unaware; yet these hidden undertakings are effective in shaping the world. God has created you, the human father, to enter His "Secret Service" and undertake the mission to secretly win the world for Christ. Over the next several reflections, make a point to accept the sufferings that come your way without grumbling or boasting, but rather offering them to God on behalf of the conversion of fathers and their families.*

* See Examen *Silence Before God* on page 445

SILENCE BEFORE GOD

51. THE REAL POWER BEHIND PRAYER

Charity, the greatest of all virtues, is friendship (communion) with God. Being a friend of God and living in communion with God is the greatest thing that you or I will ever do or experience.

There exist three foundational components of friendship: trust, communication, and self-donation. By means of communication, combined with self-donation, trust in the other is developed. If I sacrifice for my wife, yet never communicate with her (this perhaps being her wildest dream), or if I communicate with my wife, yet never sacrifice for her, our relationship will lack trust and intimacy, never achieving the full expression and stature of love. And so it is with our friendship with God.

In order for our friendship with God to express the full measure of love, it is imperative that we communicate with God, which is prayer, and donate ourselves to God, which is sacrifice. This is where our *spiritual location* (part 1) and living *our vocation* (part

PILLAR 1: LISTENING TO DISCERN YOUR MISSION [EMBRACING SILENCE]

2) meet; where silence and sacrifice merge; where prayer and action integrate. We've discussed how to pray (communicate with God), but what gives prayer power?

Our Lord, responding to His apostle's question about why they could not exorcise a demon from a young boy, said, "Only by prayer and fasting can this kind be expelled." If our prayer is to be powerful, our prayer must be animated by secret sacrifice. Prayer without sacrifice is lip service, and sacrifice without prayer is the mere submission of the body and the training of one's own will. Secret sacrifice inspires our prayer, and prayer inspires us to sacrifice in secret.

In the following sections we will discover the ways God is asking the human father to secretly sacrifice himself for his wife and children. Remember that your vocation is your path to glory. Therefore, it is within your vocation (marriage and fatherhood) that you will discover how to sacrifice truly.

> **TAKE THE LEAD** Those who work in the government's Secret Service consistently embark on and accomplish missions of which the world is unaware; yet these hidden undertakings are effective in shaping the world. God has created you, the human father, to enter His "Secret Service" and undertake the mission to secretly win the world for Christ. Over the next several reflections, make a point to accept the sufferings that come your way without grumbling or boasting, but rather offering them to God on behalf of the conversion of fathers and their families.*

* See Examen *Silence Before God* on page 445

PILLAR 2

EMBRACE YOUR ESSENCE

[Embracing Woman]

GOD ASKS EACH OF US "WHERE ARE YOU?" THIS IS THE PERENNIAL QUESTION THAT HAUNTS THE DEEP SUBCONSCIOUS RECESSES OF MAN'S HEART. THE ANSWER TO THIS QUESTION DETERMINES EACH MAN'S LOCATION IN GOD'S PLAN OF SALVATION, HIS VOCATIONAL MISSION—THE VERY FOUNDATION OF THE SPIRITUALITY OF FATHERHOOD.

YOU NEED HER

52. THE MEASURE OF A MAN: HIS RELATIONSHIP WITH WOMAN

Have you ever seen someone, perhaps a child, attempt to open a flower before it blooms? When someone attempts to pull back the petals on a rose for the purpose of peering inside, they destroy the flower. Flowers are analogous to women. A flower's petals open and spread when it receives the warmth of the gentle sunlight, without which it will never open. So it is with a woman. When a man attempts to pull back woman's "petals," when he manipulates, coerces, intimidates, pressures, forces her to expose her beauty, he can crush her confidence, purity, dignity, and ability to become vulnerable and to trust. When this happens, a woman can become ashamed, overprotective, suspicious, and resentful.

However, when a man offers his bride the warmth of the Sonlight, that is, the divine love planted within his heart, she becomes trusting, vulnerable, and more willing to unveil her exterior and interior beauty before him.

Why do so many women's' "flowers" remain shut tight? Because they have yet to experience the tender, gentle, self-giving love of the Son of God through their husbands. Because of this, the world never encounters the real gift of her person, her gift of womanhood and beauty, which remains locked up inside of her.

In a certain sense, the measure of a man is determined by how he lives in relationship to woman. Does he force her to pull back the petals or does he love her in such a way that she becomes who God has called and destined her to be. Does he protect her dignity, guarding her mystery, or does he reduce her to an object to be used to fulfill his disordered need for self-gratification?

A man's essence—what constitutes the core of his being—is how and to what level he sets the pace of self-sacrificial love for his wife and children. To truly set this pace, a man is to embrace woman in three ways: First, he is to embrace all women, their beauty, dignity, and person, by striving to defeat and overcome lust in the heart; second, he is to embrace his wife by remaining yoked to her and bearing her burdens as his own; and third, he is to embrace the Woman, the Blessed Virgin Mary, by doing what St. Joseph did: entrusting his entire vocation as a father and husband to this great lady.

Remember, the measure of a man is determined by how he embraces woman. Over the next several reflections we will meditate on what it means to embrace, protect, and cultivate the "flower" of woman, that she may reveal her awe-inspiring, God-given, beauty.

St. Joseph discovered himself, his mission, and his capacity for greatness by living in relationship to his wife, Mary. So it will be with you. You will discover your true capacity for fatherly greatness only in light of being a heroic husband for your wife.

> **TAKE THE LEAD** Often a husband's relationship with his wife can become strained, burdened, and embittered. This is sometimes a consequence of one spouse not obtaining what they want from the other. A way to combat this tendency is to begin viewing your wife as your ally; the one who God has created to "draw out" your masculine essence. Over the next several reflections, your wife will most likely say and do things that cause you frustration and consternation. Rather than reacting negatively to her behavior, try to believe that her actions are a means to make you a man of self-giving love.*

* See Examen *Embrace Dignity of Women* on page 446

PILLAR 2: EMBRACE YOUR ESSENCE [EMBRACING WOMAN]

YOU NEED HER

53. YOUR ESSENCE: SETTING THE PACE OF SELF-GIVING LOVE

From the moment that God created Eve and onward throughout the history of mankind, man has been measured by how he lives in relationship to woman and the child she bears. Which leads us to the second pillar of St. Joseph's spirituality: embracing woman.

It has been said that no woman can teach a man how to become a man—only a man can do that. As true as this may be, woman is indispensable in helping the boy become a man. Indeed, a woman cannot teach a boy how to become a true man, but rather, she affords him the opportunity to become one. In a certain sense, every man needs the woman—the bride—to become a great man and secure his salvation; and every woman needs man—the representative of the eternal bridegroom—to help her experience her feminine dignity and love of God.

Men and woman, though made of the same "stuff"—body and soul—are unique in their essence. A man's body indicates that he is different from the woman, and this sexual difference communicates a message that reveals who he is, that is, his identity, and who he is for her—his mission. Your body indicates that you are called to go forth from yourself, to initiate self-sacrificial, self-giving love. Just as a man must penetrate a woman's body in sexual intercourse, which can bear the fruit of physical life, so also his initiating self-giving love penetrates her soul with the seed of love, which brings forth the fruit of spiritual life. Your essence—every man's essence—as reflected in his body, is to set the pace of self-giving love. The test of a true man is whether he lives from his essence and sets this pace.

Many marriages and families fail and become divided because men fail to understand and live from their essence. If you ever experience the temptation to flee from the woman who will help you become true man, call upon St. Joseph and imitate his example; after initially withdrawing from Mary, he took her into his home. Taking Mary into his home, into his soul, was Joseph's first step toward becoming a true man and father of greatness.

If you, like St. Joseph, embrace woman by setting the pace of self-giving love in your marriage, you will not only discover who you are, but also allow your wife to become who she has been created to be. Your marriage will begin to image the marriage of Christ and his Church, enabling your family to experience in their humanity what God is in eternity—self-giving love.

> **TAKE THE LEAD** Often a husband's relationship with his wife can become strained, burdened, and embittered. This is sometimes a consequence of one spouse not obtaining what they want from the other. A way to combat this tendency is to begin viewing your wife as your ally; the one who God has created to "draw out" your masculine essence. Over the next several reflections, your wife will most likely say and do things that cause you frustration and consternation. Rather than reacting negatively to her behavior, try to believe that her actions are a means to make you a man of self-giving love.*

* See Examen *Embrace Dignity of Women* on page 446

YOU NEED HER

54. DO YOU NEED HER?

Why did you marry your wife? Was it her beauty that allured you? Did her personality, wit, and charm captivate you? Did you discover in her a friend who has interest in things that interested you? Now consider some of the elderly couples that you have met. Their attributes have sagged and beauty has faded; their personalities and interests have changed and memories have failed, and yet they are still together. Why are they still married?

Beauty fades, personalities shift and mature. Life's responsibilities can often cause our interests to evolve, become more practical, while former pursuits fade and diminish. You may have married your wife because of her beauty, her personality, or because you share common interests; however, we marry and remain married because of something that is more intrinsic to the soul of man—something that we really need.

In the beginning, after creating Adam, God said, "It is not good that the man should be alone." The Hebrew word for alone is *abadad*, which literally means "bad." The one and only occasion during the entire creation account that God deems anything bad is in regard to man being alone, in loneliness, and isolated from communion.

After stating this concern for Adam, God created woman, Eve, for the purpose of moving man from isolation and loneliness—which is bad—to communion and love, which God deems to be the highest good. Communion, self-giving love, marriage, the one-flesh union and its fruit—the family—are the highest goods (humanly speaking) because God created these to reflect, relive, and reveal His identity.

What God is in eternity, He desires to replicate, reveal, and relive in our humanity. God is an eternal exchange of persons whose essence is self-giving love. God desires that we share in this eternal exchange of love—even now—and therefore, He gives us marriage and the family as the context in which we can experience heaven on earth. This may not sound like your family, but this is the reason for your marriage and the existence of your family. This is why you need her, and even if you didn't understand it at the time, this is why you married her.

> **TAKE THE LEAD** Often a husband's relationship with his wife can become strained, burdened, and embittered. This is sometimes a consequence of one spouse not obtaining what they want from the other. A way to combat this tendency is to begin viewing your wife as your ally; the one who God has created to "draw out" your masculine essence. Over the next several reflections, your wife will most likely say and do things that cause you frustration and consternation. Rather than reacting negatively to her behavior, try to believe that her actions are a means to make you a man of self-giving love.*

* See Examen *Embrace Dignity of Women* on page 446

THE MYSTERY OF MARRIAGE

55. THE MISSION OF MARRIAGE

Some say that if a couple remains married they have really accomplished something. But what is this "something" that they have achieved? Survival is not really something to be proud of; thriving, however, is worthy of admiration. What does a thriving marriage accomplish?

Consider that God's intention is to create human beings (physical, fleshly creatures) who are capable of revealing His mystery, His invisible identity. Which raises the question: What is God's mystery or identity? God has revealed Himself as three distinct Persons who are one in self-giving love, and from this union proceeds life, love, joy, bliss, glory, rapture, power, beauty, creativity, and ecstasy (see CCC 1824). What God is and does in eternity He wills to reflect, relive, and reveal in our humanity. Considering this intention, He created man and woman in His image. The three main attributes of the Trinity are distinction, unity, and fruitfulness. God is three distinct Persons (distinction), Who exchange themselves with one another (unity), and from this eternal union comes forth love and life (fruitfulness).

God created man and woman as two distinct persons, who by themselves are limited in their ability to image God, but together, by means of their sexual complementarity and self-giving love, they achieve unity. This union is an actual reliving and revealing of God's self-giving love, which also produces life, both spiritual and physical: as Pope St. John Paul II says, "Man becomes an image of God not so much in the moment of solitude as in the moment of communion" (TOB 9:3).

Marriage and family has been created by God as a perpetual reminder of our identity (we are living symbols of God's love) and our destiny (we are to live in the eternal exchange of love of the Trinity). "God Himself is an eternal exchange of love; Father, Son and Holy Spirit, and He has destined us to share in this exchange" (CCC 211). In other words, your marriage and family are ordained to experience and express God's eternal self-giving love. This is a great calling!

An Olympic athlete suffers, sacrifices, and endures long hours of training for the purpose of achieving what very few people accomplish—a gold medal. Marriage is the school of self-giving love in which you and your wife, by means of much suffering, sacrifice, and endurance, achieve what so few accomplish: the experience of God's eternal love, even now on earth.

> **TAKE THE LEAD** There is a tendency among men who are goal oriented to be swallowed into the black hole of daily responsibilities and forget the real motivation for his duties. This can be applied to marriage. When we lose sight of our destiny—the Trinity—we view marriage as a chore and our role as husbands as a burden. Over the next several reflections, ask God to inspire you with the reoccurring reminder that God desires to reflect, relive, and reveal the glory of the self-giving love of the Trinity in your family. By having this mind-set, you will be granted the power to see beyond the minor setbacks and set your hopes on the real purpose of your marriage.*

* See Examen *Embrace Dignity of Women* on page 446

PILLAR 2: EMBRACE YOUR ESSENCE [EMBRACING WOMAN]

THE MYSTERY OF MARRIAGE

56. WHY IS IT SO DIFFICULT?

Have you ever wondered why there is so much tension between the sexes? Why do so many marriages end in divorce? Why do couples become entrenched in their bitterness toward one another? The very intense magnetic attraction between the sexes sometimes backfires and becomes the very power that fuels resentment and division. Why is this?

Consider that what God does in eternity—eternal self-giving love—is painless, but within our sinful context, self-giving love can often be very painful. The Crucifixion of Christ confirms this. He attempted to give Himself to humanity, but was rejected. When we attempt to authentically give ourselves away to another, we always run the risk of rejection. But such rejection should never dissuade us from this tremendous mission to love in the image of Christ.

Marriage is a tremendous calling. Indeed, it is not for the fainthearted, but for those who desire to walk the path of saints. What is a saint? One who lives and experiences communion with God. Marriage and family life have been created to be a school whose pedagogy is self-donation. Marriage and family makes saints.

To live one day in relationship with God, God must live in our relationships today—especially our marriages. Remember that little-*r* relationships lead to the big-*R* Relationship of the Trinity. Our marriages constitute a little-*r* relationship that leads to the big-*R* Relationship of God. What we do in our humanity determines our destiny. If you desire to live in union with the eternal Relationship of the Trinity, it is imperative that you learn how to live in relationship with your wife.

This is God's plan. God created man and woman, husband and wife, to be magnetically attracted to one another, to need each other—because they need God. God created your marriage to be the specific context for you and your wife to experience a foreshadowing of God's eternal exchange of persons. God gave you your wife so that the two of you could begin to reveal, relive and reflect His eternal self-giving love by learning to love one another. This is precisely what faithful, enduring, God-centered marriages accomplish.

This is the divine mission for marriage; and the devil will do anything to keep your marriage from fulfilling this purpose. And that is why marriage can be tremendously difficult.

> **TAKE THE LEAD** There is a tendency among men who are goal oriented to be swallowed into the black hole of daily responsibilities and forget the real motivation for his duties. This can be applied to marriage. When we lose sight of our destiny—the Trinity—we view marriage as a chore and our role as husbands as a burden. Over the next several reflections, ask God to inspire you with the reoccurring reminder that God desires to reflect, relive, and reveal the glory of the self-giving love of the Trinity in your family. By having this mind-set, you will be granted the power to see beyond the minor setbacks and set your hopes on the real purpose of your marriage.*

* See Examen *Embrace Dignity of Women* on page 446

THE MYSTERY OF MARRIAGE

57. UNVEILING THE MYSTERY

Your marriage is rich with meaning, significance, and mystery. Your marriage is not merely a type of social or cultural construct invented by men for the purpose of harmonizing and bringing order to society. Marriage was not created to ensure that men, who, after moving away from home, would have an ample substitute for their mother. No. Marriage is so much more.

Marriage wasn't created by man, but rather created for man by God. God created marriage as a way to communicate His plan and our participation in that plan.

According to ancient Jewish cultural traditions, a wedding feast would normally last seven days, culminating on the seventh day with the groomsmen carrying the bridegroom in procession to the *chuppah*—the wedding tent—where the bride awaited him. After the attendees witnessed the couple's vowing themselves to one another, the couple would enter the *chuppah*'s inner chamber and the bride would remove the veil from her face—and perhaps much more. The Greek word used for the act of unveiling is *apokolyspsis*, which is translated as "uncovering," "lifting of the veil," or "revelation." The pinnacle moment of the Jewish marriage feast is the unveiling, the revelation of the spouses to one another.

In other words, God created marriage to be His way to unveil the mystery of Christ's marriage to the Church, to reveal to spouses their roles, what each spouse represents (the husband represents Christ the Bridegroom and the wife represents the Church, the Bride of Christ), and how they can experience a glorious participation in God's love by revealing themselves to one another.

God created marriage, specifically your marriage, to be a revelation, an *apokolypsis*, a way to uncover God's plan for you and your wife, while also helping us lift the veil from the mystery of God. It is "[f]or this reason a man shall leave his father and mother and cleave to his wife and the two shall be one flesh. This is a great mystery—I mean in reference to Christ and his Church" (Eph 5:31). In other words, marriage is a mysterious sacrament that relives and reveals the marriage of Christ and His Church. Far from a man finding a substitute for his mother as caregiver, he rather unites himself to his wife for the purpose of experiencing the mystery of Christ's mystical marriage to His Church—heaven on earth.

> **TAKE THE LEAD** There is a tendency among men who are goal oriented to be swallowed into the black hole of daily responsibilities and forget the real motivation for his duties. This can be applied to marriage. When we lose sight of our destiny—the Trinity—we view marriage as a chore and our role as husbands as a burden. Over the next several reflections, ask God to inspire you with the reoccurring reminder that God desires to reflect, relive, and reveal the glory of the self-giving love of the Trinity in your family. By having this mind-set, you will be granted the power to see beyond the minor setbacks and set your hopes on the real purpose of your marriage.*

* See Examen *Embrace Dignity of Women* on page 446

THE MYSTERY OF MARRIAGE

58. HOW A DYING MAN CAN MAKE HIS MARRIAGE BEAUTIFUL

What is your role? To be Christ to your wife. To love your wife as Jesus loves the Church. "Husbands, love your wives, just as Christ also loved the Church and delivered Himself up for her, cleansing her in the bath of water by means of the word; in order that he may present to Himself the Church in all her glory, not having spot or wrinkle or any such thing, but that she might be holy and without blemish" (Eph 5:25–27).

Every man desires a beautiful woman, or more precisely, he desires that his woman be beautiful. Every woman desires to be beautiful, more precisely, the most beautiful woman in her husband's world. Your wife's beauty is not only external. In fact, her true internal beauty is expressed in and through her body. How often have we encountered women who have the gift of external beauty, but because they lack internal beauty they repulse us? What then makes a woman beautiful? What makes Christ's Church beautiful "without spot or blemish"? When you sacrifice your disordered selfish nature and discover the Word of God; when you live it, embody it, and share it with your wife, you wash her in Christ's self-sacrificial love, which enhances and draws out her true beauty. Your love, precisely Christ's love expressed through you, helps to make your wife beautiful.

Your marriage has been created to reveal the mystery of Christ's undying, relentless, sacrificial, fruitful love for His Church by means of your self-donation on behalf of your wife. Your marriage is intended to launch the world into the mystery of Christ and His Church; and the family that flows from the fountain of your marriage has been created to launch us into the mystery of the Trinity. As Pope St. John Paul II said, "Our God in His deepest mystery is not a solitude, but a family, since He has in Himself fatherhood, sonship and the essence of the family, which is love."

Because of St. Joseph's self-sacrificial, disinterested love for the Virgin Mary, particularly by overcoming the temptation to burden her with the expectation of fulfilling his desires for love, his "[f]amily of Nazareth shows us that every family is means to be an 'icon of God' and image the Holy Trinity to the world" (Archbishop Gomez). So it will be with you. If you love your wife in the manner that Joseph loved Mary, and in the way Christ loves the Church, your family will become what God has intended it to be: an *apokolypsis,* an unveiling of God's love to this world.

> **TAKE THE LEAD** There is a tendency among men who are goal oriented to be swallowed into the black hole of daily responsibilities and forget the real motivation for his duties. This can be applied to marriage. When we lose sight of our destiny—the Trinity—we view marriage as a chore and our role as husbands as a burden. Over the next several reflections, ask God to inspire you with the reoccurring reminder that God desires to reflect, relive, and reveal the glory of the self-giving love of the Trinity in your family. By having this mind-set, you will be granted the power to see beyond the minor setbacks and set your hopes on the real purpose of your marriage.*

* See Examen *Embrace Dignity of Women* on page 446

PILLAR 2: EMBRACE YOUR ESSENCE [EMBRACING WOMAN]

THE MYSTERY OF MARRIAGE

59. WHERE ARE YOU FROM? WHERE ARE YOU GOING?

Often when meeting someone for the first time we are asked or ask the other, "Where are you from?" Certainly this question can and is used as a means of developing conversation. However superficial it may appear, its motivation is founded in seeking to understand the other—who they are, what are their life experiences, and how their experiences and culture have helped to form them into the person they are today.

Perhaps you've heard the phrase "get back to your roots," that is, return to the place or the culture of your origin for the purpose of understanding your true identity. Remember that to achieve your destiny it is imperative that you understand and embrace your identity. Your identity does not exist in isolation from the human experience, but is intrinsically connected with all men, who find their beginning in one man—Adam, and his beginning.

By returning to the beginning, you will not only discover where you are from—your roots—but also a clue to your identity; and also discover the core of woman's identity, her origin, and how the original man's and woman's beginning can lead you and your wife to the ultimate destiny. Considering this, we will reflect upon our origin to discover who the man is for the woman, and who the woman is for the man: who you are for your wife, and your wife is for you.

On the sixth day of creation, "[t]he Lord God formed man out of the dust of the ground and breathed into his nostrils the breath of life, and man became a living being. The Lord God planted a garden in the east and he put there the man he had formed" (Gen 2:7–8). And again, "The Lord God took the man and placed him in the Garden of Eden to till it and keep it. And the Lord God commanded the man 'thus from every tree of the garden you may eat; but from the tree of knowledge of good and evil you must not eat; for the day you eat of it, you must die'" (Gen 2:15–16).

These brief words are loaded with rich significance regarding who a man is and his relationship to all women, particularly his wife. Adam was created on the sixth day. The sixth day is the day that God created the animals. It is therefore a day that symbolizes the animal, the beast, the spiritless flesh. However, Adam is separated from all the other creatures created on the sixth day when he receives the breath of God—in Hebrew, *Ruah*, which is interpreted as God's Spirit.

God gave Adam His likeness, His very Spirit, which elevated Adam from the realm of the beasts, symbolized by the sixth day. God gave man His very presence to enable him to live in intimate communion and relationship with God, symbolized by the seventh day. From this point onward, man is engaged in the battle to live according to the Spirit of God, which differentiates himself from the beasts, and the evil one who is bent on keeping man entrapped in the "sixth day."

You may be from the sixth day, but you are made for the seventh day—Heaven and communion with God. God has created your marriage as the "training ground" to help you cease living like a beast and become a man of self-giving love.

> **TAKE THE LEAD** There is a tendency among men who are goal oriented to be swallowed into the black hole of daily responsibilities and forget the real motivation for his duties. This can be applied to marriage. When we lose sight of our destiny—the Trinity—we view marriage as a chore and our role as husbands as a burden. Over the next several reflections, ask God to inspire you with the reoccurring reminder that God desires to reflect, relive, and reveal the glory of the self-giving love of the Trinity in your family. By having this mind-set, you will be granted the power to see beyond the minor setbacks and set your hopes on the real purpose of your marriage.*

* See Examen *Embrace Dignity of Women* on page 446

THE MYSTERY OF MARRIAGE

60. MOVING FROM DAY SIX TO DAY SEVEN

If your mission is to move from day six, the day of the beast, to day seven, the day of the Lord, how do you accomplish this? It is important to understand that without the *Ruah*, God's Spirit, a husband cannot attain communion with his wife or with God (day seven). Yet, with God's Spirit within him, he can experience the harmony of self-giving love in his relationship with his wife and with God.

The word "man" in Hebrew is Adam, which is related to the Hebrew word *Adamah*, which means ground. This indicates that the name Adam literally means "from the earth." This is important because Adam's name indicates his, and every man's, God-given mission, foundational identity, and essence. Adam was called to "rise from the earth." This was his destiny. This is our destiny as well. The first fundamental way we move from day six to day seven is to understand that we are called to rise from the dead, which means that we must first lay down our life.

Second, Adam was not created in the garden, but outside the garden, in the unknown, uncharted, undiscovered, undefined wilderness. Only later is he placed by God in the garden (as mentioned twice in the creation account as a way to emphasize this fact). The word "garden" was often used in Hebrew literature to describe woman, her mystery, her fruitfulness—the domestic world. Considering this, we can conclude that all men, as symbolized by Adam, stand on the horizon between the outside, exterior, hostile, competitive, world and the domestic life. The second fundamental way we are to move from day six, to day seven is the duty and responsibility to integrate these two worlds; mining, gathering and hunting the resources necessary for our family to thrive, while also protecting the domestic life from the violent, hostile, ever invading world.

Third, notice that when God gave man His Spirit and the command to till and keep the earth, and to not eat from the tree of knowledge of good and evil, woman had not yet been created. This indicates that man has another fundamental responsibility besides providing for and protecting his family: he is called to transmit the commands of God to her. This truth is confirmed in Ephesians 5: husbands "[l]ove your wives as Christ loved the Church, and delivered himself up for her, that he might sanctify her, cleansing her in the bath of water, by means of the word." Notice that this spiritual cleansing consists of baptism, but also her sanctification by God's word. This means that the third way we move from day six to day seven is by fulfilling the noble mission of transmitting God's truth and commands, particularly by our example.

You and I, like Adam, are responsible to God for the woman, while the woman is responsible to God through the man. It is your responsibility to God to transmit the Word of God to your wife, and this is accomplished by loving her like Christ loves the Church: by delivering yourself up for her.

> **TAKE THE LEAD** There is a tendency among men who are goal oriented to be swallowed into the black hole of daily responsibilities and forget the real motivation for his duties. This can be applied to marriage. When we lose sight of our destiny—the Trinity—we view marriage as a chore and our role as husbands as a burden. Over the next several reflections, ask God to inspire you with the reoccurring reminder that God desires to reflect, relive, and reveal the glory of the self-giving love of the Trinity in your family. By having this mind-set, you will be granted the power to see beyond the minor setbacks and set your hopes on the real purpose of your marriage.*

* See Examen *Embrace Dignity of Women* on page 446

DISCOVERING YOUR ESSENCE

61. THE WEIGHT OF RESPONSIBILITY

Recall that Adam was called to stand on the horizon between the outside, uncharted world and the garden, and to integrate these two worlds. Every man is commissioned by God to use what is good from the outside world for his family. But every man also has the responsibility to stand guard at the gate of the garden to ensure that the evil of the world does not penetrate or invade it. Do you sense the weight of responsibility placed upon us men?

In addition to this, God gave Adam a series of commands: "Till and keep the garden," which literally in Hebrew means that Adam was called to cherish and protect the woman, the child, and the environment. Adam was commissioned to provide by means of his hard work, but also he had the duty to protect the garden of woman and her child. Adam was told that he could eat of every tree except the tree of knowledge of good and evil. Here God draws the line in the sand, indicating that the generous Creator has given man dominion, glory, honor, and power, placing all things under his feet (see Psalm 8). But God was also communicating the message that man must never mistake himself for God.

The question arises: Where was Eve when Adam received these commands? She did not exist. As mentioned previously, Adam was called not only to provide for and protect, but also to transmit the divine truth he received from God to woman. Again, to repeat an important truth: men are responsible to God for the woman and the child. This is indicated after the fall of Adam and Eve. God did not first approach the woman asking her where she was, but rather God approached the man first, asking him, "Where are you?" Again, we can sense the tremendous pressure, and responsibility that falls upon us men.

Recall that the name Adam can be translated as meaning "from the earth." Adam was called to defend Eve and her garden from the serpent who was bent on invading and penetrating her with sin. Adam was ordained with the task, if necessary, to stand in the breach between the evil one and his bride and deliver himself up for her. Hypothetically, if Adam had done so, God would have surely resurrected him "from the earth," and thus his identity would have led to his destiny. But Adam failed. Rather than rising from the earth in glory, he returned to it in death.

Like Adam, we may be tempted to remain silent in our refusal to sacrifice for our bride. Yet, it is vital that we understand that our ultimate end is not to return to the earth in death, but rather to rise from it in glorified life. This is the weight of responsibility—and of glory.

> **TAKE THE LEAD** One of the greatest ways a husband can fail his children is by withdrawing from his wife. This does not apply only to the divorced husband whose children are in his wife's custody. A husband can be absent physically, spiritually, emotionally and personally. One reason that a man flees is because he resists being crushed by his wife's demands, her burdens, her desires, her neglect, her demeaning attitude. However, if you can embrace such "blows" and respond with love, a "holy oil" will anoint your marriage. Over the next few reflections, make it your aim to resist all forms of retaliation and rather find opportunities to anoint her with the oil of gladness.*

* See Examen *Embrace Dignity of Women* on page 446

PILLAR 2: EMBRACE YOUR ESSENCE [EMBRACING WOMAN]

DISCOVERING YOUR ESSENCE

62. SETTING THE PACE

Where was Adam when the serpent tempted Eve? The sacred text tells us that after Eve had eaten from the fruit, she turned and gave the fruit to her husband, indicating that he was by her side during the temptation account. Adam's silence is profound. His silence is not the silence of one who sacrificially suffers without complaint, but rather one who by his silence refuses to defend or sacrifice himself for another. Silence in the positive sense is a willingness to remain resolute in one's defense of the truth. Silence in the negative sense is an unwillingness to stand up for the truth for the sake of self-preservation.

Jesus, on the night of his betrayal, ironically enters a garden. Here in this garden, Judas and the temple guards, like the serpent, secretly enter the garden by night. It is at this moment Jesus says, "Let these go." In other words, "Release my bride, my church, and take me instead." From the point of Jesus' apprehension onward, He silently, resolutely, sets the pace of self-giving love, determined to deliver Himself up for his bride on Calvary. By doing so, Jesus becomes the New Adam who fulfills the destiny of the old Adam by rising from the earth on Easter Sunday.

St. Joseph stood on the horizon between the hostile, challenging, competitive world and the garden of Mary and Jesus, by protecting them from Herod, providing for them, while also communicating to them—mostly through his silent, steadfast, sacrificial example— the law and the love of God. Remember that "Joseph refused to expose Mary to shame." This can indicate that Joseph protected Mary from the threats of the outside world (such as Herod), but just as important, from the threat of himself. Joseph knew that "[t]he heart is deceitful above all things, and unsearchable; who can know it?" (Jer 17:9). "With all watchfulness guard thy heart" (Prov 4:23). And "He that trusts in his own heart, is a fool; but whoso walks wisely, he shall be saved" (Prov 28:26).

Joseph was acutely aware of the human tendency to use another, objectify another, lust for another, to coerce or dominate another. Yet Joseph, in his self-mastery, refused to expose Mary to any such thing. St. Thomas Aquinas said that God gives the grace proportionate to our office and state in life; and St. John Paul II said, "It is inconceivable that such a sublime task [Joseph being Mary's husband and Jesus' father] would not be matched by the necessary qualities to adequately fulfill it" (GR 8). St. Joseph was given the grace to protect Mary and Jesus from the serpent of sin, and even and especially from himself.

You and I—if we are to set the pace of self-giving love—are to strive to protect our wives not only from the hostile world, but also from our selfish motivations and disordered desires. By doing this in little ways, over time, and with the grace of God, we will not succumb to the tendency to be silent for the sake of self-preservation, but rather silently remain resolute in the defense of our family, our vocation, and the God who has called us to greatness.

> **TAKE THE LEAD** One of the greatest ways a husband can fail his children is by withdrawing from his wife. This does not apply only to the divorced husband whose children are in his wife's custody. A husband can be absent physically, spiritually, emotionally and personally. One reason that a man flees is because he resists being crushed by his wife's demands, her burdens, her desires, her neglect, her demeaning attitude. However, if you can embrace such "blows" and respond with love, a "holy oil" will anoint your marriage. Over the next few reflections, make it your aim to resist all forms of retaliation and rather find opportunities to anoint her with the oil of gladness.*

* See Examen *Embrace Dignity of Women* on page 446

DISCOVERING YOUR ESSENCE

63. FINDING YOURSELF IN HER

Since the earliest of times, plays, dramas, and in recent times movies have made audiences' hearts swoon with the heartrending theme of a man sacrificing his life for the woman he loves. These stories capitalize on an essential truth that resonates with the human heart: women long for the sacrificial love of the New Adam as embodied in the man they love. However, when women are not given the authentic, life-giving, self-donating love of the New Adam through a man, they are more easily tempted to seduce the old Adam in us men for the purpose of obtaining some type of affirmation—even if the affection and attention is disordered and ultimately unfulfilling. It appears that when Eve realized that Adam was neglecting to protect her from the serpent, she sought to obtain his attention by tempting him with the forbidden fruit.

A woman's heart longs for the warrior who is willing to fight and even die for her. But why would a man want to offer his life in sacrifice for a woman? What is it about a woman that could inspire a man to donate himself to and for her?

After God stated that it is not good (literally, bad) that the man is alone, he cast Adam into a deep sleep. The Hebrew word for this sleep is *tardemah*, which is interpreted as "supernatural slumber," or as translated to the Greek, *ecstasis*, which literally means "to be outside of oneself."

Before this divinely induced slumber, Adam had experienced the tremendous responsibility and weight of his God-given mission—in solitude—without a partner. However, when Adam awakes he sees the woman that God had formed from his rib in her naked glory and sings an ode of joy and adoration to God: "This is bone of my bones and flesh of my flesh!" Adam sees the completion of himself in Eve. Adam's rib in Eve indicates that he is in her and can only be complete when united with her; whereas Eve, because she is taken from the man, is always longing to return to him. From this moment onward, not only Eve, but every woman—by means of her feminine beauty and presence—perpetually reminds men of their noble mission. Woman's spiritual, emotional, physical and intellectual beauty constantly summon man to move beyond his self-absorbed microcosm and become a warrior of self-giving love.

> **TAKE THE LEAD** One of the greatest ways a husband can fail his children is by withdrawing from his wife. This does not apply only to the divorced husband whose children are in his wife's custody. A husband can be absent physically, spiritually, emotionally and personally. One reason that a man flees is because he resists being crushed by his wife's demands, her burdens, her desires, her neglect, her demeaning attitude. However, if you can embrace such "blows" and respond with love, a "holy oil" will anoint your marriage. Over the next few reflections, make it your aim to resist all forms of retaliation and rather find opportunities to anoint her with the oil of gladness.*

* See Examen *Embrace Dignity of Women* on page 446

DISCOVERING YOUR ESSENCE

64. IS SHE WORTH DYING FOR?

God knows that the weight of responsibility of fulfilling the divine mission to be guardian of the garden is too great for us. Because of this he gifts us with a collaborator, another self, a partner to aid us in our mission—he creates Eve, woman, your wife. The word "Eve" means life-giver. Yet, her ability to impart or bear life is far more than physical, biological reproduction. The Hebrew word for Eve can also convey the idea that the woman, Eve, gives the man vitality, courage, strength inspired by love.

The creation account culminates with God creating Eve last. St. Thomas Aquinas said that what is last in God's execution is first in God's intention. Woman, therefore, is first in God's intention; she is the pinnacle of His creation. She is the most delicate, fragile, beautiful, glorious, and attractive. Mary, the Mother of Jesus—the Mother of God—is the fulfillment and ideal of this pinnacle of the created order.

Woman's essence and core mission is to be a mediatrix of life and love. Symbolically she is the very garden where life and love are formed; and the Virgin Mary is the exemplar and pinnacle of this ideal in that she gives life and love in the person of Christ to the world. Your duty and mission as a man, husband, and leader is to protect, provide for, love, and cherish woman—particularly your wife—as a symbol of the pinnacle of creation, to ensure that her garden remains sacred, beautiful, unstained, and capable of giving love and life to the world. She is truly worth dying for.

St. Joseph believed Mary, his wife, to be worth his continual sacrifice and enduring self-donation. Joseph left behind lands and homes when commanded on numerous occasions by the angel of the Lord to uproot his life and move to new lands. St. Joseph surrendered any desire for sexual intimacy by loving Mary, his wife, in a celibate manner. St. Joseph accepted the humiliation of his good character as a righteous, law-abiding, God-fearing Jew, by receiving a woman who was pregnant before he took her into his home. Joseph sacrificed all for the Woman, and by doing so, he received Christ through her; for woman is the mediatrix of life and love. And so it will be with each of us. If you choose to intentionally donate yourself consistently on behalf of your wife, you will receive the God of grace, blessing, and favor through her. She truly is worth dying for.

> **TAKE THE LEAD** One of the greatest ways a husband can fail his children is by withdrawing from his wife. This does not apply only to the divorced husband whose children are in his wife's custody. A husband can be absent physically, spiritually, emotionally and personally. One reason that a man flees is because he resists being crushed by his wife's demands, her burdens, her desires, her neglect, her demeaning attitude. However, if you can embrace such "blows" and respond with love, a "holy oil" will anoint your marriage. Over the next few reflections, make it your aim to resist all forms of retaliation and rather find opportunities to anoint her with the oil of gladness.*

* See Examen *Embrace Dignity of Women* on page 446

PILLAR 2: EMBRACE YOUR ESSENCE [EMBRACING WOMAN]

DISCOVERING YOUR ESSENCE

65. AGONY AND ECSTASY

Nearly all of life's experiences consist of a combination of bitter and sweet, pleasure and pain, blessing and curse. Indeed, every blessing has its curse and every curse has its blessing. Even the Lord Jesus Himself—the greatest gift known to humanity—brought the Blessed Mother incomparable joy and unfathomable sickness of sorrow. Your wife is no different. A wife is one of God's most tremendous blessings, but also can be the source of significant angst, frustration, and heartache.

EDEN = DELIGHT   GETHSEMENE = OIL PRESS

Recall that in Hebrew literature the word "garden" was often used to symbolize woman. The name of the first garden, Eden, literally means "delight." By means of associating these terms, we discover that God created the woman as a symbol of delight; and properly speaking she affords men great delight. Recall also that Jesus, the New Adam, on the night of His betrayal, entered a garden—the garden of Gethsemane. It was in this garden that Jesus agonized over His impending torture, Crucifixion, death, and surrendered Himself and His cause over to His Father. It was in this garden that Jesus triumphed over the temptation to preserve Himself, and rather offered Himself in sacrifice for His bride, the Church. Without His sacrifice, the Church, would have never blossomed into existence.

The word "Gethsemane" means oil press. Woman, the garden—created to be a delight—can often become a place of incredible tension, and resentment. In Jesus' day the process of extracting oil from olives was called treading. Olives were set in a small cove or well of a rock and crushed by another rock, excreting the oil from the olive into the cove of the rock. This process occurred in Gethsemane—hence the name.

When you, as a husband, press forward—like Christ and St. Joseph—to set the pace of self-giving love, you will often experience the burden and sting of rejection, resistance, and perhaps even betrayal from your wife. In a sense, we husbands will be tread. But as you undergo the crushing blows to your pride and ego, if you embrace them properly, the oil of charity—forgiveness, forbearance, and freedom to love without expecting anything in return—will be squeezed from you and poured out, anointing your wife and children.

Unfortunately, such pressure and conflict can cause us, much like Jesus' disciples on the night of His betrayal, to flee the garden. Often men will remain happily in the garden, if it brings them the fruit of delight; but if the garden becomes an oil press that begins to demand that more love be squeezed from them, they flee. What a man is and does under duress is what he truly is.

This process of treading is essential for you to become the father, husband, leader, and man of greatness that God has called and destined you to be. Only by means of suffering can we reach our full capacity to love. Pope St. John Paul II said that "[s]uffering exists in order to unleash love in the human person." Suffering, particularly within marriage, if embraced, can serve to unite the couple, while also offering their children an example of heroic, enduring, self-giving love. When your wife witnesses you overcoming the temptation to retaliate against her; or flee from her, and rather begin to offer yourself in little ways to and for her, she will begin to experience an anointing with the oil of your charity, which will begin to heal her. When this happens the bitterness of Gethsemane can become truly what it should be, a garden of delight.

TAKE THE LEAD One of the greatest ways a husband can fail his children is by withdrawing from his wife. This does not apply only to the divorced husband whose children are in his wife's custody. A husband can be absent physically, spiritually, emotionally and personally. One reason that a man flees is because he resists being crushed by his wife's demands, her burdens, her desires, her neglect, her demeaning attitude. However, if you can embrace such "blows" and respond with love, a "holy oil" will anoint your marriage. Over the next few reflections, make it your aim to resist all forms of retaliation and rather find opportunities to anoint her with the oil of gladness.*

* See Examen *Embrace Dignity of Women* on page 446

LEAD | THE FOUR MARKS OF FATHERLY GREATNESS

HIS NEEDS—HER NEEDS

66. A MAP FOR MARRIAGE

Sexual difference is real. Sexual difference matters. Sexual difference indicates that man and woman, at the core of their being, are different, and in a particular way deficient—they need each other to complete one another. Sexual difference summons men and women to overcome their personal deficiencies through self-giving love. God created man and woman to fit together, to complement and help complete one another, to depend on one another in the pursuit of joy, truth, and communion with God. As Pope St. John Paul II said, "Human life by its nature is 'co-educational,' and its dignity as well as its balance depend at every moment of history and in every place of geographical longitude and latitude on 'who' she shall be for him and he for her."

HOLY TRINITY
One (Unity) in Self-Giving Love
God's Glory = Total Self-Giving Love

CHURCH (Bride - Symbolized by Mary)
"They have no wine"

CHRIST (The Divine Bridegroom)
"I thirst"

NEED 4 — Cherished as Spiritual Inspirer
NEED 3 — Cherished as Essential Counterpart
NEED 2 — Emotional Intimacy: to Be Pursued
NEED 1 — Cherished for Her Beauty

NEED 4 — Respected for Spiritual Authority
NEED 3 — Respected for His Mission
NEED 2 — Physical Intimacy
NEED 1 — Respected for His Strength

Communication Leads to Communion

WIFE   **MARRIAGE MAP**   **HUSBAND**

We men are created to be initiators of self-sacrificial love as expressed in and through our bodies. Women are created to be the essential counterpart, the completion of man, by receiving his self-donation and in return giving him and the world life and love, in a way that man himself could not have on his own. Again, St. John Paul II says, "The husband is above all the one who loves [initiator of self-donation] his wife, who by contrast is the one who is loved" (TOB 92:6). God designed men and women to need each other. This is not a weakness or character flaw per se, but unique to God's original plan.

Men need women and women need men, but often we don't understand how to harmonize our sexual difference, achieve unity, and become one as God is one. Statistical data, research studies, and psychologists remind us that the leading cause of marital breakdown is lack of communication. Communication leads to communion. According to John Gottman, there are four types of communication problems that lead to divorce: criticism of the partner's personality; contempt; defensiveness; and stonewalling (the refusal to communicate at all). Couples become hurt and resentful because certain needs are not being addressed; and usually these authentic needs are not being addressed because couples fail to exercise the humility, patience, courage, and vulnerability to communicate their needs properly.

To clarify, these are not simply wants, but rather authentic, God-given needs that exist at the core of every human being's soul. When these needs are addressed in earnest a person's dignity and call to greatness is awakened. Married couples need one another because they have an inherent need to give themselves to another in order to discover themselves by means of the other. "Man [human beings] can only discover himself by becoming a sincere gift" (GS 24). Your identity leads to your destiny, and you can only discover who you *really* are, by giving yourself away to others—particularly your wife. To become the husband, father, and leader that God has created and destined us to be it is imperative that we be purified of selfishness by means of being a gift to our wives.

TAKE THE LEAD The needs of others can be confused as being simply disordered wants. A wife can make the mistake of misinterpreting her husband's authentic desire as a perverted passion. How can you know what your wife needs? How will she know what you need? Vulnerability is the key. Set out to spend consistent time with your wife—only the two of you—and simply ask her what her heart desires. This can open a "can of worms," and yet, by attentiveness, patience, and endurance you will learn how to win her heart.*

* See Examen *Embrace Your Wife* on page 446

HIS NEEDS—HER NEEDS

67. A KEY TO A SUCCESSFUL MARRIAGE

One of the keys to an intimate, joy-filled, trusting marriage is the expression of needs; and the greatest need (besides God) that the two have is the need for one another. But how often do we men express the fact that we actually need our wives? Too often we believe that by admitting our need for our wives we appear weak, insecure, lacking strength. Yet, God's logic is that "[t]he cross is foolishness to man but it is the wisdom of God" (1 Cor 1:18), and "In our weakness God is made strong" (see 2 Cor 12:9). Jesus from the cross confessed his need: "I thirst." The eternal Bridegroom expresses to the bride His need: "I need you." "I thirst for you." "Quench Me with your love." The bride as represented ultimately by the Virgin Mary, particularly at the wedding of Cana, says to the Bridegroom, "They have no wine." In other words, "I have a need that only you can fulfill." "I need you."

When God created Adam, he was initially alone, and experienced the full weight of his solitude. God used this solitude to communicate to Adam his massive need for a partner—for a wife. Today, God is communicating to us men that we also have this need for woman. One of the keys to a successful, resilient, intimate, enduring, thriving marriage is when a husband begins to express to his wife—in one way or another—that he needs her, that she is vital to his success, that she is essential to the mission God has set before him.

Mary needed Joseph to protect and provide for her family. There existed many responsibilities that only Joseph could do for Mary. Joseph needed Mary to draw him out of himself and more deeply into the mystery of the incarnate God. In a similar way, your wife needs you and you need your wife. If your wife doesn't believe you need her and that she is essential to your mission, she will be tempted to find someone else who will need and desire her.

Communication leads to communion and is essential for any successful marriage. Even more essential is communicating authentic needs in an open, trusting, and sincere way. But even more essential is the communication of the reality that "I need you." Or as the perfect Bridegroom says to the bride, "I thirst." To admit to your wife that you need her can be most humbling. But the fact that you need her is the truth, and the truth will set us free to love like God.

> **TAKE THE LEAD** The needs of others can be confused as being simply disordered wants. A wife can make the mistake of misinterpreting her husband's authentic desire as a perverted passion. How can you know what your wife needs? How will she know what you need? Vulnerability is the key. Set out to spend consistent time with your wife—only the two of you—and simply ask her what her heart desires. This can open a "can of worms," and yet, by attentiveness, patience, and endurance you will learn how to win her heart.*

* See Examen *Embrace Your Wife* on page 446

HIS NEEDS—HER NEEDS

68. GOD'S PLAN FOR YOUR MARRIAGE

Communication leads to communion. But what if a husband doesn't know what he needs to communicate to his wife? What if we don't really understand our own needs? If you don't know what you need, or what your wife really needs, it is impossible to communicate those needs. If you are not communicating your needs to your wife, and if she is not communicating her needs to you, you will struggle in vain to achieve a deep and abiding communion with her.

To sift through the vast, nearly countless amount of wants that the human heart desires would be a daunting, overwhelming, and perhaps impossible task. Yet we don't have to look very far to discover the most fundamental needs of a husband and wife. These needs are not universal needs such as the need for God, life, love, food, water, shelter, oxygen, clothing, companionship; but more specifically they are the core needs that can and should be expressed and addressed by spouses.

Keep in mind that "[m]an became the image of God not only through his own humanity, but also through the communion of persons, which man and woman form from the very beginning.... Man becomes an image of God not so much in the moment of solitude as in the moment of communion" (TOB 9:3). The greatest joy (and the greatest challenge) on this earth is to image God—to actually participate in His essence, which is self-giving love. If this is the greatest joy for spouses, then we can conclude that one of a husband's primary goals is to break forth from his solitude and strive to live in communion with his wife.

One of the keys to living in communion with your wife is first realizing that she has innate, divinely inspired, feminine needs; second, that God has granted you the ability to address her needs; third, that you also have intrinsic authentic, masculine desires that God has planted in your soul; and fourth, that God has created your wife with the ability to address your fundamental authentic needs.

Your foundational core needs will not be exactly the same as your wife's, but rather her needs and your needs will complement and help complete the other.

The divine plan behind spouses having complementary needs is aimed at helping spouses to break free from selfishness, become gifts to one another, and by doing so begin to image God and experience His love in their lives. As the Church teaches: "Man cannot fully find himself except through a sincere gift of self" (GS 24:3/TOB 15:11).

In other words, 1) spouses have real, authentic, God-given needs; 2) spouses are called to express those needs to one another; 3) once these needs have been communicated, spouses use their creativity and generosity to attempt to address these needs by being a gift to the other; 4) by being an authentic gift to the other they begin to achieve communion with one another; and 5) in their communion they begin to experience a real participation in God's love—imaging God's eternal self-giving love to their family and the world. It's that simple—and that difficult.

> **TAKE THE LEAD** The needs of others can be confused as being simply disordered wants. A wife can make the mistake of misinterpreting her husband's authentic desire as a perverted passion. How can you know what your wife needs? How will she know what you need? Vulnerability is the key. Set out to spend consistent time with your wife—only the two of you—and simply ask her what her heart desires. This can open a "can of worms," and yet, by attentiveness, patience, and endurance you will learn how to win her heart.*

* See Examen *Embrace Your Wife* on page 446

PILLAR 2: EMBRACE YOUR ESSENCE [EMBRACING WOMAN]

HIS NEEDS—HER NEEDS

69. DO YOU KNOW WHAT YOU REALLY NEED?

Spouses are called to "[b]e subject to one another, in the fear [reverence] of Christ" (Eph 5:21). We subject ourselves to the other by understanding and addressing one another's needs. Husbands and wives have many, many needs; however, for the sake of simplicity we will be categorizing these needs into four different areas. These needs stem from a husband's overarching need and a wife's overarching need. We do not have to peer very far to discover these needs. In chapter 5 of the book of Ephesians the author says, "Men ought to love their wives as their bodies. He that loveth his wife, loves himself. For no man ever hated his own flesh; but nourishes and cherishes it, as also Christ does the Church" (Eph 5:28–29). "Let every one of you in particular love his wife as himself; and let the wife respect her husband" (Eph 5:33).

From these few words we can conclude that a woman's overarching need is to be cherished—that is protected, nurtured, cared for, and held dear. When a husband believes his wife to be a representative of the pinnacle of creation, a life-bearer, his encouragement and vitality, he realizes that by holding her dear and nurturing her he is actually caring for himself. If she is cherished she will in turn address her husband's chief core need, which, as the sacred text tells us, is to be respected.

When a man receives respect from his wife he has a sense of strength, nobility of character, boldness, courage, and a willingness to take prudential risks, to initiate and even to sacrifice for her sake. Notice that her respect for you is contingent upon you initiating love for her—cherishing her as yourself.

Mary the Mother of God, the spotless, sinless, immaculate conception, respected Joseph as "head of the Holy Family" (see Litany of St. Joseph). "The omniscient God certainly chose the best possible man to be the foster father of Jesus. In the culture of those days, all authority in the family was assigned to the father, and obedience to Joseph would have been expected of both Jesus and Mary"

(Bishop Daniel R. Jenky, CSC, St. Joseph, Sixteenth Festival Letter). In other words, Mary respected Joseph.

Let us "go to Joseph" and imitate his love for Mary, expressing the care he had for her to our own wives, cherishing them that they may in turn reciprocate love by granting us the respect that Mary gave to Joseph.

> **TAKE THE LEAD** The needs of others can be confused as being simply disordered wants. A wife can make the mistake of misinterpreting her husband's authentic desire as a perverted passion. How can you know what your wife needs? How will she know what you need? Vulnerability is the key. Set out to spend consistent time with your wife—only the two of you—and simply ask her what her heart desires. This can open a "can of worms," and yet, by attentiveness, patience, and endurance you will learn how to win her heart.*

* See Examen *Embrace Your Wife* on page 446

HIS NEEDS—HER NEEDS

70. HIS AND HER FOUR COMPLEMENTARY NEEDS

What if you knew what your wife really wanted before she had to tell you, or without you having to ask her? What if there is a way to understand your wife, comprehend her real needs, and address her desires without her becoming frustrated with you, and you frustrated with her? Much of the heartache, turmoil, tension, and frustration within marriage could be overcome if we a husband simply knew what his wife actually needs.

For most men, understanding his wife seems to be an insurmountable mystery that cannot be solved. Meeting her desires is akin to shooting at a target moving at light speed at the distance of Pluto. Yet, if we discover that man and woman, husband and wife, have four fundamental needs, and how those needs compliment and relate to one another, we husbands will be far more capable of addressing her soul's desire, and awakening her to her true identity, dignity, and mission, which will ultimately inspire her to respect you and your mission. This does not mean that we will solve the complex mystery of woman. No. Rather, it does mean that we will aid her in the unveiling of, and rejoicing in, her feminine mystery.

His and her four needs begin with the exterior, physical characteristics and abilities expressed in and through the couple's bodies, then proceed to the deeper, more spiritual needs of the human person. For our purposes, this reflection will only focus on listing his and her needs and demonstrating how they complement one another.

For example, a woman's primary core need is to be cherished for her beauty (physical, emotional, intellectual, and spiritual). Her second need is for emotional intimacy; she desires to be pursued in a properly ordered way, which simply means that her husband seeks her, and discovers ways to spend time with her, listen to her heart, and share experiences with her. Her third core need is to be cherished as his essential counterpart, his partner in "their mission"—his other self who helps to complete him and discover his true identity. Her fourth need is to be cherished in her role as the spiritual inspirer, her ability to act as a human conduit, a transmitter of divine inspiration, counsel, wisdom, and discernment.

The husband's four core needs are related to, and complement, her four needs. If her first need is to be cherished for her beauty, his first need is to be respected for his strength. If her second need is for emotional intimacy, his need is for sexual, physical intimacy. If her third need is to be his essential counterpart, then his need is to have a real sense of mission. If her fourth need is to be his spiritual inspiration (humanly speaking), then his fourth need is to be her and the family's spiritual leader.

His and her four needs are not the conclusion of conjecture or random guesswork, but rather have their origin and basis in the Sacred Scripture and are also inscribed, discovered, and expressed in our human nature. "When God-Yahweh says, 'It is not good that the man is alone (Gen 2:15), He affirmed that, 'alone,' the man does not completely realize his essence. He realizes that only by existing 'with someone'—and put even more deeply and completely, by existing 'for someone.' They point out how fundamental and constitutive the relationship and communion of persons is for man" (TOB 14:2).

St. Joseph's first step in inaugurating his call to greatness, discovering his essence, and becoming the leader that God created and destined him to be, was accomplished by virtue of embracing the Virgin Mary and existing *with* and *for* her. Indeed, by existing "for your wife" and for God "in your wife," by understanding and addressing her fundamental needs, you will discover your essence, and become the husband, father, and leader you are called and destined to be.

> **TAKE THE LEAD** The needs of others can be confused as being simply disordered wants. A wife can make the mistake of misinterpreting her husband's authentic desire as a perverted passion. How can you know what your wife needs? How will she know what you need? Vulnerability is the key. Set out to spend consistent time with your wife—only the two of you—and simply ask her what her heart desires. This can open a "can of worms," and yet, by attentiveness, patience, and endurance you will learn how to win her heart.*

---

* See Examen *Embrace Your Wife* on page 446

PILLAR 2: EMBRACE YOUR ESSENCE [EMBRACING WOMAN]

HER FIRST NEED: BEAUTY

71. ARE YOU CONVINCED OF HER BEAUTY?

What is the primal desire of every woman? For what, fundamentally, does she want to be cherished? There exist two places where we can discover the answer to this question: Sacred Scripture and the store. Scripture tells us: "Husbands, love your wives just as Christ also loves the Church, and delivered himself up for her, that he might sanctify her, cleansing her in the bath of water, by means of the word, in order that He might present to himself the Church in all her glory, not having spot or wrinkle or any such thing, but that she might be holy and without blemish."

These words afford us several key insights into woman: first, woman is an image of the Church, that is, a holy bride. Second, she is called to be beautiful, glorious, without spot, wrinkle, or blemish. Third, just as it is Christ's mission to present His bride, the Church, to His Father, so also a husband is to do the same for his own wife. Scripture indicates that an aspect of God's plan for woman is that she be beautiful, and this is the reason that she naturally longs to be cherished as such.

The second place that we can discover this intrinsic truth is in the stores. Commercial retail offers a nearly infinite array of cosmetic products, anti-aging creams, hair coloring products, nail polish, clothing, jewelry; and doctors offer plastic surgery, Botox injections, and liposuction. Though these can be disordered attempts to enhance a woman or "make" her beautiful, they all testify to the fact that women desire to be beautiful, and recognized as such.

Beauty is not only external, but primarily internal; and the external has been divinely created with the intention of expressing the internal beauty of the feminine soul. Beauty is far deeper than the flesh, and only a true man accomplishes what Christ obtains for His Church: he assists his wife in realizing her timeless spirit and true beauty that is expressed in and through her body.

Often, however, many women—including our wives—are deeply wounded, suffer from insecurity, feel criticized, objectified, and shamed by the world's impossible standard of beauty. This unrealistic perfection causes a universal anguish in the feminine soul, a fundamental disquiet that daily taunts and haunts a woman, robbing her of the freedom to reveal her true self.

Perhaps a reason wives don't believe they are beautiful is because we husbands are not convinced of their real beauty. The first step to awakening your wife to her God-given beauty is to be convinced of it yourself.

> **TAKE THE LEAD** Regardless of her age, your wife longs to be cherished for her beauty. Examine her closet, her dresser drawers, and the cosmetic goods stocked in the bathroom. This is her chief desire: to be cherished for her beauty. As we age, our physical beauty rusts and tarnishes. It is up to you to be man enough to see your wife's ever-changing, ever-aging body and discover anew her radiant God-given beauty. Over the next several reflections, be intentional about bringing attention to your wife's beauty. Compliment her. But don't overdo it. Be sincere. See God's glory in her and remind her of the glory that lives within her.*

* See Examen *Embrace Your Wife* on page 446

PILLAR 2: EMBRACE YOUR ESSENCE [EMBRACING WOMAN]

HER FIRST NEED: BEAUTY

72. IS YOUR WIFE STILL BEAUTIFUL? HER FIRST NEED (CONT.)

Scripture tells us that St. Joseph "refused to expose Mary to shame." The Greek translation of this verse can mean that Joseph refused to unveil Mary's dignity to shame—particularly his own. St. Joseph refused to expose Mary to his potential to lust, and overcame any temptation to reduce Mary to an object to be used for his self-gratification. Joseph peered through Mary's flesh and was granted the ability to perceive the beauty of her person revealed in and through her body. Joseph perceived Mary as a living tabernacle of God's presence, and therefore dedicated his life to the mission of being the admirer and protector of her dignity and beauty.

A true husband, like Joseph, peers beyond his wife's (exterior) body to see her interior beauty. He perceives in her stretch marks, cellulite, wrinkles, age spots, and C-section scars her sacrificial beauty as life-bearer—a living tabernacle of God's presence who bears in her body the marks of the demands of giving life to the world.

Often, the blemishes, scars, and weight gain are our wife's war wounds that testify to the fact that she has endured the stress of loving her husband faithfully. Your wife is a living symbol of the Church that Christ gave Himself up for, that she may be beautiful without spot or blemish. The Church has blemishes in the members of her body, and in a similar way our wife's bodies have imperfections which we are all too quick to notice. But even more so, their souls have been wounded, scarred, and disfigured by the stressors and lusts of men. Yet Christ washes away the Church's blemishes in His love; for "love covers a multitude of sins." You also are called to be a transmitter of Christ's healing power to your wife. How is this accomplished? By washing her in the Word.

TAKE THE LEAD Regardless of her age, your wife longs to be cherished for her beauty. Examine her closet, her dresser drawers, and the cosmetic goods stocked in the bathroom. This is her chief desire: to be cherished for her beauty. As we age, our physical beauty rusts and tarnishes. It is up to you to be man enough to see your wife's ever-changing, ever-aging body and discover anew her radiant God-given beauty. Over the next several reflections, be intentional about bringing attention to your wife's beauty. Compliment her. But don't overdo it. Be sincere. See God's glory in her and remind her of the glory that lives within her.*

* See Examen *Embrace Your Wife* on page 446

HER FIRST NEED: BEAUTY

73. WASH YOUR WIFE IN THE WORD–A NONNEGOTIABLE

Are you fearful of reading, meditating on, or praying with the Bible? Does Scripture intimidate you or bore you? If so, then you are like many men. It is common for a man to be uncomfortable with the Word, but even more common is the trepidation and resistance to read the Bible and pray with his wife. Why is this? Most men have the instinct to protect and defend their ego and to do nearly whatever is demanded to avoid humiliation—particularly being humiliated in front of his wife. Your wife knows you better than anyone else. She knows your strengths and your weaknesses, and almost nothing is as painful as when she notices and comments on your failings.

A man may avoid praying or reading the Bible with his wife, or sharing the Word with his family for fear that his limited knowledge of God and His Word will be discovered. But even more than feeling inadequate is the fear that his wife or children will view him as a hypocrite who "say one thing and do another." When a husband considers these obstacles, he often disregards the Bible and sharing the Word with his family, particularly his wife, accounting it as an extra, a negotiable, and not necessary to the success of his marriage or fatherhood.

But what if the Word, and your transmission of the Word, is one of the nonnegotiables, one of the essentials that could breathe life, vitality, and newness into your marriage and vocation as a father? Consider that "all scripture is inspired by God, is profitable to teach, to reprove, to correct, to instruct in justice, that the man of God may be perfect, furnished for every good work" (2 Tim 3:16). All Scripture is inspired, including the aforementioned statement. The Word of God is one of the most powerful tools that will aid you in your spiritual growth while also helping you raise a family that will participate and transmit God's love and joy to our aching world.

Would you like to have the ability to teach, reprove, correct, instruct, and help protect your family? Sacred Scripture is one of the most effective tools in a father's spiritual toolbox. To teach, however, he must allow himself to be taught. To correct his children, he must accept correction; to instruct he must be instructed; to help perfect others, it is imperative that he be one who strives for perfection. To wash your wife in the Word, you must also be washed in the Word, which means that you read the Word and embody it in your marriage.

> **TAKE THE LEAD** Regardless of her age, your wife longs to be cherished for her beauty. Examine her closet, her dresser drawers, and the cosmetic goods stocked in the bathroom. This is her chief desire: to be cherished for her beauty. As we age, our physical beauty rusts and tarnishes. It is up to you to be man enough to see your wife's ever-changing, ever-aging body and discover anew her radiant God-given beauty. Over the next several reflections, be intentional about bringing attention to your wife's beauty. Compliment her. But don't overdo it. Be sincere. See God's glory in her and remind her of the glory that lives within her.*

* See Examen *Embrace Your Wife* on page 446

HER FIRST NEED: BEAUTY

74. HOW TO WASH YOUR WIFE IN THE WORD

Today's culture rejects the reality, the need, and the primacy of male headship as something antiquated, a product of a chauvinistic patriarchal culture. The idea of a husband transmitting the Word to his wife is viewed as male tyranny and a grave insult to the dignity of women. This rejection has caused many a man to cower in shame and neglect to act upon his God-given right and mission to lead his family to salvation and communion with God.

But consider again that when God gave Adam the commands regarding the protection and provision for the garden, Eve did not yet exist, which implies that God expected Adam to transmit these divine ordinances. Consider that Jesus, the New Adam, was called Rabbi and taught His Bride, the Church. Consider also that Joseph, the husband of Mary, though he was the least qualified and least perfect member of the Holy Family, was ordained by God to transmit the Torah to them, leading them to observe the Law and its ordinances.

To be a man, father, husband, and leader who is capable of transmitting God's instructions and inspirations to his family demands courage, humility, and above all trust that he will encounter Jesus, who is waiting for him in the Word.

This does not mean that you must be a theologian, a biblical scholar, an academic, or an historian. It does mean that you make meeting Jesus in the Word a personal priority. When you are formed by the Word you will become capable of forming others by the transmission of the Word you have received, thus you will become capable of transmitting God's mercy, truth, and the traditions of your faith through your word and example.

Your role and mission to transmit the Word doesn't mean that your wife cannot teach you or your children; or that she doesn't share her counsel, offer her wisdom, or be a source of inspiration. No. Often a wife is more intelligent, gifted, talented, faithful, compassionate, and love Jesus more intensely than we husbands do. Nevertheless, you, as a husband, father, and leader are responsible to God to take the initiative to wash your wife in the Word. Remember, God does not call the qualified; He qualifies the called. When we reflect on the docility of Mary full of grace, and Jesus full of grace and truth, under Joseph's leadership we cannot help but conclude that the father-leader dynamic in the Holy Family is the paradigm for all families.

There are many ways that you can share the Word with your wife and family: schedule family prayer, pray privately with your wife, lead a prayer of thanksgiving before meals, read and reflect on the upcoming Sunday readings with your family. Regardless of what method you use to transmit the Word to your family, when your wife notices how God is transforming you by your own personal encounter with Jesus, she will not only be more receptive to your transmission of God's truth, but she will also become more receptive to you and more apt to reveal herself to you. Hence, washing her in the Word allows you and your wife to witness her unveiled beauty.

> **TAKE THE LEAD** Regardless of her age, your wife longs to be cherished for her beauty. Examine her closet, her dresser drawers, and the cosmetic goods stocked in the bathroom. This is her chief desire: to be cherished for her beauty. As we age, our physical beauty rusts and tarnishes. It is up to you to be man enough to see your wife's ever-changing, ever-aging body and discover anew her radiant God-given beauty. Over the next several reflections, be intentional about bringing attention to your wife's beauty. Compliment her. But don't overdo it. Be sincere. See God's glory in her and remind her of the glory that lives within her.*

* See Examen *Embrace Your Wife* on page 446

PILLAR 2: EMBRACE YOUR ESSENCE [EMBRACING WOMAN]

HIS FIRST NEED: STRENGTH

75. WHAT MAKES YOU STRONG?

Why is smallness or weakness so embarrassing? From the earliest of age, every boy instinctively desires not to be weak, but strong. Why is it when you greet a guy and grasp his upper arm, he instinctively flexes? Why do many men's sports involve high levels of intense physical contact? Whether it's cage match fighting, football, rugby, ultimate fighting, arm wrestling, boxing, or martial arts; men gravitate toward intense physical competition, relentlessly testing their limits and admiringly watching others do so. It has been said that when a woman becomes depressed she goes shopping; when men become depressed they invade countries. If depressed men invade countries, it is because they feel the need to prove something. Man's disdain for weakness and his attraction to physical competition testify to an essential truth: a man's primary, innate need is to be respected for his strength—particularly by woman. Just as woman's primary, natural, innate need is to be cherished for her beauty, man's complementary need is to be respected by his wife for his strength.

But what is true strength? Is having the ability to bench press more than one's body weight, or lift heavy objects true strength? We admire those with external strength because it demonstrates an internal reality: self-mastery, discipline, and perseverance. Human beings are subconsciously impressed by people who master themselves in pursuit of a goal.

Often a man will question his own strength and find that the only way to measure it is by competing or fighting against another—and if he is victorious, he deems himself to be more of a man than the man he defeated. But is defeating another always the mark of true strength? There are many muscle heads, Super Bowl champions, and professional fighters who have succumbed to the temptations of womanizing, abusing their own wife and children, or committing acts of violence. No one respects them. Do we respect the class bully who intimidates his smaller classmate into surrendering his lunch? No. Yet nearly every human being respects the man who sacrificed his seat on a lifeboat in order to save a woman and children, while he and the *Titanic* sank to the bottom of the ocean. There isn't a man who doesn't respect the soldier who risks his life to get his injured comrade out of harm's way.

Considering this, we can conclude that it demands more strength to give one's life for the purpose of saving another's life, than to take another's life so that one may live. Man, whose core desire is to be respected, continually lives in the tension between obtaining respect by exercising brute power and domination, and exercising self-control for the purpose of being a gift to another. Often the Christian ideal of self-mastery for the purpose of self-giving can become warped in a man, having the character of pusillanimity (faintheartedness). Such a man holds the "form of religion while denying the power of it" (2 Tim 3:5). Such a man avoids confrontation, he plays it safe, wearing the face of niceness, while neglecting to protect woman—particularly his wife. He often appears soft; he is compromising and believes that the essence of being a Christian man is doing whatever it takes to "get along." By doing so, he appears to be self-giving, but is interested only in protecting himself from confrontation, defeat, and being disliked.

Man desires that woman respect him for his strength. However, women, though attracted to men of physical strength, are not primarily interested in a man's physical strength, but rather respect a man for his deep, abiding, unshakable confidence and inner strength. St. Paul articulates the mission of the true man of strength: ". . . a husband is head of the wife just as Christ is head of the Church, being Himself *savior of the body*" (Eph 5:24). "Husbands love your wives, just as Christ loved the Church, and *delivered Himself up for her*" (Eph 5:26). "Let each one of you also love his wife as he loves himself; and let the wife respect her husband" (Eph 5:33).

These words encapsulate and convey the vision and description of a man of strength: he loves her as he loves himself; he expresses this love by delivering himself up for her, and by doing these things he wins her respect as a man of great strength.

If a man embarks upon the mission to be an image of Christ the Savior he cannot afford to play it safe, avoid confrontation, or be fainthearted. No. He will need the strength of the strongest man who ever lived—Jesus Christ, who appeared weak in submitting to the cross, but by embracing it, became the "strong one of Jacob" who wins the Bride.

> **TAKE THE LEAD** The following several reflections demand a mental shift from the conditioning of the world to the divine reality. Strength is expressed by heroic self-giving love. Lust crushes self-giving. Be honest with yourself and examine your heart. Are you bound by lust, do you masturbate, use pornography, evaluate a woman by her body? If you find lust in your heart, you are like most men. But what will separate you from these fallen men? Rise and return to the Lord. Go to confession. Confess your disordered desire and set out to sacrifice your lustful tendencies for your wife, that she may begin to see her beauty and value.*

* See Examen *Embrace Your Wife* on page 446

HIS FIRST NEED: STRENGTH

76. WHAT UNDERMINES YOUR STRENGTH?

Have you ever been humble enough to question whether you are indeed a man of strength, a man who is willing and capable of delivering himself up for his wife and family? If you have, you may have noticed how challenging it is to be honest with yourself and assess truly your internal strength. It is easy to make excuses for ourselves, to focus only on the good that we do; but by doing so we fail to change, progress, and become the man and husband we are called to be. Fortunately, there is a simple three-point self-examination that can assist you in calling attention to those things that are holding you back from being a true leader.

There exist three enemies that undermine and betray our strength, that should serve as alarms alerting us to the reality that we may not be as strong as we think. The first enemy is mistrust, particularly of God, which is expressed by doubt. The second enemy that sabotages your strength is complaining, whining, and grumbling—again, particularly against God. The third enemy of your strength is lust, which is a tendency toward selfish gain—using others for your personal benefit; consistently desiring more and more.

These three enemies are intimately connected and gain potency and power by building upon one another. Let's examine each of them individually.

Distrust of God, or doubt, begins when we encounter a challenge that appears outside of our control and ability to remedy. When encountering such a difficulty we may present our dilemma to God, but receive no immediate or apparent response. When God delays action or intervention we begin to believe that He isn't listening, doesn't care, or worse, has abandoned us, or that He is against us, and His divine wrath has fallen upon us.

When we succumb to doubt we become suspicious of God's benevolence, question His generosity, and begin to distrust His love and good will toward us. When a man distrusts the most generous God, he cannot help but to mistrust others and their motives—particularly his wife's.

PILLAR 2: EMBRACE YOUR ESSENCE [EMBRACING WOMAN]

When doubt gains hold of our soul we tend to grumble, complain, resist, and whine about our current situation. This is expressed in little, as well as big, ways: "It's too humid out." "Is this all of the fries they gave me?" "Why is my wife tired all of the time?" "Why isn't the house clean?" "Why can't I hit it big like my friends?" "Why isn't my wife like his?" "I hate my job—my life." Does any of this sound familiar? When we complain we extinguish our ability to be thankful. We no longer believe anything is worthy of our gratitude. We can only see our circumstances, relationships, finances, employment, and the like as deficient, full of problems and obstacles. We tend to blame the people and circumstances around us—particularly the people closest to us.

Thankfulness is the secret to having a healthy relationship with God and unlocking the favors He desires to grant us. When we neglect to be thankful, we begin to believe that we deserve more, the more we don't already have. Rather than rejoicing in what we have been given, we complain about what we do not have. This disposition causes us to desire (covet) our neighbor's car, his house, his lawn, his life, his wife. This is jealousy, envy, greed, which ultimately manifests itself in lustful patterns—patterns that destroy people's lives.

> **TAKE THE LEAD** The following several reflections demand a mental shift from the conditioning of the world to the divine reality. Strength is expressed by heroic self-giving love. Lust crushes self-giving. Be honest with yourself and examine your heart. Are you bound by lust, do you masturbate, use pornography, evaluate a woman by her body? If you find lust in your heart, you are like most men. But what will separate you from these fallen men? Rise and return to the Lord. Go to confession. Confess your disordered desire and set out to sacrifice your lustful tendencies for your wife, that she may begin to see her beauty and value.*

* See Examen *Embrace Your Wife* on page 446

HIS FIRST NEED: STRENGTH

77. WHAT UNDERMINES YOUR STRENGTH?, PART 2

Satan is continually belittling us, tempting us, taunting us, coercing us for the purpose of keeping us sissified. His strategy is simple: First, he plays with our mind, convincing us that we are inferior, weak, and that we must counteract that feeling of inadequacy by doing something that will make us feel like a real man. This is where doubt and mistrust of God begin. He skews our vision of reality, convincing us that we are failures, pathetic, and destined for doom. He then goads us to complain about our lives, especially our wives, their behavior, their lack of attention and responsiveness to us. He whispers things like, "You can do better. You don't need her. She's holding out on you and she's holding you back. Look at her, she's not even trying to be beautiful for you."

It is at this point that the demonic attack gains traction and power, and lures us with the consoling thought of using women for our disordered gratification. We subconsciously begin to believe that controlling, objectifying, manipulating, and lusting after a woman will make us feel like a real man. For many men, lust is not as much about physical gratification as it is a failed attempt to obtain power and masculine strength.

Pornography is typically the baseline method for men to fulfill their desire to conquer woman. It is a man's way to use a woman who cannot and will not deny him. Ironically, the very motivation of desiring not be a sissy, which lured him into using woman, betrays him. Rather than controlling woman with his lust, he is now controlled by his lust for woman. In the end, a man who wanders down this road of temptation is left with the nagging sense of his smallness.

St. Joseph's silence—even amidst the most challenging circumstances that a husband and father can face—testifies to his resilient, enduring trust in God. In moments of crisis, Joseph turned to the Lord and waited patiently for His divine counsel. It was his faith and trust in God that enabled him to lead Jesus and Mary to the temple, on many occasions, to offer his thanksgiving sacrifice.

Notice that it was Joseph's faith that granted him the ability to be grateful, and from his grateful heart he was given the strength to love Mary purely.

Do you desire to be like St. Joseph, a man of resilient, enduring strength? Overcome doubt with trust in God; being "thankful in all circumstances" (1 Thess 5:18) that He is building you into a man of greatness, and in believing this truth you will become a man who loves all women, especially your wife, purely.

> **TAKE THE LEAD** The following several reflections demand a mental shift from the conditioning of the world to the divine reality. Strength is expressed by heroic self-giving love. Lust crushes self-giving. Be honest with yourself and examine your heart. Are you bound by lust, do you masturbate, use pornography, evaluate a woman by her body? If you find lust in your heart, you are like most men. But what will separate you from these fallen men? Rise and return to the Lord. Go to confession. Confess your disordered desire and set out to sacrifice your lustful tendencies for your wife, that she may begin to see her beauty and value.*

* See Examen *Embrace Your Wife* on page 446

LEAD | THE FOUR MARKS OF FATHERLY GREATNESS

HIS FIRST NEED: STRENGTH

78. WHAT GIVES YOUR STRENGTH POWER?

Has there been a time in your life when you attempted to deny yourself some consolation or gratification without really understanding why you were doing it? What happens when we sacrifice something without comprehending why we are giving that pleasure up? How often, as kids, and even as adults, have we made a resolution on Ash Wednesday to give up this or that, only to fail miserably within the first week of Lent? The project of fasting ultimately fails when we don't understand the true motivation behind the sacrifice.

When no actual goal exists, or we lack understanding of the goal, our motivation begins to wane, and when our motivation is lacking, we lose the ability to be thankful for the opportunity to sacrifice for that goal; and when this occurs, inevitably our commitment is surrendered.

This dynamic also applies to sexual purity. If we don't understand the goal of chastity, our motivation to be sexually pure will be lacking; and if we aren't motivated to be chaste and pure, we will certainly struggle in vain to be thankful for the opportunity and ability to endure sexual challenges. When the character of thankfulness is deficient, it is only a matter of time before we succumb to the temptation to lust.

Lust is destructive in that it attempts to divorce love from sacrifice. Lust wants the benefits of love without submitting to its radical demands to offer oneself for the sake of others—while never using the other. Where sacrifice exists not, love does not exist. And if sacrifice is lacking in the man, he is not a man really, but rather a boy trapped in a man's body. The man of strength is a man of sacrifice.

Unfortunately, we can often appear to be loving sacrificially only for the purpose of acquiring something from the other; and when that something is not given, our true motive becomes apparent by our resentment toward the one who is not giving us what we desire.

From where does a man derive the power and motivation to love sacrificially? With this question in mind, we will turn to Jesus, the

PILLAR 2: EMBRACE YOUR ESSENCE [EMBRACING WOMAN]

perfect example of strength, in our next reflection. But for now, let us examine our motive for attempting to be sexually pure. What is your motive? Your motive matters.

> **TAKE THE LEAD** The following several reflections demand a mental shift from the conditioning of the world to the divine reality. Strength is expressed by heroic self-giving love. Lust crushes self-giving. Be honest with yourself and examine your heart. Are you bound by lust, do you masturbate, use pornography, evaluate a woman by her body? If you find lust in your heart, you are like most men. But what will separate you from these fallen men? Rise and return to the Lord. Go to confession. Confess your disordered desire and set out to sacrifice your lustful tendencies for your wife, that she may begin to see her beauty and value.*

* See Examen *Embrace Your Wife* on page 446

HIS FIRST NEED: STRENGTH

79. THE MOTIVATION TO BECOME PURE

On the night that He was betrayed by Judas, Jesus offered the first Eucharist. The word "Eucharist" in the Greek means "thanksgiving." In other words, Jesus' last will and testimony to His Church was His thanksgiving sacrifice—"This is my body given for you; do this in remembrance of Me"—which began in the Upper Room at the Last Supper, and culminated on Calvary where it was ultimately completed. This raises the question: What could Jesus have been thankful for? He knew that within hours after completing the Last Supper He would be betrayed, tortured, condemned, and murdered.

Our Lord expressed thanksgiving to His Father for the strength, courage, endurance, and love He would be given in order to deliver Himself up for His bride. Jesus was thankful that He could stand in the place of condemned sinners, delivering them—by means of His sacrifice—*from* eternal damnation, and *for* eternal communion with God.

Recall that the evil one undermines our strength by first instilling doubt and mistrust of God. Second, he convinces us that we are being slighted and induces complaining—the opposite of thanksgiving. Third, to compensate for our lack of consolation and feeling of inadequacy, he lures us into lust instead of being a gift to others. Notice that Jesus, during His agony in the garden of Gethsemane, entered the tenacious battle to trust in His Father. This battle was so intense that while considering His impending death He sweated blood and cried out, "Abba, Father, you can do all things; but not my will, but thine be done" (Lk 22:42). Jesus overcame doubt and exercised perfect trust in His Father.

Notice also that Jesus gave thanks to His Father, accomplishing His sacrifice without complaining or grumbling. Our Lord's trust and thanksgiving is expressed ultimately in self-giving love for mankind—the polar opposite of lust.

How painfully difficult it must have been for Christ to see his bride's beauty amidst her rebellion, neglect, infidelity, sinfulness, and selfishness. Yet, He understood fully that it was His mission and responsibility to look beyond her marred, sinful character, and deliver Himself up for her—to take on her ugliness, to ensure that she would obtain that beauty.

You and I are responsible for seeing our wives' potential beauty and delivering ourselves up for her that she may attain that beauty. "A woman needs her man to be strong enough to deliver himself up for her daily that she may receive from him a vision of her own beauty and person. When the man does this, his wife begins to believe her worth, value, and beauty. Men must be strong to face the enemy and overcome the temptation to lust—especially the use of pornography. Satan is trying to incapacitate men from seeing reality. This is where the wife needs her husband most. A husbands is responsible for seeing his wife's beauty and falling to this temptation will debilitate him from doing just that" (Kathy Schluter, *What Your Wife Wants*).

When you understand clearly that you are not simply suppressing your sexual desires, but rather are motivated to overcome lust to ensure that your wife may attain her beauty, you will be strengthened to deliver yourself to God to accomplish this noble goal.

> **TAKE THE LEAD** The following several reflections demand a mental shift from the conditioning of the world to the divine reality. Strength is expressed by heroic self-giving love. Lust crushes self-giving. Be honest with yourself and examine your heart. Are you bound by lust, do you masturbate, use pornography, evaluate a woman by her body? If you find lust in your heart, you are like most men. But what will separate you from these fallen men? Rise and return to the Lord. Go to confession. Confess your disordered desire and set out to sacrifice your lustful tendencies for your wife, that she may begin to see her beauty and value.*

---

*   See Examen *Embrace Your Wife* on page 446

HIS SECOND NEED: PHYSICAL INTIMACY

80. YOUR SECOND NEED: PHYSICAL INTIMACY

What is your natural, instinctive reaction to the idea of admitting and discussing your needs with your wife? Often, a man experiences an internal aversion to the confession of his needs to his wife for fear that he will appear weak or be taken advantage of. But perhaps this is part of God's plan. Not that we be taken advantage of, but rather that we encounter and admit our personal weakness. The paradox of the true man is that if he is to become great, he must first admit and believe that he is little; if he desires to be strong, he must first be convinced of his weakness; to be exalted, he must first humble himself before God. Often God calls a husband to humble himself before his wife by discussing his needs.

The Latin word for "need" or to "have need" (as expressed in Matthew 6:32: "For your Father knows that you *have need* of all these things") is *indigetis,* which is comprised of the root words *indu,* which means "in," and *egere,* meaning "to need," or "to lack." The English translation for this word is "indigent," which can be defined as being poor, impoverished, even a beggar. Spouses, in a certain sense, are naturally impoverished, but by addressing one another's poverty they begin to experience the love of God as expressed through the human person of their spouse.

The challenge is that a man does not want to appear weak or impoverished, or to admit that he needs his wife. It is vital that you understand that needing your wife or having needs that only your wife can address does not indicate that you are objectively deficient, or that something is inherently wrong with you. No. This is God's design. God intentionally created and crafted spouses to need each other and express their needs to one another as a means for the two to become humble, pure, unified, and mutually glorified.

This is important because you have needs that at times can make you feel like a beggar—as though you are deficient, or perhaps unholy, if not perverted. Besides being respected for your strength, you have an inherent, authentic secondary need that is closely related to your need to be respected for your strength: physical intimacy as expressed in conjugal relations. This desire is not simply a superficial or base longing for selfish gratification (although it can become that), but rather, man's authentic, God-given need for communion; and if this need is not addressed by his wife, his marriage will be besieged by serious tension and undergo incredible duress.

Why? Physical intimacy is more than sexual enjoyment or a way to relieve stress. The one-flesh union is for many men an ultimate expression of his strength, and it is in this particular area that a man experiences his wife's respect or disrespect for his strength acutely. Quite often when a husband's sexual initiation is declined by his wife, he interprets her action as rejection.

But as Kathy Schluter says, "Physical intimacy is not woman's primary need, especially when she is spending her days tending her children or feels worn down. The last thing she is interested in is renewing her marital vows. There are many good wives, good Catholic moms, who believe that intercourse with their husband is simply one more chore to do. They distance themselves from sexual intimacy and allow the thief, Satan, to steal, kill, and destroy their marriage; they allow Satan to separate sexuality from holiness. He convinces them that the sexual act is either profane, or a burden. Women often become trapped in the belief that 'this is one more thing I have to do.' She needs a man who can transmit a vision of what the two are actually participating in when they come together in the marital embrace."

Remember, the husband has a certain responsibility to transmit the divine truth to his wife, particularly when it comes to sexual intercourse. As difficult as this task may appear to be, God has granted you and me an intense need for physical intimacy, and this longing has the power to humble us and compel us to discuss this challenging topic with our wives. To do this effectively, you will need to understand what married couples are participating in when they have sexual intercourse. In other words, you will need to have a divine vision of conjugal love.

TAKE THE LEAD You and I are challenged to understand sexual intercourse as more than a biological function, but rather as a theological gift. It is up to you, as the man who sets the pace of self-giving love, to initiate the conversation that sheds light on the true joy and meaning of the conjugal union. You and your wife may be wounded—if not severely wounded—in this area, and therefore raising this subject could cause further tension. Things will often appear worse before they become better. Stay the course and humbly share God's vision for your marriage and the sexual act. Then, if the two of you engage in conjugal relations, love her with the attention, tenderness, and selflessness of God who created sexual intercourse and sexual climax.*

* See Examen *Embrace Your Wife* on page 446

PILLAR 2: EMBRACE YOUR ESSENCE [EMBRACING WOMAN]

HIS SECOND NEED: PHYSICAL INTIMACY

81. HOW TO DISCUSS "SEX" WITH YOUR WIFE

Recall that the marriage bond between a man and a woman is a sacrament, that is, a real, active, participation in and revelation of Christ's marriage to His Church. To many of us this sounds too lofty, academic, lacking passion, eros; and at the very least does not sound enticing. Granted, the concept doesn't seem very appealing if we don't understand that at the heart of marriage is an incredible exchange not only of bodies, but of persons through acts of total self-giving love. As Pope St. John Paul II said, "All married life is a gift; but this becomes most evident when spouses, in giving themselves to each other in love, bring about that encounter which makes 'them one flesh'" (LF 12).

The one-flesh union has been divinely designed to be the pinnacle, symbolic, human expression of Christ's love for His Church. "This is my body, given for you." We hear these words proclaimed during every Holy Mass. This means that there is a deep connection between the Eucharist (which means "thanksgiving") and the sexual union between spouses. St. John Paul II says, "In that sign [the sacrament of marriage] through the 'language of the body' man and woman encounter the 'great mystery.' In this way conjugal life becomes in a certain sense liturgical" (TOB 380). "The language of the body reread in 'subjective' and 'objective' dimensions . . . becomes the language of the liturgy" (TOB 377). In other words, the eucharistic liturgy is God's expression of His self-giving love, which culminates in Christ the Bridegroom giving the Church, His Bride, His Body. Similarly, the one-flesh union between spouses is meant to be liturgical, meaning that by exchanging their persons as expressed through their bodies, they offer God thanksgiving for their marriage. This is a type of eucharistic (thanksgiving) feast.

Rather than pressuring your wife to "do this duty," or neglecting sexual intercourse with your wife, it is your holy obligation to communicate to her this liturgical vision, that is, that the one-flesh union is one of the greatest expressions of self-giving and thanksgiving to God.

We may have difficulty experiencing the fact that at Holy Mass there is the mystical union of heaven and earth—the union of God and man. Likewise, couples may often miss the mystical nature of the marital act. Conjugal union is a renewal of the sacrament of marriage; it is efficacious—that is, it transmits grace to the couple to unify the two as one flesh; and it is an actual living in the mystery of Christ's self-giving love. It is a husband's responsibility to communicate this vision and initiate self-giving love for the purpose of granting his wife a spiritual backdrop to sexual union.

An all-too-common objection to the idea that sexual intercourse in marriage has been designed by God to communicate His love for His Church is that it is too fleshy, it feels too good, and that Christianity and its practices are created for the intention of mortification and to make us uncomfortable. But we must keep in mind that Christ did not invent the torture of crucifixion—men did. Yet God, on the other hand, did invent sexual union, and God Himself is an eternal exchange of persons—infinite self-giving love—and wills to share that infinite, glorious love with humanity.

This is the good news of the Gospel. You and your wife's sexual union unleashes incredible amounts of grace that heals and elevates your marriage and your family. Though it may feel awkward, you—as husband and leader—are called to communicate this glorious good news.

> **TAKE THE LEAD** You and I are challenged to understand sexual intercourse as more than a biological function, but rather as a theological gift. It is up to you, as the man who sets the pace of self-giving love, to initiate the conversation that sheds light on the true joy and meaning of the conjugal union. You and your wife may be wounded—if not severely wounded—in this area, and therefore raising this subject could cause further tension. Things will often appear worse before they become better. Stay the course and humbly share God's vision for your marriage and the sexual act. Then, if the two of you engage in conjugal relations, love her with the attention, tenderness, and selflessness of the God who created sexual intercourse and sexual climax.*

* See Examen *Embrace Your Wife* on page 446

HER SECOND NEED: EMOTIONAL INTIMACY

82. PURSUING HER

How does a husband effectively communicate the mystical vision of the one-flesh union to his wife? Only a man who has discovered his strength in Christ can honestly address woman's second need: emotional intimacy—to be pursued. If you hope that your wife authentically desires to address your need for physical intimacy, it is important to refrain, at all cost, from any type of verbal bullying, coercion, or manipulation. Though these methods may initially wear her down and cause her to surrender into giving you what you desire, real intimacy and true spousal bonding will not occur. She will feel used.

There is a profound connection between a woman's need for emotional intimacy and man's need for physical intimacy. So how does a husband address his wife's need for emotional intimacy, while also helping her understand his authentic need for physical intimacy?

Many women, from the time of girlhood, whether or not they were consciously aware of it, desired to be pursued—much like a princess desires to be pursued by a prince. There are many ways to properly pursue your wife, but for the sake of simplicity, we will mention three: first, consistently express your gratefulness for your wife. It is vital that we sharpen our vision to recognize what our wives offer, who they are, and their heroic daily efforts, and intentionally thank them for these things. Your consistent acts of gratitude will allow the dignity of her soul to be reawakened and her person to find meaning and value.

Second, it is important to express delight in your wife's beauty. Often a husband will refrain from affirming his wife's beauty for fear that she will become too confident and leave him; or perhaps she will begin believing she has power over him. On the other hand, there are husbands who refrain from expressing adulation for their wife's beauty because they choose no longer to see it; and because of this, she also struggles to see her own beauty. Both disordered tendencies will cause a wife to seek confirmation of her beauty from other men. Whether your wife is "put together," or she is disheveled, it is vital that "she believes that you believe her to be the most beautiful woman in your world" (Kathy Schluter).

Third, it is essential that you pursue your wife by intentionally finding ways to spend time with her. This perhaps is the most important way to pursue your wife. When a husband purposefully carves out time to be with his wife, to look in her eyes, to listen to her recount her day, to discuss her hopes and desires or her health problems, or to exercise or enjoy some form of entertainment together, his wife will begin to believe that she is not an afterthought, but rather important to him.

There is an important qualifier regarding a husband's motivation for pursuing his wife: A husband does not offer his wife emotional intimacy as a means of manipulating or coercing her into giving him physical intimacy. If this is your hidden motive, your wife will eventually discover your true intentions and distance herself from you. No woman desires to truly be manipulated, but many a woman allow herself to be used in her attempt to obtain love. Woman is not a project but a person. Our motives matter. Instead of our motivation primarily being to obtain self-gratification at the least cost to ourselves, our intention should be to pursue her as an act of love for God, as a way for the both of you to achieve and experience union with God through the other.

Unfortunately, when a man strives to love his wife authentically and overcome the temptation to lust for, or to use his wife, his marriage and sexual desire can become the "dark night" of a husband; the refiner's fire that purges him of self-attachment and impure motives. However, by loving her for her own sake, and striving to be a disinterested (not with a disordered self-interest) gift, over time your wife will begin to see you as a man of strength and desire you all the more.

> **TAKE THE LEAD** True love is willing the good of another—particularly your wife. The ultimate defining factor of such love is to will your wife's good, even at your own expense. Your wife longs to be important, valued, cherished, and pursued. One way to demonstrate

your desire and love for her is to schedule a consistent "date night." Make a commitment to spend at least one hour a week being together, listening to her, looking deeply into her eyes, and awakening her heart to the reality that you still desire her.*

* See Examen *Embrace Your Wife* on page 446

HER SECOND NEED: EMOTIONAL INTIMACY

83. RESPONDING TO REJECTION

We all, at some point in our lives, have experienced the sting of rejection. Whether you were overlooked by your employer for a promotion, not selected for the varsity team, marginalized by your peers, or whether that special girl declined your invitation to prom, the pain stemming from rejection is painful and memorable. If we are not watchful, those occasions of rejection can catch us off guard, tempt us to become angry, resentful, and bitter. This is true in marriage. There will be numerous occasions when your wife will not respond positively, affirming and receiving your initiation to intimacy—and this rejection stings.

But what if there are times when not having sexual intimacy with your wife is better for you in achieving what really matters—union with God? The one-flesh union between spouses has been divinely created as a way to launch us into the very heart of God—that's the purpose of sexual intercourse—regardless of whether we experience physical intimacy. How can this be?

Abstinence from sexual intercourse—if embraced—purifies a man of his tendency toward selfishness and grants him the opportunity to love his wife for who she is—not for what she can give him. There will be many occasions in which you will desire to consummate your marriage with your wife and she, for whatever reason, may not. How you respond affects not only your relationship with her, but also with your children, as well as your relationship with the Father.

> **TAKE THE LEAD** True love is willing the good of another—particularly your wife. The ultimate defining factor of such love is to will your wife's good, even at your own expense. Your wife longs to be important, valued, cherished, and pursued. One way to demonstrate your desire and love for her is to schedule a consistent "date night." Make a commitment to spend at least one hour a week being together, listening to her, looking deeply into her eyes, and awakening her heart to the reality that you still desire her.*

* See Examen *Embrace Your Wife* on page 446

PILLAR 2: EMBRACE YOUR ESSENCE [EMBRACING WOMAN]

HER SECOND NEED: EMOTIONAL INTIMACY

84. WHEN SHE'S NOT GIVING WHAT YOU NEED

The trailhead of the family is marriage, and the most evident act of God's glory, life-giving power, and self-giving love in marriage is the one-flesh union. The grace, the life in the form of babies, and the blessing of becoming a family has tremendous potential to heal not only marriages, but entire families. The sacred liturgy of the Eucharist transmits grace from Christ to His body—all believers; and in a similar way the "liturgical" act of the one-flesh union transmits grace from the couple to the entire body of the family. Which raises another question: how is grace transmitted when a couple does not consummate their marriage by engaging in sexual intercourse?

When you initiate or desire to have sexual intercourse with your wife and she doesn't reciprocate that desire, it is important to reflect upon the spiritual significance of your abstinence. If the marital act is a symbol of the Mass—particularly the Eucharist—consequently the bed becomes a symbol of the altar. Upon the altar Christ lays down His Body and expresses this sacrificial offering with the words, "This is my body given for you." In a similar way, when your wife declines your initiation to intimacy, you are to lay yourself on the altar of your bed, praying from the heart, "This is my body given for you." This prayer is a way to express your offering of self on behalf of your wife to God. In this way you offer your desires to God for your wife by "offering your body to God as a holy and living sacrifice. This is your spiritual worship" (see Rom 12).

St. Joseph offered his body as a holy and living sacrifice to God on behalf of Mary. By continually striving to overcome any temptation to resent her for his celibate state of life, he became the "most chaste spouse," a real man, the pure and noble husband who experienced the first fruits of Christ's redemption.

TAKE THE LEAD True love is willing the good of another—particularly your wife. The ultimate defining factor of such love is to will your wife's good, even at your own expense.

> Your wife longs to be important, valued, cherished, and pursued. One way to demonstrate your desire and love for her is to schedule a consistent "date night." Make a commitment to spend at least one hour a week being together, listening to her, looking deeply into her eyes, and awakening her heart to the reality that you still desire her.*

* See Examen *Embrace Your Wife* on page 446

PILLAR 2: EMBRACE YOUR ESSENCE [EMBRACING WOMAN]

HER SECOND NEED: EMOTIONAL INTIMACY

85. BEGINNING THE CYCLE OF HEALING AND RESTORATION

The effects of offering yourself on the altar of your bed during times of abstinence on behalf of your wife are significant and worth your sacrifice. First, God knows and sees the sincerity of your efforts to love your wife as a person and not as an object, and because of your faithfulness He will grant you the gift of purity—the ability to heroically overcome lustful desires. Second, eventually your wife will realize that your love for her is authentic and sincere. Third, you will begin to experience the effects of Christ's redemptive grace—even and especially in your body—which will enable you to be a shining example of a man who sets the pace of self-giving love. Fourth, grace will be transmitted to your entire family, which gradually lifts them from the gravity of selfishness to the heights of self-giving love.

Much healing and restoration within marriages can be derived from a husband's offering himself in this manner; but this healing is dependent on him setting the pace of self-giving love. If he chooses not to set the pace, this healing and restoration will not occur. As Pope St. John Paul II says: "From the beginning man was to have been the guardian of reciprocity of donation [self-offering] and its true balance. Although maintenance of the balance of the gift seems to be entrusted to both, a special responsibility rests with the man above all, as if it depended more on him whether this balance was maintained or broken, or even if already broken reestablished" (TOB 33:2).

> **TAKE THE LEAD** True love is willing the good of another—particularly your wife. The ultimate defining factor of such love is to will your wife's good, even at your own expense. Your wife longs to be important, valued, cherished, and pursued. One way to demonstrate your desire and love for her is to schedule a consistent "date night." Make a commitment to spend at least one hour a week being together, listening to her, looking deeply into her eyes, and awakening her heart to the reality that you still desire her.*

*   See Examen *Embrace Your Wife* on page 446

HER SECOND NEED: EMOTIONAL INTIMACY

86. THE TWO EXPRESSIONS OF LUST

Are you attracted to your wife? For some husbands the response to this question is not entirely positive. There are times when wives, due to stress, childbirth, hormone imbalance, health difficulties, psychological difficulties, and the like, begin to lose the luster of their youth, gain unwanted weight, lose hair in places that they desire it to grow, and grow hair in places that they don't want it to grow. They develop age spots, wrinkles, and are often wanting for energy and vitality. This type of situation can prove to be a real test for the husband. When his desire for his wife decreases, his vulnerability to temptation—lust—increases. The evil one works tirelessly to convince us that lusting after other women is acceptable and justified, especially when a man's wife appears to be "letting herself go."

Jesus warns us, "If you lust after a woman in your heart you have already committed adultery" (see Mt 5:28). Pope St. John Paul II reflects on this warning: "Are we to fear the severity of Christ's words, or to believe in their salvific power?" In other words, our Lord would not demand us to overcome lust in the heart, unless He would provide us aid to defeat it.

Before we proceed with the idea of "defeating lust in the heart," it will be helpful for us to consider the two forms of lust: positive and negative. The apparently positive character of lust masks itself by complimenting a woman for her beauty with the sole purpose of manipulating her and using her to fulfill a man's disordered desire for self-gratification. It is often said that men will use love to get sex and women will use sex to get love. Though this is a generalization and may not apply to all persons, this dynamic is evident in our culture. The main point is that the positive form of lust masks its ill motives by means of elevating the woman by means of affirming her.

The negative form of lust is expressed when a man looks to his wife to fulfill his lustful desires, but after he analyzes her, he finds her wanting in beauty, unattractive, and not meeting the world's impossible standard of beauty, and because of this he shuns her.

Both forms of lust are deadly. Why? Because lust is taking rather than giving. It is the exact opposite of God's glory, which is self-giving love—which is also our glory. Whether we are battling the temptation to use woman solely to satiate our lustful desires or are unwilling to engage her because we believe that she is beneath our standards, or are tempted to objectify and use other women, it is imperative that we offer ourselves, manifesting Christ's total self-giving love as expressed in the words "This is My Body given up for you." By offering yourself in this way, you will be "delivering yourself up for her," and become "her savior," and she will gradually desire to respect you for your true strength—the capacity to love like Christ.

TAKE THE LEAD True love is willing the good of another—particularly your wife. The ultimate defining factor of such love is to will your wife's good, even at your own expense. Your wife longs to be important, valued, cherished, and pursued. One way to demonstrate your desire and love for her is to schedule a consistent "date night." Make a commitment to spend at least one hour a week being together, listening to her, looking deeply into her eyes, and awakening her heart to the reality that you still desire her.*

* See Examen *Embrace Your Wife* on page 446

HER SECOND NEED: EMOTIONAL INTIMACY

87. DEFEAT LUST IN THE HEART

The key to being respected by your wife as a man of strength is to deliver your body for her. To accomplish this, you will need nothing less than Christ's redemptive grace, which presupposes that we understand clearly that by relying solely on our own power we will fail ultimately.

Consider that in the beginning, Adam's soul and body were harmoniously integrated without any rupture or division. His body did what his spirit desired. After Adam's fall into sin, his body and spirit warred with one another. This tension between our souls and our bodies is a universal reality that we all know too well. St. Paul expresses this tension powerfully: "For I do not that good which I will; but the evil which I hate, that I do. For I am delighted with the law of God, according to the inward man [spirit]: But I see another law in my members fighting against the law of my mind, and captivating me in the law of sin, that is in my members . . . . Unhappy man that I am, who shall deliver me from this body of death? . . . The grace of God, by Jesus Christ our Lord" (Rom 7:24).

Jesus accomplished what no man could: He healed the tension between body and soul. He sacrificed Himself on behalf of the human race as the completely integrated New Adam. He died, yet without ever experiencing a rupture between his body and spirit. He became sin for us. This sin had to be obliterated. Jesus offered His body, as sin, to be destroyed by the Father. Yet Jesus and the Father knew that Christ could overcome the destruction of sin because He was fully integrated body and soul. In other words, Jesus' two natures of divinity and humanity were fully integrated and because of this He was able to defeat sin and death in His body and rise from the grave—something that no man could accomplish. It is through Jesus' Resurrection, and the imparting of the Holy Spirit to us, that our souls and bodies gradually become reintegrated, that we may become new men, capable of defeating lust in our bodies. This is the salvific power hidden in Christ's words regarding adultery in the heart.

According to Pope St. John Paul II, St. Joseph was a man who by receiving this redemptive grace became an integrated man: "Are we not to suppose that [Joseph's] love as a man was also given new birth by the Holy Spirit? Are we not to think that the love of God which has been poured forth into the human heart through the Holy Spirit, molds every human love into perfection?" (GR 19).

The same Spirit that molded St. Joseph into perfection will also perfect you, provided that you desire to defeat lust in your heart and are determined to rediscover your wife's true beauty.

> **TAKE THE LEAD** True love is willing the good of another—particularly your wife. The ultimate defining factor of such love is to will your wife's good, even at your own expense. Your wife longs to be important, valued, cherished, and pursued. One way to demonstrate your desire and love for her is to schedule a consistent "date night." Make a commitment to spend at least one hour a week being together, listening to her, looking deeply into her eyes, and awakening her heart to the reality that you still desire her.*

* See Examen *Embrace Your Wife* on page 446

HIS AND HER THIRD NEED: THE NEED FOR MISSION

88. IS THERE SOMETHING MORE?—HIS THIRD NEED

Do you know someone who has experienced or is experiencing a midlife crisis—that moment in a person's life when he becomes aware of the passage of time, and senses that to this point, his life has had little impact or significance and lacks real meaning. Why is it common for men in their forties to begin asking questions like: "Is this all there is?" "Why am I doing this?" "What is the point of life?" Or more specifically: "What is the point of my life?" When men don't find real answers to these confounding questions they begin to compare themselves with more successful friends and acquaintances. They turn toward created things from which they hope to derive value and purpose. Why do so many men experience the midlife crisis?

Recall that the first man, Adam, was created outside the garden—a symbol of the secure, loving, safe, environment of the domestic life—in the undiscovered, uncharted, unformed wilderness. Being descendants of Adam, there will always exist in the hearts of men an innate need and longing for adventure, challenge, conflict, risk, and discovery. In a word, a man is meant for mission. If men do not address this fundamental need, or dismiss or repress it as being immature daydreaming, they may begin to experience such a crisis. If a man doesn't have a sense of mission his spirit will hibernate, languish, and eventually die. A man's third primary need is to be respected for his sense of mission. This sense of mission, though, rather than being respected by a wife, can often be an object of resentment, disdain, or envy.

But before you venture out to purchase a new motorcycle, mountain-climbing gear, or a new boat, or to begin training for the upcoming triathlon, it is important to understand clearly where your mission is born and the context in which it will thrive.

Remember that the quest for your identity is an essential aspect of every man's journey toward his ultimate destiny. Your identity can only be discovered in light of the one who created you. "God

PILLAR 2: EMBRACE YOUR ESSENCE [EMBRACING WOMAN]

alone knows the plans that He has for you" (see Jer 29:11). Your identity is directly related to your mission, and your identity and mission can only be discovered by listening to and waiting on the *Vox* (voice) of God; and the voice of God speaks to us primarily and powerfully through our vocation. In other words, your mission is not arbitrary, based on whims and trends, or a product of your imagination; but rather it is born in God's heart and transmitted through His *Vox*, and will only thrive and be fulfilled within the context of your vocation.

Rather than fleeing from your vocation to discover an adventure, you will discover your true mission by returning to your vocation as father and husband.

> **TAKE THE LEAD** There is a difference between sharing your hopes, dreams, and desires with your wife, and burying her in your burdens, setbacks, and failures. Identify areas in your marriage in which the two of you can reconnect, collaborate, and help complete each other. Perhaps the two of you could exercise together, mentor other couples, or landscape the yard. Whatever you do, keep in mind that you and your wife's mission is to have a marriage that radiates Christ's magnetic love to this world. Over the next several reflections restrain yourself from burdening her with your burdens, and rather bless her with your presence.*

* See Examen *Embrace Your Wife* on page 446

HIS AND HER THIRD NEED: THE NEED FOR MISSION

89. DISCOVERING YOUR MISSION

Very often, many men blame their family, their marriage, or their responsibilities for their lack of mission. However, God has created marriage and family to be the fertile soil in which your mission germinates, grows, and bears fruit that will last. It is not that uncommon for a man to shuck the context of his vocation and seek an altogether unrelated or arbitrary adventure that is based on personal, passing passions. If your mission is not born within, or at the service of, or discovered through your vocation, it may not be your God-given mission.

For example, because of the confidence a man derives from his marriage, he may strike out in a business venture or a career change that alters the trajectory of his life. After having children, a man begins to work diligently and intentionally to provide for his family, and doing so increases his capacity for knowledge, talent, and work ethic. The combined talents and gifts of a man's wife and children can lead his family to serve their community in different ways. By means of his desire to raise his children to holiness, a father begins to become holy himself, not only leading his family members to salvation, but also discovering his ability to lead others to God. The opportunities that the vocation of marriage and fatherhood afford are nearly limitless.

It was within the context of his vocation that St. Joseph received his mission. The angel directed Joseph, "Do not be afraid to take Mary, *your wife*, into your home, for that which is conceived in her is of the Holy Spirit." By means of Joseph's marriage with Mary, he discovered his mission to be the guardian of the redeemer. In fact, Joseph's role as protector and patron of the Church was born within his vocation as a father. To those who have been faithful in small responsibilities more will be given; and Joseph was continually faithful in protecting, providing for, and leading his family on earth, and therefore God has given him the greater responsibility of being the patron and protector of God's family, the Church.

PILLAR 2: EMBRACE YOUR ESSENCE [EMBRACING WOMAN]

If you and I are faithful to the primary mission of our vocation as fathers, the Holy Spirit will enlighten us to the fullness of our divinely ordained mission—a mission truly worthy of respect.

TAKE THE LEAD There is a difference between sharing your hopes, dreams, and desires with your wife, and burying her in your burdens, setbacks, and failures. Identify areas in your marriage in which the two of you can reconnect, collaborate, and help complete each other. Perhaps the two of you could exercise together, mentor other couples, or landscape the yard. Whatever you do, keep in mind that you and your wife's mission is to have a marriage that radiates Christ's magnetic love to this world. Over the next several reflections restrain yourself from burdening her with your burdens, and rather bless her with your presence.*

* See Examen *Embrace Your Wife* on page 446

HIS AND HER THIRD NEED: THE NEED FOR MISSION

90. YOUR WIFE IS NOT THE MISSION—HER THIRD NEED

Do you remember when you first fell in love with your wife? Perhaps she was all that you could think about. Often, when a man meets the woman he hopes to spend the rest of his life with, he strategizes ways to win her. In a sense, she becomes his goal. To describe it in crude terms, she becomes his mission. The truth is that woman is not an end in herself, but a means to a greater, more glorious end. Your wife is not the mission; she is not the adventure. This truth can be especially difficult for younger, unmarried men to embrace. But most married men quickly discover that by making his wife the mission he suffocates her spirit, while also limiting his spirit from desiring even greater things.

We men have a primal instinct to be hunter-gatherers. We are goal-oriented. Because of this a man can often confuse woman as being the mission, the goal, the adventure. Even if a woman feels affirmed initially by this, she eventually becomes bored with being her husband's mission. A woman desires not so much to be her husband's mission, but to be on mission with her husband. This is woman's third primary need, which complements his third need, to be respected for his sense of mission: a wife desires to be cherished as the essential partner of her husband. She desires to be a part of a greater mission with him.

Scripture tells us that God created Eve as Adam's helpmate. As most women will express emphatically, helpmate doesn't sound very appealing or important. However, the Hebrew word for "helpmate" is *ezer chenegdo*, which can be translated as "essential counterpart," a "completion of self." Your wife desires to be your essential counterpart, the completion of you. Without his wife and her partnership, a husband lacks a certain power, vitality, and encouragement. Your wife will often provide essential wisdom that pertains to your mission. She may be the encouragement that enables you to risk doing something that transcends your marriage.

Your mission could be as simple as remodeling your home, starting a business venture, flipping houses, serving the Church, helping

PILLAR 2: EMBRACE YOUR ESSENCE [EMBRACING WOMAN]

the poor. Regardless, the greatest mission that you and your wife share is that your marriage proclaims to the world Jesus' undying, relentless, self-giving love; and the best way to accomplish this is by working together.

A wife can feel as though she is in competition with, or cannot compete with, her husband's mission. This is because she feels as though the mission is "his" mission, and not "their" mission. This is an important distinction. To have a successful marriage, it is vital that you determine ways to collaborate and support one another in *the* mission; or at the very least harmonize each other's mission to ensure that they complement and enhance the other.

Mary, the wife of Joseph was given the mission of bearing the Christ Child to the world and be an intimate sharer in His redemptive work. Joseph was given the mission of protecting Mary and Jesus to ensure that the world would have a savior. Mary was Joseph's inspiration, encouragement, and reason for his mission. Mary was Joseph's *ezer chenegdo*, his essential counterpart, and in a certain sense, the two complemented and completed each other, and by means of their partnership, salvation has come to the world.

Like Mary and Joseph, when you and your wife decide to partner in the mission, God will afford you the blessed experience of participating with him in bringing others to Jesus and His salvation.

> **TAKE THE LEAD** There is a difference between sharing your hopes, dreams, and desires with your wife, and burying her in your burdens, setbacks, and failures. Identify areas in your marriage in which the two of you can reconnect, collaborate, and help complete each other. Perhaps the two of you could exercise together, mentor other couples, or landscape the yard. Whatever you do, keep in mind that you and your wife's mission is to have a marriage that radiates Christ's magnetic love to this world. Over the next several reflections restrain yourself from burdening her with your burdens, and rather bless her with your presence.*

* See Examen *Embrace Your Wife* on page 446

HIS AND HER FOURTH NEEDS

91. YOUR FOURTH NEED: SPIRITUAL AUTHORITY

We've discussed his and her needs that begin from the exterior—such as strength and beauty—and proceed to the interior, or the intrinsic needs that constitute the core identity of both the husband and wife. Imagine a triangle with the left-hand side representing his needs, and the right side representing her needs (see diagram on page 176). Both begin at the baseline of the triangle with those needs that have more of an exterior character; but as one ascends the sides of the triangle the needs become more spiritual in character. Notice also that the two lines eventually converge, forming an apex, a point of harmony and unity.

The apex symbolizes the point in marriage when spouses' needs converge and become nearly indistinct. The husband's ultimate need is to be respected as having spiritual authority, while her ultimate need is to be cherished as his spiritual inspirer. When couples consistently address one another's needs, they eventually reach the summit where their needs and roles become unified and almost indistinct; where they truly become one.

For example, someone may refer to God as the divine mind. Another may say that God is love, and yet another might suggest that God is truth. In God these attributes are one and the same. God's mind is His love, and His love is His mind, and His mind and love are His truth. If God has created married couples to become an image of Him then it makes sense that as couples reach the summit of understanding and addressing one another's needs through self-giving love, that his spiritual authority and her spiritual inspiration become unified and harmonized, and that they become a united front of love, wisdom, counsel, and authority.

If this is indeed your greatest need—to be respected as having spiritual authority—why should your wife respect you? Scripture attests to the husband's spiritual authority with those highly contentious words, "Let wives be subject to their husbands as to the Lord; because a husband is head of the wife, just as Christ is head of the Church, being Himself savior of the body" (Eph 5:23).

PILLAR 2: EMBRACE YOUR ESSENCE [EMBRACING WOMAN]

Some have interpreted these words as meaning that the husband is the spiritual leader, but what does that actually mean? Too often, the term spiritual leader is misunderstood as the husband being holier than his wife or having a deeper spirituality than she does. But how do we interpret this idea of a man's spiritual leadership if his wife is holier than her husband, or if she has a more profound and intimate relationship with Jesus than he does? Does this undermine his role as spiritual head?

A husband is the spiritual "head" in that he has an "office" of authority that God appoints to him when he enters marriage. This authority becomes intrinsic to his being, his very identity; it is who he is. It cannot be earned, but if he neglects his office, he can be disrespected. However, even if he abuses his office, the office remains. Much like inhabitants of a kingdom who respect the son who inherited his father's throne, even before he has exercised his full power; or like neighbors who respect the rights of a landowner who received his property by means of inheritance; a wife respects her husband for what he is—as having the spiritual authority that he inherited from her father when he married her.

The pope has an office. Even if he is a scoundrel, nevertheless his office of authority exists. So it is with fatherhood. This is good news. For if we have been scoundrels, neglecting our vocation as fathers and husbands, we can repent and return to that office and lead by loving and love by leading,

> **TAKE THE LEAD** A husband can err in one of two ways in relating to his wife: domination or abdication. On one hand a husband can misuse his gift of authority for the purpose of deriving what he wants from his wife. On the other hand, out of fear of confrontation, or sheer unwillingness to fight for what he believes is right, a husband can allow his wife to rule over and manipulate him. The golden mean between domination and abdication is self-donation. This is the essence of authority. It may be beneficial to ask your wife if she trusts your leadership. But be ready for brutal critique. (If you want to grow, you want this critique.) Though her critique could become condemnation or become exaggerated, nevertheless, there exists an element of truth in her response. Listen carefully; withhold your response. Take to prayer what she has disclosed. Make the changes needed and become a man worthy of being trusted with authority.*

* See Examen *Embrace Your Wife* on page 446

HIS AND HER FOURTH NEEDS

92. WHY SHOULD SHE RESPECT YOU? YOUR FOURTH NEED (CONT.)

Does your wife respect your authority? Why should she? Many men struggle with envisioning themselves as spiritual leaders for numerous reasons. Some men simply don't want the pressure that comes with being a spiritual leader; while others don't understand how to lead their wives; and still others do not believe they have earned the right to be acknowledged as the "spiritual leader" of the family. For these reasons and others, many men do not believe that they have a need to be respected as a spiritual leader. Whether we realize it, or are willing to admit it, the need to be respected as one who has spiritual authority is real; and it is the pinnacle, the ultimate need, of the masculine soul.

There exists form and substance. The form is the office of authority. This is an objective reality that exists whether the character of the substance—that is, the subjective spirit and action that comes forth from the office—is good or bad. Your wife may have "more substance," but regardless of how "good" she is, she can never replace your divinely ordained role of spiritual authority. Your office of husband, father, leader is essential to your being. Today, many men deny the very essence of their nature by neglecting their office of having spiritual authority. Yet the office remains. This should give you and me hope that if we have neglected our spiritual authority we can change our ways and return to our office.

In the biological sphere, if a man does not sow his seed, life cannot exist in his wife's womb. In a similar way, if a man does not exercise his authority to sow the seed of self-giving love, his wife will struggle to experience the fullness of spiritual fruitfulness. As Pope St. John Paul II said, "The husband is above all the one who loves and the wife, by contrast, is the one who is loved. One might even venture the idea that the wife's 'submission' to the husband, understood in the context of the whole Ephesians 5:22–23, means above all 'the experiencing of love'" (TOB 92:6). This means that your spiritual authority is expressed by discovering ways to initiate

PILLAR 2: EMBRACE YOUR ESSENCE [EMBRACING WOMAN]

acts of self-donation on behalf of your wife to ensure that she experiences love.

Does this mean that you will initiate every good idea? Does this indicate that you dictate a rule of life and your wife silently submits to you? No. It simply means that you use your office of spiritual authority to plant the seed of self-donation in your wife's soul. To deny or misuse your spiritual authority would be a denial of your essence—who you really are.

Why do some wives neglect to respect their husband's spiritual authority? Very often it is because the husband neglects to respect and revere his office as a spiritual author who crafts a vision of love and life for his family. Why should your wife respect you? Because of your God-given office of having spiritual authority. When you begin to recognize your need to be respected for your spiritual authority, you will begin to envision yourself as a spiritual leader; and envisioning yourself in this way you will begin to respect your office of spiritual authority and be respected for your spiritual leadership.

> **TAKE THE LEAD** A husband can err in one of two ways in relating to his wife: domination or abdication. On one hand a husband can misuse his gift of authority for the purpose of deriving what he wants from his wife. On the other hand, out of fear of confrontation, or sheer unwillingness to fight for what he believes is right, a husband can allow his wife to rule over and manipulate him. The golden mean between domination and abdication is self-donation. This is the essence of authority. It may be beneficial to ask your wife if she trusts your leadership. But be ready for brutal critique. (If you want to grow, you want this critique.) Though her critique could become condemnation or become exaggerated, nevertheless, there exists an element of truth in her response. Listen carefully; withhold your response. Take to prayer what she has disclosed. Make the changes needed and become a man worthy of being trusted with authority.*

* See Examen *Embrace Your Wife* on page 446

HIS AND HER FOURTH NEEDS

93. DOES SHE INSPIRE YOU? HER FOURTH NEED

From the first moment that original man, Adam, awoke from his *tardemah*, his supernatural slumber, and witnessed—with complete purity—the awe-inspiring, naked beauty of Eve, he was inspired by the Holy Spirit to praise God in an ode of joy: "This is bone of my bones and flesh of my flesh!" Adam's response is what every woman, at a deep, subconscious level, desires: she desires and deserves to be cherished for her beauty. Daughters of Eve have been created by God to draw out, summon, a man's spiritual authority, that is, his ability and desire to protect and cherish what he loves.

During the act of sexual intercourse, a woman's beauty literally draws out the man's seed, which in turn makes her fruitful. In a spiritually analogous way, woman has been created with the unique ability and power to draw out a man's spiritual authority. Every woman has the innate need, indeed her pinnacle need, to be the spiritual inspirer that draws out man's spiritual authority, that she may "experience love."

Which raises a question: Does your wife inspire you?

The word inspire literally means "in" and "to breathe"; or more clearly, "to influence, move, or guide by divine or supernatural inspiration." Woman, in a certain sense, helps her husband "breathe in" the Holy Spirit. Adam was created by the *Ruah*, the breath of God. When God created Eve from Adam, Adam unknowingly participated in donating the "matter" that God animated by His breath. Yet, when Eve returns the fruits of what she has received from both Adam and God, it is in a magnified and inspired form. This is precisely woman's role as spiritual inspirer: she magnifies her husband's gift of spiritual authority by returning it in a magnified form. Much like the servants who provided the water that Jesus transformed into wine at the wedding feast in Cana, analogously, woman receives her husband's water, and in a certain sense, makes it wine.

As a husband, you use your spiritual authority to plant the seeds of divine love in your wife's soul. You cultivate the seed, protect her garden, and allow her vine to flourish and bear fruit (see Psalm 128:3) and she returns your gift magnified. Much like St. Paul who planted the seed of the Gospel but realized that only God could make the seed grow (see 1 Cor 3:6–8), so also we husbands have a certain level of contribution. We sow the seed of our spiritual authority, and God, in woman, makes it grow.

Mary, the mother of Jesus, received the seed of divine life into herself, and by carrying and sharing this life with the world, she can humbly yet boldly proclaim, "My soul doth magnify the Lord." She magnifies the gift of the Holy Spirit—she magnifies God!

A man who uses his spiritual authority properly implants confidence in his wife that enables her to flourish in magnifying the gifts that God has given to her. Perhaps more importantly, he receives this magnified gift from her and cherishes it. This reception of the magnified gift is a vital action of the husband, for your wife desires to be needed, affirmed, and lauded for her unique ability to be a source of inspiration.

> **TAKE THE LEAD** A husband can err in one of two ways in relating to his wife: domination or abdication. On one hand a husband can misuse his gift of authority for the purpose of deriving what he wants from his wife. On the other hand, out of fear of confrontation, or sheer unwillingness to fight for what he believes is right, a husband can allow his wife to rule over and manipulate him. The golden mean between domination and abdication is self-donation. This is the essence of authority. It may be beneficial to ask your wife if she trusts your leadership. But be ready for brutal critique. (If you want to grow, you want this critique.) Though her critique could become condemnation or become exaggerated, nevertheless, there exists an element of truth in her response. Listen carefully; withhold your response. Take to prayer what she has disclosed. Make the changes needed and become a man worthy of being trusted with authority.*

* See Examen *Embrace Your Wife* on page 446

HIS AND HER FOURTH NEEDS

94. HOW THE TWO BECOME ONE SPIRITUALLY

Sacred Scripture poetically describes woman as a garden enclosed, a fountain sealed. This fountain is symbolic of the Holy Spirit that lives within her. As Jesus said, "From within you shall well up springs of living water." He was speaking of the Holy Spirit welling up from within the human person. This is true for all baptized Christians, but in a particular way Jesus' words apply to women who "magnify" those streams of living water. Mary transmitted the Presence of Jesus within her to Elizabeth, and because of this transmission, John the Baptist leapt with joy and is sanctified in the womb. God chooses to speak to husbands through their wives in a way that He chooses not to speak to us directly.

Your wife's pinnacle need is to be cherished as your spiritual inspirer. She longs to share her wisdom and guidance with you. She desires to be taken seriously. Perhaps the reason so many wives verbally bite at their husbands, ridiculing and demeaning them, is because the husband has forgotten or neglected to factor in his wife's wisdom and counsel to his decision-making process.

It is vital that you and I be intentional about allowing our wives the "space" to contribute their wisdom, counsel, and perspective. If you listen and act upon your wife's wisdom, she will be far more inclined to respect your spiritual authority.

St. Joseph protected Mary from shame, cultivating her person, tending her vine to ensure that the gift of God would be magnified. Your wife receives the seed of your love, and magnifies this gift, returning to you nourishment, wisdom, and love. She becomes your advocate, counselor, and inspiration—provided that you, like St. Joseph, become the protector of your spiritual inspirer.

Without a doubt, St. Joseph cherished the wisdom, counsel, guidance, and inspiration that Mary continually offered; and Mary reciprocated his love for her by respecting his spiritual authority—an authority that Jesus also submitted to. Mary and Joseph experienced the pinnacle of the union of persons. When this dynamic

PILLAR 2: EMBRACE YOUR ESSENCE [EMBRACING WOMAN]

occurs within your marriage, you and your wife will experience a unity of persons, the pinnacle of married life, wherein the two truly become one.

> **TAKE THE LEAD** A husband can err in one of two ways in relating to his wife: domination or abdication. On one hand a husband can misuse his gift of authority for the purpose of deriving what he wants from his wife. On the other hand, out of fear of confrontation, or sheer unwillingness to fight for what he believes is right, a husband can allow his wife to rule over and manipulate him. The golden mean between domination and abdication is self-donation. This is the essence of authority. It may be beneficial to ask your wife if she trusts your leadership. But be ready for brutal critique. (If you want to grow, you want this critique.) Though her critique could become condemnation or become exaggerated, nevertheless, there exists an element of truth in her response. Listen carefully; withhold your response. Take to prayer what she has disclosed. Make the changes needed and become a man worthy of being trusted with authority.*

* See Examen *Embrace Your Wife* on page 446

COMMUNICATING NEEDS

95. HOW TO COMMUNICATE WITH YOUR WIFE, PART 1

Recall that God created your marriage to relive, reveal, and reflect His love. God designed marriage in this way for many reasons, three which are well worth mentioning: First, God's intention is for you and your wife to begin experiencing His eternal love right now on earth. Second, God wills that you be purified and prepared by means of your marriage for the eternal life of bliss ultimately experienced in God's eternal exchange of persons—the Trinity. Third, God has created your marriage to be a bold witness that participates in saving souls. Keep in mind that the evil one hates you and your marriage because God created your marriage to be a reminder to others of their heavenly destiny.

God designed you and your wife to have authentic—God-given—needs that only your spouse can address. These needs are divinely designed to help spouses complement and, in a sense, complete each other. Not only are these needs to be acknowledged and understood, but also discussed. Why? Because communication leads to authentic communion. Expressing needs enables the couple to express their tender dependence upon the other. By doing this, both spouses truly understand that they are needed and important to the other.

To discuss one's needs charitably is a tremendous challenge and has the potential to cause significant pain. Why? Most often we are willing to share our needs because we feel that those needs are not being addressed or fulfilled by our spouse. Because of this, when expressing needs, we are tempted to resort to blaming, criticizing, and condemning the other for not meeting our needs. This is not communication that leads to communion, but rather condemnation that has the potential of leading to divorce.

There exist several key principles that if applied to our efforts of communicating with our wife will help us experience authentic communion with them. Over the following several reflections, we will outline these core principles of communication. For now, let us, as husbands, ask God for the grace to open our hearts that we may be willing to communicate compassionately with our wife.

> **TAKE THE LEAD** You now have the "big picture" of marriage. You understand, at some level, the meaning and mystery of your marriage. God gave us needs—authentic spousal needs. The purpose of those needs is to unite you and your wife. This unification can only come through communication. For men, communication and sharing needs can be most difficult, and yet the communication of needs is essential to achieve authentic, lasting communion and joy. Whether you and your wife have been arguing, forgiveness is still needed for some past betrayal, or one of you is distant, take the first step and initiate communication with her. But do so with humility. Humility is like the sun. Flowers open for the sun. A wife opens her heart to a humble husband.*

* See Examen *Embrace Your Wife* on page 446

COMMUNICATING NEEDS

96. HOW TO COMMUNICATE WITH YOUR WIFE, PART 2

Do your discussions with your wife seem to turn into arguments? Do simple comments unexpectedly digress into marital conflict? If so, you are like the majority of married couples who struggle to communicate with their spouse. There exist a number of practical ways that, if applied, will enable couples to communicate in a way that fosters true communion.

First, we as husbands must strive to never blame our wife for not addressing our needs. Blaming, criticizing, condemning only lead to stonewalling—the refusal to communicate honestly. This cannot be stressed enough. Stonewalling is a foreshadowing of Hell, where the damned are entrenched in their own self-pity, bitterness, and resentment, expressed in a refusal to honestly and openly communicate.

Second, we can only express our needs and should not attempt to determine our wife's giftedness—or response—to our expressed needs. This indicates that you become vulnerable, honest, and pure by expressing your needs without attempting to coerce, manipulate, bully, or force her to address your needs. Your wife alone—not you—can determine how she chooses to respond to your needs and become a gift to you.

Third, it is important not to reduce communicating and addressing needs to marital bargaining: "You scratch my back, I'll scratch yours." "I do this for you, you do this for me." This is not the "dynamic of the gift" that always gives space for the person to freely give themselves to one another. Unfortunately, after the fall of Adam, the ability to be a gift freely given has been compromised by our selfish desires. "From the moment in which man 'dominates' her, the communion of persons—which consists in the spiritual unity of the two subjects who gave themselves to each other—is replaced by a different mutual relationship, namely a relationship of possession of the other as an object of one's own desire (TOB 31:3). This can be defined as marital bargaining, which only leads to disappointment because one of the spouses will eventually feel as though they receive less while giving more. In other words, they feel used.

Fourth, you and your wife are not bargaining over needs as though they are objects separated from the person. For example, a man who needs physical intimacy may say, "I want *it*," *it* referring to sexual intercourse. In this case the husband has separated the "object" of his desire from the "subject," his wife—whom he ought to purely desire. This can be defined as lust—the objectification of the person. Our approach must always be "I need you," rather than "I need it."

Fifth, a husband's ability to listen and discern his wife's sentiments ought to be heightened. This means that you listen for her heart and discern what her soul is saying. She may be saying one thing, but if you listen carefully to her body language you may discover that she is communicating something quite different. Asking her "I heard you say *this*. Is that what you mean?" may help to draw out her true feelings, so long as it is said in a compassionate manner.

Overall, be patient with her style of communication. Women are beautifully complex creatures, and sometimes what they say and what they mean are very, very different.

Sixth, and perhaps most vital to spousal communication, is forgiveness. Forgiveness is the very heart of marriage. No forgiveness—no marriage. At the heart of Christ's marriage to His bride, the Church, is ongoing, perpetual, relentless, intentional forgiveness, mercy, and reconciliation.

The word "mercy" is derived from the Latin word *misericordia*, or *miserum cor*. *Miserum* means "compassion" and *cor* means "heart." In other words, mercy is to have a compassionate heart. In addition to this, the Latin word *merces* means to "pay the price." Mercy, then, is the action of paying the price for the purpose of liberating another from misery. This is a powerful description of marriage: a liberation of spouses from misery by their being merciful to one another.

Too often, however, marriage is miserable rather than merciful. Make mercy you measure, and mercy will be measured to you. Indeed, blessed are the merciful for mercy shall be theirs. Again, no mercy—no marriage.

When Mary was discovered pregnant without St. Joseph's cooperation, Joseph applied mercy in a tangible way. He was compassionate from the heart, and in the end, he paid the price for Mary's fiat to the

Lord, sacrificing his good reputation, his sexual desires, and his financial future to liberate Mary from the consequences of being a teenage girl who is pregnant before the final stage of their marital vows.

By communicating with your wife in the ways outlined above, you will become like St. Joseph, a man who liberated his wife for love.

> **TAKE THE LEAD** You now have the "big picture" of marriage. You understand, at some level, the meaning and mystery of your marriage. God gave us needs—authentic spousal needs. The purpose of those needs is to unite you and your wife. This unification can only come through communication. For men, communication and sharing needs can be most difficult, and yet the communication of needs is essential to achieve authentic, lasting communion and joy. Whether you and your wife have been arguing, forgiveness is still needed for some past betrayal, or one of you is distant, take the first step and initiate communication with her. But do so with humility. Humility is like the sun. Flowers open for the sun. A wife opens her heart to a humble husband.*

* See Examen *Embrace Your Wife* on page 446

PILLAR 2: EMBRACE YOUR ESSENCE [EMBRACING WOMAN]

COMMUNICATING NEEDS

97. THE GREATEST SCANDAL

Perhaps you've heard those words of Jesus that often give us a sense of uneasiness and a holy fear: "But he that shall scandalize one of these little ones that believe in me, it were better for him that a millstone should be hanged about his neck, and that he should be drowned in the depth of the sea" (Mt 18:6).

Jesus warns us that whosoever causes scandal to children will be held accountable. This is a challenging admonition.

The Greek word for "scandal" is *scandalon*, which literally means "bait trap." The evil one's bait trap that ensnares our children in disbelief is the scandal of spouses persisting in resentment, bitterness, and unforgiveness. When children witness the two people—a father and mother—who in their innocent estimation are either like God, or the closest representation of God's love, remain entrenched in unforgiveness, they begin to believe that Christians are hypocrites; that God's grace is not effective, and that religion is pointless. This is a great scandal—if not the greatest scandal—to our children.

A man remains entrenched in his unforgiveness when he blames another rather than being compassionate from the heart toward his wife for the purpose of liberating her from her pain and misery. This is how a husband pays the price for his wife: he stops blaming her and begins claiming the compassion of Christ as his own by expressing it to his wife.

Jesus once asked, "Why do you try to remove the speck in your brother's eye when you have a beam in your own. First remove the beam from your own eye, then you can remove the speck in your brother's eye" (Mt 7:5). The visual is powerful: when the man who has the large beam extruding from his own eye turns his head, he inadvertently pummels those around him. He wonders why those with specks in their own eyes can't see well enough to move out of his way.

The seventh key to communication that leads to communion is the key to marital forgiveness: the husband initiates forgiveness and reconciliation. You and I, as husbands, men, are created to set the pace of self-giving love. In dancing, we men lead. In forgiveness we lead. We initiate self-giving love—that is our essence.

One of the greatest scandals to our children is when their parents refuse to forgive one another. This also indicates that one of the most valuable lessons you can give to your children is initiating forgiveness with your wife.

> **TAKE THE LEAD** You now have the "big picture" of marriage. You understand, at some level, the meaning and mystery of your marriage. God gave us needs—authentic spousal needs. The purpose of those needs is to unite you and your wife. This unification can only come through communication. For men, communication and sharing needs can be most difficult, and yet the communication of needs is essential to achieve authentic, lasting communion and joy. Whether you and your wife have been arguing, forgiveness is still needed for some past betrayal, or one of you is distant, take the first step and initiate communication with her. But do so with humility. Humility is like the sun. Flowers open for the sun. A wife opens her heart to a humble husband.*

* See Examen *Embrace Your Wife* on page 446

COMMUNICATING NEEDS

98. INITIATING THE DANCE OF FORGIVENESS

A very practical way to set the pace of self-giving love is to ask for forgiveness first. Even if in the particular dispute, dilemma, confrontation, or relational tension we are only culpable for 1 percent of the problem, nevertheless we are to ask for forgiveness—authentically and sincerely—for that 1 percent.

When we ask for forgiveness, rather than saying "I'm sorry," we ask "Will you forgive me?" Why the distinction? When we say "I'm sorry," we are not completely humbling ourselves. We are simply expressing how we feel without asking for anything. In that case, we retain control. When we ask, "Will you forgive me," we are humbled, perhaps humiliated, vulnerable—much like a beggar. We figuratively place our heart in our wife's hands, while running the risk of rejection.

In addition to this, when your wife asks you for forgiveness, try never to respond by saying, "I forgive you, but you did . . ." When we forgive, there are no buts. Our Lord Jesus, while enduring His torturous Crucifixion, forgave His enemies, His future bride, for killing Him. Jesus did not say, "Father forgive them . . . but they did this, or that"

Receiving God's Forgiveness is conditional. The Our Father, the prayer that Jesus gave us, contains an important condition regarding forgiveness: God forgives us if we forgive others, as testified by the words, "Forgive us our trespasses *as we forgive* those who trespass against us" (see Mt 6:12). In other words, you and I are to forgive our wife for her sins, faults, even betrayals, if we desire that God forgives us.

Your wife will hurt you. But hurts, if they are forgiven, can make your marriage grow stronger. Communication leads to communion. During moments of marital trials, tests, strife, anguish, and bitterness, we husbands are to be the first to ask for forgiveness for our culpability regardless of how small that culpability is. Second, we ought to communicate our hurt. This is difficult because we have an inherent need to be respected for our strength. A man's first reaction to being hurt is to bury the pain. Yet, the truth will set you free. Third, a husband is to be intent on being merciful, determined to pay the price of his wife's sins.

Remember, perhaps the greatest satanic trap set for children is persistent unforgiveness between spouses. But if you are determined to set the pace of self-giving love and initiate forgiveness by admitting your fault, you have a much better chance of transmitting the love of God not only to your wife, but also to your children.

> **TAKE THE LEAD** You now have the "big picture" of marriage. You understand, at some level, the meaning and mystery of your marriage. God gave us needs—authentic spousal needs. The purpose of those needs is to unite you and your wife. This unification can only come through communication. For men, communication and sharing needs can be most difficult, and yet the communication of needs is essential to achieve authentic, lasting communion and joy. Whether you and your wife have been arguing, forgiveness is still needed for some past betrayal, or one of you is distant, take the first step and initiate communication with her. But do so with humility. Humility is like the sun. Flowers open for the sun. A wife opens her heart to a humble husband. *

* See Examen *Embrace Your Wife* on page 446

COMMUNICATING NEEDS

99. YOU CAN'T DO IT YOURSELF

To forgive another from the heart, particularly your wife, is one of the most challenging things you will ever do. In fact, to forgive your wife from the heart is impossible for a man who relies solely on his own powers. Often within marriage spouses do terrible things that not only undermine their vows, but crush their ability to trust and reconcile with one another. Infidelity, betrayal, misunderstandings, using one another, harsh criticism of the other's body, personality, and behavior all weigh heavily on a married couple; without the grace of God, many of us are simply gritting our teeth and enduring the time remaining in the marriage.

The good news is that Christ came, became one of us, died in place of us, rose from the grave to conquer the effects of sin (ultimately death), and ascended into heaven to present all of humanity in Himself to the Father so that the Holy Spirit could be sent to each of us.

One of the greatest powers the Holy Spirit offers is the ability to forgive from the heart. Christianity is not a mere imitation of Christ—as if we live on the outside of Jesus, looking upon Him—but rather a participation with Christ in us. We are to collaborate and participate with God within us and allow His power, particularly to forgive, to be expressed in and through us.

When a husband throws in the towel, gives up the fight, when he refuses to forgive his wife, he "grieve[s] the Holy Spirit" that dwells within us (see Eph 4:30). We "have an appearance indeed of godliness, but denying the power thereof" (2 Tim 3:5). We may pray, attend Mass, listen to Christian music, while all the while believing that Christ—God within us—cannot heal our heart, our marriage, and grant us the ability to forgive. When we believe such things, we lack faith in the power of God's presence within us; and "[w]ithout faith, no one is acceptable in the sight of God" (Heb 11:4).

We often overlook the truth that baptism is not merely a symbol, or a mere washing away of original sin—though it does accomplish this. At baptism the Holy Spirit knits the divine and human nature of Christ into our being. From that point onward, we contain within us the power to love, to forgive, to be compassionate and truly merciful as Christ is merciful. In other words, we don't simply imitate Christ, we participate with Christ who dwells within us.

By participating with Christ in loving your wife, you become, in Christ, her savior (in a qualified sense), for it is Christ in you who is saving her. When this occurs, you and your wife participate in saving the world for Christ by your example in Christ. If there is no dying with Christ, your marriage will not rise with Christ. Die to yourself for you wife and the two of you will rise in glory.

> **TAKE THE LEAD** You now have the "big picture" of marriage. You understand, at some level, the meaning and mystery of your marriage. God gave us needs—authentic spousal needs. The purpose of those needs is to unite you and your wife. This unification can only come through communication. For men, communication and sharing needs can be most difficult, and yet the communication of needs is essential to achieve authentic, lasting communion and joy. Whether you and your wife have been arguing, forgiveness is still needed for some past betrayal, or one of you is distant, take the first step and initiate communication with her. But do so with humility. Humility is like the sun. Flowers open for the sun. A wife opens her heart to a humble husband.*

* See Examen *Embrace Your Wife* on page 446

PILLAR 2: EMBRACE YOUR ESSENCE [EMBRACING WOMAN]

THE ENEMY OF INTIMACY

100. GOD ACTING IN THE SEXUAL ACT

Have you ever purchased a cheaper, less expensive model of an item because the item that you really wanted was too expensive—only to regret it later? Have you ever purchased a cheap piece of furniture only to replace it repeatedly with other pieces of cheap furniture, finally discovering that the cost of all the furniture previously purchased far surpasses the cost of the one you actually wanted?

Whether we are updating our homes, purchasing shoes, or choosing vacation destinations, all too often we settle for less because we assume that the cost of our true desire will be unaffordable.

While it is admirable to live modestly and beneficial to be thrifty, there are occasions when we restrain God's intention to grant us more, because of our lack of faith. We may have the exterior mark of Christian character by seeming to be modest and conservative; but with a bit more labor, a little more time, some sacrifice, and faith in our Father's benevolence, we can often experience those heavenly blessings for which our soul desires.

Regarding our sexual life, married couples often settle for less. We often fail to recognize that a little more labor and a little more sacrifice can make sexual intimacy so much more than what the world offers. The world offers an exchange of goods, wherein persons are treated as objects—things to be used for pleasure. God created man and woman to need each other, to desire each other, and to give themselves to one another by exchanging their bodies that they may ultimately exchange their persons, and in doing so, experience the bliss of authentic union. This exchange of persons, as its character and motive are made purer, becomes an actual participation in God's exchange of persons in the Trinity. In fact, God, who is an eternal exchange of persons, is in each of the spouses who give themselves to one another. In other words, God is *in* the sexual act, and His presence elevates the significance of this act of love to a divine level.

247

TAKE THE LEAD For many men, this next set of reflections will be very challenging and could irritate old wounds. Whether it is the use of contraception, the use of pornography, a spouse's stonewalling, a wife refusing to "have sex" with her husband, it is vital that the both of you expose your wounds to the Wounded Healer, Christ, who can heal your wounds, and make them shine with glory. Approach your wife with the idea of praying together for your marriage. It may feel awkward at first—very awkward. However, by worshipping God together, you will open your hearts to one another and to the healing power of God.*

* See Examen *Embrace Your Wife* on page 446

PILLAR 2: EMBRACE YOUR ESSENCE [EMBRACING WOMAN]

THE ENEMY OF INTIMACY

101. ARE YOU SETTLING FOR LESS?

One of the purposes of sexual intercourse is that the couple become one as God is one; and in their union, spouses experience a glimmer of the joy, ecstasy, and glory of the Trinity's self-giving love. This is one of the reasons why God created sexual climax—that we may humanly experience a very, very, very small taste of divine love that stems from self-donation.

In addition to this, man and woman become co-creators with God, the "Lord and Giver of Life." This ability to co-create with God is astonishingly sacred. Woman's fertility is sacred. Your wife's sexuality, femininity, and fertility are sacred, beautiful, life-giving, and demand protection. But not the *protection* that the world offers. God has created you and I, as husbands, to be guardians of woman's deepest mystery—her ability to conceive and bear life to the world.

The Church teaches us that the "ends" of marriage are procreative and unitive, or as some say, babies and bonding. But there is another end that is as important as the other two. Marriage is not only procreative and unitive, but also redemptive; meaning that it has, by God's grace, the ability to redeem us, to make us whole—to unite our body with our soul (which is united with God's Spirit). In other words, the one-flesh union and our striving to uphold the sacredness of this union by engaging in it without lust, and by abstaining from it without lust, is intended to purify us, redeem us, make us whole, and make us one with God.

Mary and Joseph, by their union of wills with one another and their openness to God, "drew down" divine life into Mary's virginal womb. Their marriage was not only procreative and unitive, but also redemptive. The sufferings, misunderstandings, anguish of Mary's virginal conception; the consequences of bearing the Son of God to the world; the demands placed upon Mary and Joseph to adore, reverence, and protect this mystery of God made flesh—all served to make them whole, complete, and unified with God's will. Though the Blessed Virgin Mary was perfectly sinless, she nevertheless grew in that perfection. Much of her growth occurred in her marriage to Joseph. The trials, tests, and determination to love Mary at all costs provided St. Joseph the context for his redemption. He refused to settle for less.

It is easy to settle for less. It's the seemingly painless path. But if you embrace your wife's procreative ability and are open to receiving the children that she could bear, you will experience a profound communion with your wife, and redemption in your life.

> **TAKE THE LEAD** For many men, this next set of reflections will be very challenging and could irritate old wounds. Whether it is the use of contraception, the use of pornography, a spouse's stonewalling, a wife refusing to "have sex" with her husband, it is vital that the both of you expose your wounds to the Wounded Healer, Christ, who can heal your wounds, and make them shine with glory. Approach your wife with the idea of praying together for your marriage. It may feel awkward at first–very awkward. However, by worshipping God together, you will open your hearts to one another and to the healing power of God.

* See Examen *Embrace Your Wife* on page 446

PILLAR 2: EMBRACE YOUR ESSENCE [EMBRACING WOMAN]

THE ENEMY OF INTIMACY

102. TRUE OR FALSE MERCY

There exist two types of pain: one that makes you stronger and another that makes you weaker. For example, after exercising a person may experience pain. Usually, this pain is caused by the tearing down, rebuilding, and thickening of the body's muscle tissue, which ultimately thickens the muscles and makes you stronger and more capable of competing. When a person neglects to exercise they can experience the pain of never playing, or if they play, they often experience the debilitating pain that stems from injury.

There is a difference between "good pain," which causes sexual strength, and "bad pain," which causes sexual weakness. Another way of saying this is that there is true mercy and false mercy. False mercy avoids the good pain up front, but eventually encounters bad pain. False mercy masks itself as being safe, not risky, secure, and pain-free—like war lords assuring their enemies that if they surrender before battle, they will be able to save their own lives and their family's lives. Yet, the warlords will systematically take their land, pillage the first-fruits of their crops, and rape their women. Though these victims retain their life, they are not living.

False mercy enslaves us in our fears and restrains us from becoming a threat to the evil one. False mercy keeps us manageable. The last thing that the evil one wants is a man who risks his life to love in a radical way.

Contraception is a form of false mercy. Contraception convinces us to play it safe, to avoid the risk of loving radically and sacrificially. Contraception offers the enticing ideal of "spontaneous sex," "sex on demand," "sex without consequences," but it is a diabolical trap, an empty hope that promises a good without pain—without sacrifice.

Our Lord offers real mercy, liberty from sexual captivity, a way to experience the fullness of joy in the one-flesh union in an ongoing, consistent manner.

God's plan is not contraceptive, nor does it involve barriers; but rather it replicates the pattern of His divine love in marriage. This is one reason He created the one-flesh union: to draw men and women together to relive and reflect the attributes of the Trinity: distinction, unity, and fruitfulness.

Natural Family Planning—NFP—is a way to apply this pattern of divine love to our marriages. As St. Teresa of Calcutta said, "NFP is nothing more than self-control out of love for each other." NFP, if used correctly, is 99 percent effective in planning pregnancies and spacing children. Couples who use NFP have an astonishingly low divorce rate of under 3 percent. NFP is not easy. It is challenging, but also rewarding. It is challenging because it demands that a man pay close attention to his wife's cycles, hormones, her body, and her person. In other words, NFP empowers the couple to communicate in a way that leads to authentic communion.

To love your wife authentically demands determination to love at all times, especially during times of abstinence. Rather than applying false mercy and taking the easy way out and using contraceptives to avoid pregnancy during a woman's fertile period, a man chooses to master himself and his desires for the purpose of conquering his lusts and to love his wife, regardless of what he does or doesn't receive from her.

NFP demands communication between spouses. This communication develops a deep appreciation of the other, a natural, mutual tenderness and respect that makes future acts of sexual intercourse alive, vibrant, intimate, and God-inspired. This is true mercy. Of course, this type of love is demanding, but also worthy of you. It is worth fighting for. If we cut corners, in the end our marriages lose. "If we can't say no to sex, our yes means nothing" (Christopher West).

> **TAKE THE LEAD** For many men, this next set of reflections will be very challenging and could irritate old wounds. Whether it is the use of contraception, the use of pornography, a spouse's stonewalling, a wife refusing to "have sex" with her husband, it is vital that the both of you expose your wounds to the Wounded Healer, Christ, who can heal your wounds, and make them shine with glory. Approach your wife with the idea of praying together for your marriage. It may feel awkward at first—very awkward. However, by worshipping God together, you will open your hearts to one another and to the healing power of God.

* See Examen *Embrace Your Wife* on page 446

PILLAR 2: EMBRACE YOUR ESSENCE [EMBRACING WOMAN]

THE ENEMY OF INTIMACY

103. WILL YOU SET THE WORLD ABLAZE?

You and I are to become guardians of the sacred mystery of woman, and the one-flesh union. To be a protector demands three things: self-knowledge, self-mastery, and self-giving. Self-knowledge leads to self-mastery, and self-mastery leads to self-giving. For example, by becoming aware of and admitting our weaknesses we are growing in self-knowledge. This self-awareness grants us the opportunity to acknowledge the areas in which we need to change and grow. When we identify the areas in our lives that need to be changed and strive to overcome our vices and embrace the virtue needed, we are gradually practicing self-mastery. Finally, when we begin to master ourselves, overcoming our selfish tendencies for the purpose of selflessly giving to another that they may experience the love of God, we are practicing self-giving.

To paraphrase St. Augustine, to give yourself away you must possess yourself; for you cannot give what you do not possess. Self-knowledge, particularly in the sphere of our sexual desires, can lead to self-mastery, which will enable you to give yourself to your wife in a way that is disinterested—that is, free of the idea of using the other. Self-knowledge, self-mastery, and self-giving will afford incredible intimacy with your wife.

Self-knowledge is the trailhead to self-giving. Why? By knowing and admitting his weakness, a man learns to depend upon God and His grace to help master his disorders; and by mastering his disordered passions, a man can truly be a gift without resorting to selfishness.

"Man can only discover himself by becoming a sincere gift" (see GS 24). When you truly give yourself to others—particularly your wife—and your wife affirms your gift of self, you will have a deeper understanding of who you are and the gifts you have in your possession. When we come in contact with this deeper understanding of ourselves, we grow further in self-mastery and self-giving.

Recall that the Virgin Mary became pregnant after she and St. Joseph were betrothed to each other. St. Joseph understood his identity as a son of the Father as testified by his willingness to submit the perplexing situation of Mary's pregnancy to God before he took any action. There is little doubt that Joseph was keenly aware of his weaknesses. His self-knowledge consequently afforded him self-mastery. Joseph mastered any temptation to react to the situation rashly or passionately. Rather, he submitted the confounding dilemma to God. St. Joseph expressed his self-giving love to Mary by refusing to expose her unexpected pregnancy to the religious authorities and villagers of Nazareth. Joseph's self-knowledge led to his self-mastery, which consequently afforded him the ability to express self-giving love.

It is in the silence, before God, that this cycle of self-knowledge leading to self-mastery leading to self-giving begins again, as the angel of God says: "Joseph son of David do not fear to take Mary thy wife into your home . . ." Joseph receives from the angel a confirmation of his identity: "You are a king, a son of David. You have a power within you that you may not be aware of." God, through the angel, inspires Joseph to understand his kingly power, master himself, and return to Mary, and thus, make of himself a perpetual self-donation to Mary.

You, like Joseph, will discover, and rediscover, your identity through your continual self-donation to your wife, and by discovering who you *really* are you will set the world ablaze.

> **TAKE THE LEAD** For many men, this next set of reflections will be very challenging and could irritate old wounds. Whether it is the use of contraception, the use of pornography, a spouse's stonewalling, a wife refusing to "have sex" with her husband, it is vital that the both of you expose your wounds to the Wounded Healer, Christ, who can heal your wounds, and make them shine with glory. Approach your wife with the idea of praying together for your marriage. It may feel awkward at first—very awkward. However, by worshipping God together, you will open your hearts to one another and to the healing power of God.

* See Examen *Embrace Your Wife* on page 446

PILLAR 2: EMBRACE YOUR ESSENCE [EMBRACING WOMAN]

THE ENEMY OF INTIMACY

104. TREATING YOUR WIFE LIKE A SISTER

If given the choice, would you desire your wife to be more like your sister, or more like a lover? The truth is that the two choices are not mutually exclusive, but rather depend upon one another. If you desire your wife to be your lover, you will first need to see her as your sister. Unfortunately, this doesn't sound very erotic or romantic, but, if lived, this will afford you and me entrance into the heart of the erotic and romantic.

In the erotic love poetry contained in the divinely inspired Scriptures, the Song of Songs, the Lover says to his beloved, "You have ravished my heart, my sister, my bride, you have ravished my heart with one glance of your eyes . . . . How sweet is your love, my sister, my bride! (Song 4:9–10).

By referring to his beloved as sister before calling her bride, the lover demonstrated that he is her guardian first, and her lover second. This is challenging for us men, in that we often desire to play the role of lover first, and rarely consider being our wife's brother—her protector. To envision your wife as sister demands intentional self-mastery. When you begin to master yourself, your passions, your temptation to lust, it is then that you will be capable of being your wife's lover.

Pope St. John Paul II says, "The groom's words, through the name 'sister,' tend to reproduce . . . the history of femininity of the person loved. They see her still in the image of girlhood and they embrace her entire 'I,' soul and body, with a *disinterested tenderness*" (TOB 371, emphasis added). This disinterested tenderness expressed by a husband enables his wife to thrive in a dynamic of trust.

Trust is the foundation and basis of any relationship. If no trust exists between spouses, consequently no real relationship exists. Spouses can claim that they love one another, but if they do not trust one another, love has no foundation. If a wife struggles to trust her husband, his sexual desires, and that his motivations are pure, she will struggle to love him genuinely.

Again, the lover in the Song describes his beloved as "A garden locked is my sister, my bride, a garden enclosed, a fountain sealed" (Song 4:12). In other words, the lover cannot force his way into his beloved's garden. He may only enter if she "unlocks the gate." This indicates that a man must refrain, at all cost, from pressuring his wife to have intercourse. A husband is to "entrust himself to her freedom; she may refuse. This puts the man at risk" (Christopher West).

Entrusting yourself to your wife's freedom, mastering your sexual desires, and building trust in your relationship with her may be one of the most challenging, demanding, and yet rewarding things you will ever do. However, if you rise to the challenge and risk being your wife's brother first, you will eventually win her trust and love that lasts.

> **TAKE THE LEAD** For many men, this next set of reflections will be very challenging and could irritate old wounds. Whether it is the use of contraception, the use of pornography, a spouse's stonewalling, a wife refusing to "have sex" with her husband, it is vital that the both of you expose your wounds to the Wounded Healer, Christ, who can heal your wounds, and make them shine with glory. Approach your wife with the idea of praying together for your marriage. It may feel awkward at first—very awkward. However, by worshipping God together, you will open your hearts to one another and to the healing power of God.

* See Examen *Embrace Your Wife* on page 446

PILLAR 2: EMBRACE YOUR ESSENCE [EMBRACING WOMAN]

THE ENEMY OF INTIMACY

105. MASTER OF HER OWN MYSTERY: DO YOU HAVE ANY SAY?

What is a husband supposed to do when his wife—the garden enclosed and fountain sealed—chooses to keep the gate to her garden locked? Is he supposed to repress his sexual desires? Is he called simply to "stuff" or repress his authentic desire for physical intimacy? Couples who choose to love radically—rather than conforming to the world by using contraception—by using Natural Family Planning, encounter tremendous challenges in their efforts to trust that their spouse is being generous.

Often, it is the wife, who having the experience of being pregnant, giving birth, enduring bodily changes and fluctuating health and hormones, nursing the baby through the night, and possibly remaining home to ensure that home life is balanced, is the one who primarily determines whether the couple will or won't engage in sexual intercourse. This of course is understandable in that the wife bears the burden of bearing life to the world.

Yet, in bearing this burden, a wife can develop an attitude that her husband has little or no influence or right to discuss whether the couple ought to engage in sexual intercourse. If this attitude persists, the wife will begin to be conditioned by her fear of becoming pregnant and will eventually lack generosity in giving herself freely to her husband. If this attitude persists, she could fall into the trap of viewing her husband as a weapon that may cause her "harm" rather than a lover who can grant her harmony. If or when this occurs, tension will build, and the husband and wife will most likely experience resentment toward the other and neglect addressing each other's needs.

On the other hand, a husband who is conditioned by lust and his disordered desire for self-gratification will refuse to take into account his wife's physical and emotional need for rest and peace. His lack of compassion, or neglect in sharing the responsibilities of family life, and his inability to master himself, all participate in reducing his wife to an object for his pleasure, or a producer of children.

In these cases, it would seem that the use of contraception would alleviate some—if not all—of the sexual tension between couples, and NFP would only exacerbate the tension.

However, the divorce rates among married couples who use NFP as compared with those who use contraception is significantly lower. The reason for this is that NFP fosters communication and provides a context in which the couple—nearly out of necessity—discusses their sexual challenges together.

When this occurs, the husband becomes aware of his wife's needs, her sensitivity to her situation, and he is offered the opportunity to be generous by respecting his wife's "garden enclosed," and also by being determined not to crash down her door. On the other hand, the wife is offered the opportunity to be generous by determining times and ways that she can "unlock her garden" and freely give herself to her husband.

Gradually, couples, by expressing their needs, their fears, and their desire to be loved, and perceiving their spouse's attempts to be generous, will begin to develop a foundation of trust upon which their marriage will be built. When this dynamic becomes a reality, the generosity and ability to freely give themselves to one another only increases and bonds the couple in self-giving love.

> **TAKE THE LEAD** For many men, this next set of reflections will be very challenging and could irritate old wounds. Whether it is the use of contraception, the use of pornography, a spouse's stonewalling, a wife refusing to "have sex" with her husband, it is vital that the both of you expose your wounds to the Wounded Healer, Christ, who can heal your wounds, and make them shine with glory. Approach your wife with the idea of praying together for your marriage. It may feel awkward at first—very awkward. However, by worshipping God together, you will open your hearts to one another and to the healing power of God.

* See Examen *Embrace Your Wife* on page 446

THE ENEMY OF INTIMACY

106. WHAT IF YOU ARE STUCK?

What if you are stuck in a marriage in which your wife is not responding in love to your authentic needs? What if your marriage has grown cold, insensitive, and lifeless? The truth is that there is no magic formula that will instantly bring life, vitality, and eros into your marriage.

Yet, St. John of the Cross offers a piece of wisdom that could aid those of us who are in this situation: "Where there is no love, put love, and there will be love."

Your acts of love are to be like the soft showers that eventually saturate the earth that it may flower and bear fruit. The more that you "put love" into that place where there "is no love" by drenching your wife's furrows (those spiritual ditches that lack the soil of love and life), there will one day "be love."

When a person waters a garden by flooding it with water the seedlings drown and die. So also, if you depend on and wait for special days, such as birthdays, anniversaries, or Valentine's Day to flood your wife with love, your affection will simply run off her hardened soil.

The key is to soften her calloused soul little by little, drop by drop, day in and day out, with simple acts of love; and hopefully, by means of your humility, patient endurance, and the grace of God, the two of you will no longer be stuck in a dying garden, but rather, be able to rejoice in a flourishing marriage.

> **TAKE THE LEAD** For many men, this next set of reflections will be very challenging and could irritate old wounds. Whether it is the use of contraception, the use of pornography, a spouse's stonewalling, a wife refusing to "have sex" with her husband, it is vital that the both of you expose your wounds to the Wounded Healer, Christ, who can heal your wounds, and make them shine with glory. Approach your wife with the idea of praying together for your marriage. It may feel awkward at first–very awkward. However, by worshipping God together, you will open your hearts to one another and to the healing power of God.

* See Examen *Embrace Your Wife* on page 446

EMBRACING THE WOMAN

107. DOES A "REAL MAN" NEED A MOTHER?, PART 1

One of the most demeaning and belittling insults a man could receive from another man is being called a "mama's boy." No man relishes being referred to as a mama's boy because the title connotes weakness, softness, and a dependence on the feminine.

At a deep subconscious level every boy intuits that one of the benchmarks for being a man is leaving the garden, the comfort and safety of a mother's care. Traditionally, boys, particularly in primitive tribal cultures, upon reaching the peak of adolescence, participate in an "initiation rite," in which the older men of the community remove their sons from their mother's care and engage these young men in a series of painful tests that give them the opportunity to prove their character—to prove that they are ready to enter the stage of manhood. The son leaves his home a boy, but returns a man. It appears that once a boy reaches manhood he no longer has need of a mother, lest his manhood be compromised.

But is this true for the Christian man?

John the Evangelist was the only apostle who was "man enough" to remain by our Lord's side during his Crucifixion. John's faith and courage testify to the heroic character of his manhood. Yet, our Lord, while on the cross, seeing John standing next to his mother, commanded the apostle to "Behold your mother." On the surface, it appears that Jesus wanted to be certain that John would care for his mother. But, when we consider that John's Gospel soars beyond the others in theological insight, depth, and profundity, we can conclude that Jesus' gift of His mother to John was a tremendous benefit to the apostle.

In addition to embracing all women by striving to defeat lust in the heart, and embracing your wife by bearing her burdens as your own, the third way to embrace woman is by doing what John did—taking Mary into your home; that is, entrusting yourself and your fatherhood to the woman, Mary.

Consider that the first step, humanly speaking, in Christ's initiative to save fallen mankind from the peril of sin was to entrust Himself to the Blessed Virgin (see Lk 1:28). Consider also that St.

PILLAR 2: EMBRACE YOUR ESSENCE [EMBRACING WOMAN]

Joseph's first step in inaugurating his call to fatherly greatness was entrusting his life and vocation to Mary. When we consider that even prior to these, the heavenly Father was the first to entrust His most precious gift, His Son, to this woman, and that countless hosts of saints, martyrs, preachers, missionaries, popes, bishops, priests, and religious sisters have entrusted their lives to her, the idea of a real man needing this Woman is indispensable.

Mary is the nexus of salvation, the mother to whom both divine and human persons entrust themselves. To become great fathers, we need the greatest Mother; to become great men, we need the greatest Woman.

Entrust yourself to Mary, and like Joseph you will quickly become a man of glory.

TAKE THE LEAD Many men struggle with the idea of Marian devotion. Why would a man need the help of a woman? A man might think, "I have one mother, isn't that enough?" Yet, devotion to the Blessed Virgin Mary is one of the most powerful ways to achieve true glory. Even if you have an aversion to Mary, set yourself to the task of inviting her into your life daily. If you do, she will certainly bring the life and love of the Trinity to you. A simple way to offer your heart to her is to pray, "Mother I am yours, now and forever; through you and with you, I want to belong always and only to Jesus."*

* See Examen *Embrace Mary* on page 447

EMBRACING THE WOMAN

108. DOES A "REAL MAN" NEED A MOTHER?, PART 2

Though we have said that a real man needs a mother—particularly the Mother of God—nevertheless there is an element of truth to the idea that if a boy is to become a man he must leave the safe confines of the garden—that is, he must leave his mother to become a man. Yet there is a caveat to this reasoning: once the boy becomes a man, he is to return home to his mother as her brother in Christ, as her defender, protector, and even cooperator in the redemption of mankind.

Consider that at the wedding of Cana, the wine ran out, and Mary turned to Jesus and said, "They have no wine." To which Jesus responded, "Woman, what concern is this between you and me, my hour has not yet come" (Jn 2:4).

Though some have interpreted Jesus' response as a terse rebuke, His words, if meditated upon, are rich with meaning and significance that reveal how a son who has become a man is to live in relationship with his mother.

Notice that Jesus asks Mary, "What is this between you and me?" And He follows this question with the mysterious statement, "My hour has not yet come." Jesus' words indicate that there will be something between Jesus the Son and Mary His Mother when His hour comes. In other words, when the time is right, Mary and Jesus will work together for the purpose of the redemption of mankind.

Jesus' hour arrived. While on the road to Calvary, bearing the burden of the cross, he encountered His Mother. It was in that hour that Mary climbed Calvary with her Son; and ultimately while standing at the foot of His cross, she united herself to His sacrifice. Jesus the Son, drew Mary, His Mother, into his act of redeeming the world.

It was in that hour, in a certain sense, that Jesus returned to Mary as man, brother, a bridegroom to his Mother who had become a sister and bride. It was by their sacrificial union that the two gave birth—spiritually—to sons and daughters of God—the Church.

This also is an aspect of our mission as men: we leave home as boys, only to one day return as men to aid our mothers in giving themselves in sacrifice to God on behalf of this sinful world.

> **TAKE THE LEAD** Many men struggle with the idea of Marian devotion. Why would a man need the help of a woman? A man might think, "I have one mother, isn't that enough?" Yet, devotion to the Blessed Virgin Mary is one of the most powerful ways to achieve true glory. Even if you have an aversion to Mary, set yourself to the task of inviting her into your life daily. If you do, she will certainly bring the life and love of the Trinity to you. A simple way to offer your heart to her is to pray, "Mother I am yours, now and forever; through you and with you, I want to belong always and only to Jesus."*

* See Examen *Embrace Mary* on page 447

EMBRACING THE WOMAN

109. THE DEVIL INSIDE

Independence, the idea of being liberated from needing anyone, is celebrated and often enshrined in our modern world: "I'll find a way myself"; "I'll do it my way"; "I don't need anyone's help"; "I don't need anyone telling me what to do." The figure of the Lone Ranger riding off alone into the sunset, with no obligations, no one "holding him back," and with the promise of freedom from being burdened by human responsibilities can be very appealing. Regardless of the media and Hollywood's attempts to convince us of the glory of individualism, no man is an island—and if he happens to be stranded on that island by himself he becomes vulnerable, and highly susceptible to isolation, fear, and failure.

History's greatest men were consistently surrounded by a cohort who shared in their passion and dreams. They were collaborators who were part of or surrounded by a team who aided them in their achievement, advancement, and initiatives. The most heroic men were humble enough to trust and depend upon others.

Recall that our Lord Himself did not save humanity from its sins apart from human beings, but became dependent on a mother and father to raise him to adulthood, and relied on apostles to transmit his message.

The success of a father's vocation is determined by his humility; for the Lord "[o]pposes the proud but exalts the humble" (see Lk 1:52; James 4:6; Proverbs 3:34). Pride is the human father's most malicious enemy, for it reduces him to becoming an enemy of self-giving love, which is the pinnacle expression of fatherhood. "Pride goes before destruction, and a haughty spirit before a fall" (Prov 16:18). So how do we overcome this insidious devil inside, which we call pride?

To remedy man's tendency toward pride, God granted us a powerful way to humble ourselves, in the way that Jesus, St. Joseph, John the Evangelist, and the great saints did: entrust yourself to the queen whom "[a]ll generations shall call blessed" (see Psalm 45;

Lk 1:48). Mary is this queen, the woman foretold in Genesis who crushes the head of the serpent, and not only the devil, but also the serpent of our pride, ego, and self-delusion. When a man admits his need for this Woman, He is exalted by her Son, who did the same.

If you want to be a great man, you need to give yourself to the greatest woman; if your mission of being a great father and husband is to be successful, you will need to be "with Mary" so that Mary may be "with you"; for the "Lord is with [her]" (see Lk 1:28). In other words, where the Mother is, there also is the Son; where Jesus is, there also is Mary; and if we humble ourselves as Jesus did by entrusting ourselves to Mary, we will also be lifted up with Christ. To be great fathers, we need the greatest Mother.

Therefore, "Humble yourself before the mighty hand of God and in due time He will exalt you" (1 Peter 5:6).

> **TAKE THE LEAD** Many men struggle with the idea of Marian devotion. Why would a man need the help of a woman? A man might think, "I have one mother, isn't that enough?" Yet, devotion to the Blessed Virgin Mary is one of the most powerful ways to achieve true glory. Even if you have an aversion to Mary, set yourself to the task of inviting her into your life daily. If you do, she will certainly bring the life and love of the Trinity to you. A simple way to offer your heart to her is to pray, "Mother I am yours, now and forever; through you and with you, I want to belong always and only to Jesus."*

* See Examen *Embrace Mary* on page 447

PILLAR 3

ASSUMING YOUR AUTHORITY

[Embracing Charitable Authority]

GOD ASKS EACH OF US "WHERE ARE YOU?" THIS IS THE PERENNIAL QUESTION THAT HAUNTS THE DEEP SUBCONSCIOUS RECESSES OF MAN'S HEART. THE ANSWER TO THIS QUESTION DETERMINES EACH MAN'S LOCATION IN GOD'S PLAN OF SALVATION, HIS VOCATIONAL MISSION—THE VERY FOUNDATION OF THE SPIRITUALITY OF FATHERHOOD.

LEAD
THE FOUR MARKS OF FATHERLY GREATNESS

PILLAR 3: ASSUME YOUR AUTHORITY [EMBRACE CHARITABLE AUTHORITY]

AUTHORITY PROPERLY UNDERSTOOD

110. STRIKE THE SHEPHERD

Threaded throughout the historical accounts of wars, conquests, dominions, and kingdoms is the reoccurring theme of armies fleeing, strongholds toppling, troops surrendering, cities being plundered, when their king, their leader, has been slain. Why is it so infrequent that after a king is killed in battle, his armies rally, persevere, and press on toward victory?

A modern example of this dynamic is Adolf Hitler and his Nazi regime. When the Nazis realized that their commander was dead they ceased attacking and surrendered to their enemies. Why is this? Jesus' words reveal an important truth regarding leadership: "Strike the shepherd and the sheep of the flock will be scattered" (Mt 26:31). When the shepherd, leader, commander is struck down, missing in action, rendered powerless, or captured, his flock loses confidence, direction, hope, vision and courage—and because of this, they flee or surrender.

So it is with you and every father: when the enemy, the evil one, strikes you down with sin, renders you powerless by enslaving you in addictions, or distracts you from your vocation, thus making your absence and lack of leadership felt, your family loses confidence in their personal mission and call. They falter in the hope of achieving and living for something greater than this passing world; they lose the courage to fight for what is true, good, and beautiful. When a father is struck down, his family eventually flees from God and His Church—their very life source.

No one will argue that when a king is struck down in battle, his subjects are overthrown. Yet when we proclaim the necessity, vitality, authority, and power of the father-leader, the radically feminized, politically correct, culture objects, and accuses the messengers of this truth as being discriminatory male chauvinists, thus attempting to strike down the father-king.

In a sense, the human father is condemned if he leads, and condemned if he doesn't.

If he leads, he is ridiculed and perceived by the world as a domineering tyrant who clings to an antiquated, patriarchal authority that enslaves and overpowers women and children. On the other hand, if a father neglects to lead his family, reducing his life's purpose to chasing vain pursuits, self-absorbed hobbies, and the hunt for worldly pleasures, he is disdained as a slothful, weak, selfish, man who is utterly useless.

Considering these two options, which would you want to be condemned for? For being the leader who assumes his charitable authority, or the coward who neglects or flees from his post for the purpose of remaining comfortable and politically correct?

St. Joseph is heralded as "head of the Holy Family" (see Litany of St. Joseph). The greatest woman in the world not only followed his lead but flourished because of it. And so it will be with you. If you choose to assume your authority and lead, your family will not be scattered, but rather gathered unto the Lord, under whose care they will flourish.

> **TAKE THE LEAD** At this point, you have realized that your authority is a great gift and has tremendous power. God has willed that you LEAD. You may also be realizing that such authority and leadership involves being persecuted for Christ's sake. There is a real tendency among men to be ashamed of their masculine essence, their authority and leadership. Over the next several reflections, try to identify those areas where you have compromised your God-given authority to LEAD for the sake of not "rocking the boat." Select one of those areas and make a commitment to relentlessly stand your ground.*

* See Examen *Lead by Loving, Love by Leading* on page 448

PILLAR 3: ASSUME YOUR AUTHORITY [EMBRACE CHARITABLE AUTHORITY]

AUTHORITY PROPERLY UNDERSTOOD

111. ARE YOU PREPARED TO BE MISUNDERSTOOD?

Have you ever had the experience of being wrongfully misunderstood? Perhaps you said or did something that was misinterpreted as meaning the opposite of your real intention. Misunderstandings lead to disputes, anger, and resentment, and can be the eventual cause of broken relationships. There are few things as painful as when your actions, words, or motives are misunderstood, and receive the blame and condemnation of others. Yet these experiences, as painful as they are, if embraced can unite us to Jesus—the most misunderstood man—and His mission.

To strive to save mankind from its errors is to be misunderstood. This is the lot of the prophet. This is the lot of a father. The human father and his leadership is often misinterpreted by society—and by his family—as a restraint rather than a remedy.

Of the four components of a father's spirituality (LEAD) assuming your authority may be the most important and perhaps the most misunderstood and contested. Charitable authority is often misunderstood because authority itself, as it is defined in the modern age, is understood as the power to control. If this is the case, how can this idea of authority be reconciled with the idea that human beings are not to be used and hyper-controlled.

Though the modern definition of authority is "power to control," the word "authority" actually originated in the twelfth century and is derived from the Latin word *auctoritas*, which is derived from the Latin word *auctor,* which means "author." The word "author" is defined as "to originate, create, write, invent, influence and command."

The word "charity" is derived from the Latin word *caritas*, which can be interpreted as "to value, esteem, love, or agape." When the truest definition and meanings of these two words are combined, charitable authority can be defined as the father's divinely ordained role to be the author and influencer of the story of God's love—the story of God's salvation—in his family's life. It is your responsibility as a father to coauthor, with the divine Author and Father—and with your wife—the story of the Trinity's self-giving love to your family.

Today's culture proposes that the story of God's love is preposterous, a fairy tale, and that any reality behind it is to be despised as ineffectual. Modernism and its proponents have undermined patriarchal authority, misrepresenting it as tyrannical, restrictive, domineering, and controlling. Ironically, by vilifying patriarchal authority, it is the modernists who act in a tyrannical, domineering, controlling way. But as Janet Smith says, "When fatherhood is absent from society, society is left with chaos."

Charitable authority is the very foundation of cultures, political societies, the Church, and the family. Without men who assume their divinely ordained authority and fulfill its demands, then marriages, families, societies, cultures, and nations implode into black holes of selfishness, licentiousness, and vainglory. This is precisely why fatherhood is misunderstood and attacked. Whatever is essential to God's plan in saving mankind is always vehemently rejected and maligned by the evil one.

Because St. Joseph answered God's call to assume and live his charitable authority, the Holy Family flourished, Christianity was eventually born, and societies, cultures, and families are even today given new hope. If you desire to participate in Christ's great mission of redeeming mankind by means of exercising your fatherly authority, be prepared to be misunderstood by the world—and rewarded by God.

> **TAKE THE LEAD** At this point, you have realized that your authority is a great gift and has tremendous power. God has willed that you LEAD. You may also be realizing that such authority and leadership involves being persecuted for Christ's sake. There is a real tendency among men to be ashamed of their masculine essence, their authority and leadership. Over the next several reflections, try to identify those areas where you have compromised your God-given authority to LEAD for the sake of not "rocking the boat." Select one of those areas and make a commitment to relentlessly stand your ground.*

*   See Examen *Lead by Loving, Love by Leading* on page 448

AUTHORITY PROPERLY UNDERSTOOD

112. THE TRUE PURPOSE OF AUTHORITY

What is the purpose of authority? Before attempting to answer this question, it may be beneficial to discuss one of the ways authority is misunderstood by contemporary society.

Society values "diversity," which, if translated into truth, is nothing more than modern man's exaltation of the individual and his or her distinct character. Diversity empowers the individual with a personal sense of authority that enables the person to be and do as they please. This type of personal authority stands in opposition to other authorities that may infringe upon their personal right to express themselves; or those authorities that proclaim or protect characteristics different than their own.

The person who claims diversity, yet opposes those who think differently, attempts to level all forms of authority by claiming that such authorities are bigots against "equality." In other words, the person who proclaims and desires "equality" refuses to submit to any authority outside of itself, including moral and divine authority.

This type of individualistic authority proclaims distinction without unity. If unity is likened to a symphony, then individualistic authority is like a cacophony—a chaotic combination of incongruous, harsh, jarring sounds that lack real harmony.

There exist few things as beautiful as a symphony, in which various musicians playing diverse instruments complement and in a sense complete each other. This combination of instruments, sounds, rhythms, and melodies all contribute to creating a glorious harmony that blesses the ears with uplifting pleasure and delight.

The harmony of a symphony does not neglect the distinct beauty of a violinist. Nor does a violinist eclipse the distinct character of the cellist; nor does the cellist deny the distinct character of the flutist. Each are distinct, while living simultaneously in unity. We can call this type of harmony distinction in unity, and unity in distinction. Each person, with their unique, distinct character, combined with others, form a harmonious union. Their distinction in unity and unity in distinction is ultimately a participation in the Trinity: three distinct, divine Persons, Who are a single, perfect unity.

At the head of a symphony is the conductor, a leader who harmonizes the instruments and persons of distinction into a musical score the elevates the soul. Without the conductor, there is no symphony.

The role of the human father is like a conductor of a symphony. A father identifies and affirms each family member's distinct gifts and "conducts" them in a way that helps the family complement and complete each other.

This is the purpose of fatherly authority: to lead his family to become like the Trinity—distinction in unity, unity in distinction. By doing this, the world's soul—much like one who hears a great symphony—is elevated beyond its individualistic notion of personal authority and equality to an authority that glorifies all in One, and One in all.

> **TAKE THE LEAD** At this point, you have realized that your authority is a great gift and has tremendous power. God has willed that you LEAD. You may also be realizing that such authority and leadership involves being persecuted for Christ's sake. There is a real tendency among men to be ashamed of their masculine essence, their authority and leadership. Over the next several reflections, try to identify those areas where you have compromised your God-given authority to LEAD for the sake of not "rocking the boat." Select one of those areas and make a commitment to relentlessly stand your ground.*

* See Examen *Lead by Loving, Love by Leading* on page 448

AUTHORITY PROPERLY UNDERSTOOD

113. ARE YOU REALLY WORKING AT THE OFFICE?

If there is none to lead, none will follow. A father must lead his family from evil, or evil will lead his family. Consider that the majority of millennials label themselves as "nones," that is, they are either atheist, agnostic, or have no religious affiliation. Why is this? One of the most significant factors that contribute to the escalating number of "nones" is that their fathers, and their fathers' fathers, failed to lead their families to God. When the father is absent, there is an absence of faith in his children.

St. Augustine, during one of his famous homilies, addressed the fathers in the congregation regarding the essential role of fathers: "My fellow bishops, fulfill my office in your homes." Augustine's words contain two insights of major importance: first, every father is called by God to be bishop of his home; second, his fatherhood is an office.

An office is a special duty, charge, or position of authority. The word "office" is derived from the Latin words *opis*, which means "power, ability," or *oper*, opus, which means "work, effort"; and *facere*, which means "to make, do, or bring about." In other words, the father has a unique position of authority, and is endowed with the special power to fulfill the charge of leading his family to salvation. This office has a permanent character, even if a father's character shifts. If a father neglects the duties of his office, nevertheless his office remains an objective reality.

In addition to this, Augustine gives fathers the title "bishop." A father is bishop of his domestic church, his family. The word "bishop" means supervisor. The Latin word *super* means "above," and the meaning behind *visor* is to have vision. You and I as fathers are to have a supernatural vision; we are to understand and teach others how to love as God loves.

Fatherhood is not only biological, but primarily and ultimately spiritual. Far from being reduced to a practical, pragmatic "role" that a man or woman or anyone can fulfill, fatherhood is a divine calling, an ordination. He is called to be the bishop who exercises authority as leader and priest of his home. This truth runs in opposition to the politically correct culture in which we are immersed.

St. Joseph was ordained to use the unique position of his office of father, and the power, ability, and authority associated with that office, to lead the Holy Family to fulfill God's will. So powerful was his silent, hidden authority that his twelve-year-old son, Jesus, who was intent on being about his Father's business in the temple of Jerusalem, submitted to Joseph's fatherly authority and returned to Nazareth with his parents. Jesus' obedience to Joseph's office as father demonstrates that God not only approves of this authority, but also testifies to its humble power.

> **TAKE THE LEAD** At this point, you have realized that your authority is a great gift and has tremendous power. God has willed that you LEAD. You may also be realizing that such authority and leadership involves being persecuted for Christ's sake. There is a real tendency among men to be ashamed of their masculine essence, their authority and leadership. Over the next several reflections, try to identify those areas where you have compromised your God-given authority to LEAD for the sake of not "rocking the boat." Select one of those areas and make a commitment to relentlessly stand your ground.*

* See Examen *Lead by Loving, Love by Leading* on page 448

AUTHORITY PROPERLY UNDERSTOOD

114. WHO DO YOU ANSWER TO?

The saints and holy Doctors of the Church explain that if a person desires to be holy, it is essential that he be obedient to his superiors, regardless of how trivial the matter may appear to be. The parish priest, for example, is obedient to his bishop; the bishop is to be obedient to the pope; the cloistered brother to his abbot; the religious sister to her superior; children to parents; and wives to their husbands (1 Peter 3; Eph 5).

Which raises the question: to whose authority do you, the human father, submit?

Within the context of the family, the father is the person vested with authority as priest and king over his domestic church. As countercultural, unpolitically correct, and antiwoman this may appear to be, within the hierarchy of the family, there is no greater authority than that of a father.

There exists a divinely inspired wisdom behind this idea: "Wives are to be subject to [their] husbands, as is fitting to the Lord. Husbands [should] love [their] wives and not be harsh with them. Children [are to] obey [their] parents in everything, for this pleases the Lord" (see Col 3:18–21). Wives submit to your husbands in all matters (see Eph 5:22).

To receive authority presupposes that another has granted that authority. If one expects obedience to one's authority, one must be obedient to the source of that authority. Your hierarchal position is unique within the order of creation. As to faith and morals, you, as a father, are to live under the authority of the Church, but as to the daily governance of your household, the Church and Sacred Scripture bear witness that the human father receives his authority from God alone (see Gen 2; Eph 5; I Peter).

There is an important qualification to all the aforementioned truths: God the Father, who invests the human father with his authority, commands through the apostle that he and his wife are "to subject themselves to one another out of reverence for Christ."

By subjecting yourself to God, God directs you to subject yourself to your wife; and by subjecting yourself in service to her authentic God-given needs, you are led more fully to God.

Your unique authority culminates in its fullest expression and most vibrant power when you use it to submit to your wife's and children's authentic needs—out of reverence for Christ—without denying your office of leader.

St. Joseph used his God-given authority to serve Mary. This did not deny his unique authority over his family, but rather proved it. Like Joseph, when you use your power to serve rather than to be served, you demonstrate a strength and authority that is magnetic and admirable.

> **TAKE THE LEAD** At this point, you have realized that your authority is a great gift and has tremendous power. God has willed that you LEAD. You may also be realizing that such authority and leadership involves being persecuted for Christ's sake. There is a real tendency among men to be ashamed of their masculine essence, their authority and leadership. Over the next several reflections, try to identify those areas where you have compromised your God-given authority to LEAD for the sake of not "rocking the boat." Select one of those areas and make a commitment to relentlessly stand your ground.*

* See Examen *Lead by Loving, Love by Leading* on page 448

PILLAR 3: ASSUME YOUR AUTHORITY [EMBRACE CHARITABLE AUTHORITY]

AUTHORITY PROPERLY UNDERSTOOD

115. THE RISK OF RESPONSIBILITY

The word "responsibility" can be interpreted in many ways by many people; and can often evoke a variety of emotional reactions. Some understand responsibility as being tasked to deal with something. Others interpret responsibility as having control over someone; or as the authority to act independently and make decisions without authorization; or as being held accountable or blamed for something.

Ironically, synonyms often used for responsibility are authority, control, power, leadership; but also blame, fault, guilt, culpability, and liability. Responsibility is a double-edged sword. On one hand it contains the power of authority, and on the other hand it receives the blame when that power fails.

Adam is the masculine icon of the double-edged sword of responsibility. Adam was commanded by God to be responsible for cherishing and protecting the garden, woman, and the future of the human race. As discussed previously, Adam was given this responsibility prior to Eve's existence. In a certain sense, man derives his authority from God, and woman derives her authority in union with, and from, the man. Man is responsible to God for his wife, while woman is responsible to God through her husband.

Responsibility, as some have described it, is having the ability to respond to God. This responsibility of the man is further emphasized when after the first couple's fall from grace, God doesn't initially address the woman, but rather addresses the man first. Why? Because the man, more than the woman, has the primary responsibility to cherish the woman and her child.

In Adam we encounter the paradox and risk of responsibility: authority is power, and the person of authority is blamed when its strength fails.

St. Joseph risked being responsible and was victorious in fulfilling his vocation. Regardless of our potential to fail, it is imperative that we embrace our responsibility by responding to God's call to embrace our authority.

TAKE THE LEAD   At this point, you have realized that your authority is a great gift and has tremendous power. God has willed that you LEAD. You may also be realizing that such authority and leadership involves being persecuted for Christ's sake. There is a real tendency among men to be ashamed of their masculine essence, their authority and leadership. Over the next several reflections, try to identify those areas where you have compromised your God-given authority to LEAD for the sake of not "rocking the boat." Select one of those areas and make a commitment to relentlessly stand your ground.*

* See Examen *Lead by Loving, Love by Leading* on page 448

HOW TO EXERCISE YOUR AUTHORITY

116. UNLOCKING GOD'S FAVOR

How can a father use his authority in a way that "unlocks" God's favor in his life? The truth is that God has already granted His grace and favor to men, and no man can unlock God's grace. So how does a man step out in faith, into this grace and favor, and begin walking in the works that God has prepared for him (see Eph 2:10). We discover a way to tap into God's already given favor in the scriptural account of the centurion who interceded on behalf of his servant, begging Jesus for his healing.

The Roman centurion was a man of great authority. According to historians, a "century" was approximately equal in size to a company in the United States Army; a centurion was roughly equivalent to an Army captain. Centurions "were chosen for their size and strength, their abilities at swordplay and at throwing missiles, and the quality of their discipline, which was partly shown by how well their soldiers kept their own armor polished."

The centurion in Matthew's account begs Jesus to heal his servant, who had become paralyzed and was in miserable agony. As Jesus expressed His intention to go to the centurion's home, the centurion responds by saying that he is not worthy for Jesus to enter under his roof, and then proceeds to say something that is highly significant regarding authority and leadership: "For I also am a man subject to authority, having under me soldiers . . ."

Notice that the centurion does not say, "I am a man of authority," but rather, "I also am a man subject to authority." "The centurion indeed is a man of authority, but more importantly, he understands that he is subject to another's authority. In addition to this, he recognizes that Jesus also has the authority to heal and transmit grace, and yet is also subject to a greater authority—the authority of His Heavenly Father" (Dr. Louis Joseph Hébert).

Considering this, we realize that a person who is a leader understands and acknowledges that his authority is always subject to someone greater. The human father subjects his authority to the person of Jesus, and in Jesus to His Father. Authority only has power when it subjects itself to the one who has granted the authority.

Why is this important? Trust in God is the key attribute of one who taps into the favor of God. If we continually trust in Jesus, subjecting our authority to Him, like the centurion, we can step out of spiritual darkness and blindness and begin walking in the works and graces God has prepared for us from all of eternity.

St. Joseph never testified on his own behalf as being a "just man"—a man of authority; but rather, he fell asleep praying over the dilemma of his wife being pregnant without his cooperation. In this moment of silence, Joseph subjected his authority to God, and by doing so, he "unlocked" God's favor, which animated his fatherly vocation. So also, if you submit your own authority, with humility and faith, to Jesus, God's favor, blessing, and guidance will be available for the taking.

> **TAKE THE LEAD** Often, we fathers wonder why our leadership is ineffective. The answer is often very simple: we fail to lead because we fail to follow. Jesus tells us that if we love Him we will keep His commands. To be a leader is to be a disciple, "a learner." To lead others to Christ, you must first follow Christ. Pray and ask God to reveal to you the areas in which you are being disobedient to Him. Then, after the Lord reveals these things to you, resolve to follow Christ with the motivation of becoming an authentic leader.*

* See Examen *Lead by Loving, Love by Leading* on page 448

HOW TO EXERCISE YOUR AUTHORITY

117. LEADING: AN EXPRESSION OF LOVING

Would you consider a center on a football team's offensive line—who consistently allows his quarterback to be sacked by the defense—as strong, responsible, and dependable? Would a nation's president, who allowed foreign countries to invade its territory and occupy his country, be regarded as a defender and protector of his country? Should a mother who neglects to care for her children be considered a loving parent? Should a professor who uses class time to play games and socialize with his students rather than to instruct them be considered a good teacher?

In each of the aforementioned cases, the people highlighted would either be fired from their job, impeached, or imprisoned. Yet, when a father exercises his charitable authority and uses his office to protect, provide for, and teach his children, he is often characterized as domineering, chauvinistic, patriarchal, and as suffocating and suppressing women's rights. Nevertheless, the human father as bishop and shepherd of his family exercises charitable authority—that is, he leads by loving and loves by leading. Much like a teacher who neglects to teach, a president who refrains from defending his nation, or a mother who neglects to care for her children, a father who does not lead is not loving.

Your position (office) of fatherly authority does not imply a denial of the equal dignity of both spouses, but rather testifies to that dignity. How can this be? Male headship upholds female queenship. Being a servant leader indicates that the leader is upholding his subject's dignity by serving that subject; thus raising that subject to, or above, his own level.

This is the essence of true leadership: to help those who are following you become leaders—even to lead more effectively than you. A true leader uses his authority to serve his subjects. He participates in and with the authority of Christ, who said, "I did not come to be served but to serve and give my life as a ransom" (Mt 20:28). A true leader uses his charitable authority by "counting all others as better than himself" (see Phil 2:3). (including his wife and children), while also fulfilling Jesus' command, "Let the greatest among you become the servant" (see Mt 20:26, 23:11; Lk 22:26; Mk 10:43).

St. Joseph, the member of the Holy Family who was invested with the heavenly Father's authority, became the least, the servant of Mary and Jesus, to ensure that they would achieve their destiny. It can be said of Joseph that he consistently counted Jesus and Mary—his subjects—as better than himself, and therefore God has exalted him as the exemplar of all fathers.

When you lead by loving and love by leading, exercising your charitable authority, you who are greatest (the one invested with authority over your subjects) will become the least, and by humbling yourself as the least—as the servant—God will elevate you to greatness.

> **TAKE THE LEAD** Often, we fathers wonder why our leadership is ineffective. The answer is often very simple: we fail to lead because we fail to follow. Jesus tells us that if we love Him we will keep His commands. To be a leader is to be a disciple, "a learner." To lead others to Christ, you must first follow Christ. Pray and ask God to reveal to you the areas in which you are being disobedient to Him. Then, after the Lord reveals these things to you, resolve to follow Christ with the motivation of becoming an authentic leader.*

* See Examen *Lead by Loving, Love by Leading* on page 448

PILLAR 3: ASSUME YOUR AUTHORITY [EMBRACE CHARITABLE AUTHORITY]

HOW TO EXERCISE YOUR AUTHORITY

118. CAN YOU SURRENDER YOUR GLORY?

Perhaps you've heard the accounts of saints who deprived themselves of their status, their riches, their health—in a word, their glory—for the purpose of living in solidarity with those less fortunate than themselves. Blessed Pier Giorgio Frassati, born into one of the most affluent, prominent and influential families in Italy, deprived himself of his wealth, status, and eventually his health for the purpose of secretly helping thousands of people who lived in destitution.

Fr. Peter Damian deprived himself of his health and secure position as a diocesan priest to live among the lepers who were quarantined on the island of Molokai. St. Francis of Assisi deprived himself of his father's house, riches, and prosperous business and instead chose to love "lady poverty" and answer God's call to rebuild Christ's church.

In each of these cases—and can we daresay in every case in which a man deprives himself of his glory—God elevates him to greatness. God will never be outdone in generosity.

Though "[t]he married man is concerned about how to please his wife, and therefore is divided" (1 Cor 7:33), he can also follow the heroic examples of the aforementioned saints by emptying himself of the glory that is associated with his office for the purpose of "lowering himself" to the level of his subjects. However, a father must not remain at his subject's level, but rather raise his subjects to his level—to personal greatness.

Charitable authority embodies the self-emptying, self-giving character of Jesus Christ, Who by emptying Himself and depriving Himself of His former glory with the Father, became the Son of a human father.

Indeed, this was the example of "Christ, who, although He existed in the form of God, did not deem equality with God a thing to be grasped, but emptied Himself, taking the form of a bond-servant, and being made in the likeness of men. Being found in the appearance as man, He humbled Himself by becoming obedient to the point of death, even death on a cross. For this reason also, God highly exalted Him, and bestowed on Him the name which is above every name, so that at the name of Jesus every knee will bow, of those who are in heaven and on earth and under the earth, and that every tongue will confess that Jesus Christ is Lord, to the glory of God the Father" (Phil 5:2–11).

Though being God (see John 1; Titus 2:13; Habakkuk 3:15; Isaiah 9:6), and before time sharing God's glory, Christ did not cling to this glory, but emptied Himself by becoming the lowest of all men—even becoming sin (see 2 Cor 5:21). Because Jesus did this, God the Father exalted Him so that at His name all knees shall bend in worship.

Christ's condescension that leads to exaltation is the key to your greatness. If you, like Christ, empty yourself and become a servant to your family, they and God will one day exalt you. If you surrender the glory you think you possess and embrace the lowliness you instinctively avoid, you will one day possess a glory far beyond what you can hope for or imagine (see Eph 3:20)

> **TAKE THE LEAD** Often, we fathers wonder why our leadership is ineffective. The answer is often very simple: we fail to lead because we fail to follow. Jesus tells us that if we love Him we will keep His commands. To be a leader is to be a disciple, "a learner." To lead others to Christ, you must first follow Christ. Pray and ask God to reveal to you the areas in which you are being disobedient to Him. Then, after the Lord reveals these things to you, resolve to follow Christ with the motivation of becoming an authentic leader.*

* See Examen *Lead by Loving, Love by Leading* on page 448

PILLAR 3: ASSUME YOUR AUTHORITY [EMBRACE CHARITABLE AUTHORITY]

HOW TO EXERCISE YOUR AUTHORITY

119. WHY DO FAMILIES FAIL?

What is the secret behind a joy-filled, harmonious, self-giving family? Why do some families, end up divided while others remain united? We discover one of the secrets behind a family's success by peering into the mystery of Jesus Christ's kingship.

Consider that Jesus, during his Passion, is questioned as to whether He is a real king. Jesus testified before Pilate that He indeed is a king, and because of this testimony and reality, Satan drives the cohort of Roman soldiers to assail, destroy, and disprove the kingship of Christ.

They crowned with thorns the Creator Who created man as the crown of his creation (see Ps 8). They placed a reed, as a mock scepter, in His right hand to mock Him Who would rule them with an iron rod (see Ps 2). The evil one was intent on breaking the king of creation to prove that Jesus was not king or master of Himself, or of creation.

However, the devil's mockery, rather than destroying Jesus' kingship, became the very means by which it was proved.

Without complaint, resentment, or retaliation, Jesus "[w]as oppressed and afflicted, yet He did not open His mouth; He was led like a lamb to the slaughter, and as a sheep before its shearer is silent, so He did not open His mouth (Is 53:7).

From Jesus' example we learn the meaning of authentic kingship: to be king is to be master of one's passions—even, and especially, while enduring one's own Passion.

To give power, a king must possess power. To rule others, a king must first rule himself. To be master, a man must master himself; for a king cannot give to his subjects what he does not first possess.

A father who makes his passions subject to himself is worthy of his subjects. A man who masters himself is worthy of being known as master. A father, priest-king, who rules his own power is capable of ruling with power, without power overruling him.

When St. Joseph lost his twelve-year-old son, Jesus, he did not succumb to venting his anger, sorrow, or frustration, but rather exercised mastery over himself and his passions, which afforded him to the title "Master of the Master," for Jesus "[w]ent down with them and was subject to them." Joseph's mastery over self, proved to unite his family when they appeared to be separated.

Joseph's example demonstrates the fundamental requisite and secret to fatherhood: to be master of your household you must strive to be master of your person.

> **TAKE THE LEAD** Often, we fathers wonder why our leadership is ineffective. The answer is often very simple: we fail to lead because we fail to follow. Jesus tells us that if we love Him we will keep His commands. To be a leader is to be a disciple, "a learner." To lead others to Christ, you must first follow Christ. Pray and ask God to reveal to you the areas in which you are being disobedient to Him. Then, after the Lord reveals these things to you, resolve to follow Christ with the motivation of becoming an authentic leader.*

* See Examen *Lead by Loving, Love by Leading* on page 448

PILLAR 3: ASSUME YOUR AUTHORITY [EMBRACE CHARITABLE AUTHORITY]

QUALITIES OF THE MAN OF AUTHORITY

120. DO YOU HAVE TO BE PERFECT?

Often when a man is faced with the tremendously challenging call to lead, many excuses why he should not lead come to his mind. Perhaps the most cunning and persuasive excuse is that a man is not qualified or lacks the experience to exercise his authority. This excuse is cunning in that it masks itself in the character of humility while avoiding the risk of failure, which would afford many opportunities to learn and grow in virtue.

Perhaps you have thought something like, "I am a terrible sinner. How can I lead others to be saints?" Or, "I'm not perfect and have no right to call others to perfection." While there may indeed be a quality of humility in each these statements, the truth is that if a person needed to be perfect to encourage others to perfection, no one would be encouraging. If sinners had to become sanctified saints before leading other sinners to sanctity, there would be very few, if any, saints.

The apostles weren't perfect—far from it—and yet, Jesus called them to lead and establish His Church. As one bishop said, "The Church ceases to be perfect when we join it." The Church in her Spirit is always perfect, but the Church in her members is broken, wounded, and in need of redemption. God does not call the qualified, but rather qualifies the called. Consider that St. Joseph was the "least perfect" member of the Holy Family, and yet the Church hails him forever as "head of the Holy Family" (see Litany of St. Joseph). From the beginning of creation, the human father has been endowed with the distinct character of authority and the role of leader, regardless of whether he is the least qualified member of his family.

You, as a human father, in your essence, and in your office, have nothing to be ashamed of. To be ashamed of your God-given authority is to be ashamed of the God Who imparted that authority to you. Why? As fatherhood exists in the divine Godhead, so also does fatherhood exist and function in the created order. In the Godhead, the Father is the Begetter of the Begotten One, the Son.

As the Father is the "source" in the Trinity, so also fatherhood and its authority—in a certain sense—is the source of life in the family, in society, and in the Church.

You don't have to be perfect to be a great father. You only need to be striving to live for the Father of all perfection. When you persevere in the quest of perfection, by facing and embracing your own imperfection, you will be following the path of St. Joseph, who became a father on earth like the Father in heaven.

> **TAKE THE LEAD** When encountering a trial, test, suffering, or inconvenience, rather than complaining or drawing attention to yourself, secretly surrender it to God, uniting it to a prayer for the needs of your wife and children. Strive to maintain this spirituality. You will discover that over time your silent example and secret sacrifices will obtain peace in your home.*

---

* See Examen *Lead by Loving, Love by Leading* on page 448

PILLAR 3: ASSUME YOUR AUTHORITY [EMBRACE CHARITABLE AUTHORITY]

QUALITIES OF THE MAN OF AUTHORITY

121. THE PRIESTLY FATHER

Have you ever been accused of not following Jesus and His teaching to "[c]all no man on earth your father, for you have one father in heaven?" (Mt 23:9) Catholics refer to priests as "father," and by doing so they appear to be disobeying and disregarding Christ's command to call no man on earth father.

On numerous occasions the apostles, the first priests, referred to themselves as fathers of their spiritual children. St. Paul said, "For though you have countless guides in Christ, you do not have many fathers. For I became your father in Christ Jesus through the gospel" (1 Cor 4:15).

Paul's words imply his authority as spiritual father. "Since the Bible frequently speaks of this spiritual fatherhood, we Catholics acknowledge it and follow the custom of the apostles by calling priests 'father'" (Catholic Answers, "Call No Man Father?"). In other words, the priesthood is closely associated with spiritual fatherhood.

A priest is a father in that he offers himself, in union with Christ's sacrifice, for his spiritual children; and in a similar way, every father is called to be a spiritual father by offering himself in sacrifice for his family. A priest is a father of his spiritual family; and though a biological dad does not offer the Eucharistic sacrifice like a priest, he nevertheless is called to be a spiritual father by being the priest of his family, his domestic church.

You and I are called by God to be the priests of our families. It may sound formal and awkward; and perhaps the vision of you in clerical gear comes to mind. Be at peace, you need not be adorned in liturgical garments.

What is a priest and what is his function? It is more than his exterior garment, but rather his interior function. A priest offers sacrifice. Though we have not the sacrament of Holy Orders, you and I have been ordained to offer a priestly-fatherly sacrifice—the offering of ourselves.

All men suffer; few men sacrifice. Recall that the word "sacrifice" consists of the two Latin words: *sacer*, which means "sacred," and *facere*, which means "to make." Sacrifice is the art of making something sacred; that is, setting aside something or offering something to God for the purpose of making it holy unto the Lord. The point is that a true leader, a priestly-father, converts his sufferings into a sacrifice, an offering, a prayer on behalf of his subjects (his wife and children).

This is your spiritual worship, your priestly act, to offer your body as a holy and living sacrifice unto the Lord.

As you grow older, experience the pains of an aging body, encounter financial hardships, familial tensions, the loss of loved ones and valued friendships, personal and emotional setbacks, sickness and the loss of health, you will have the opportunity that many men neglect—or simply are unaware of: the opportunity to convert all of these sufferings into sacrifices by setting them aside as an offering to God in hopes that He will transform them into grace for your family.

Your fatherly priesthood, though not at the level of the ordained priest, is a powerful gift, and by using it, you will earn the respect of being known as father.

> **TAKE THE LEAD** When encountering a trial, test, suffering, or inconvenience, rather than complaining or drawing attention to yourself, secretly surrender it to God, uniting it to a prayer for the needs of your wife and children. Strive to maintain this spirituality. You will discover that over time your silent example and secret sacrifices will obtain peace in your home.*

* See Examen *Lead by Loving, Love by Leading* on page 448

PILLAR 3: ASSUME YOUR AUTHORITY [EMBRACE CHARITABLE AUTHORITY]

QUALITIES OF THE MAN OF AUTHORITY

122. YOUR GREATEST TREASURE

Has there ever been an occasion when you wondered why your children aren't responding to your authority; why they rebel in defiance or disobey your commands? Though we fathers are not the sole reason for our children's disobedience, our faith in God and obedience to Him is a significant influence on their behavior.

Your fatherly authority is marked by power and responsibility. If you expect and hope for your children to be obedient, and for your wife to respect you, it is essential that you use your ability to respond to God by being faithful to what he has entrusted to you.

Our children, our family, are similar to the talents that the master in Jesus' parable entrusted to His servants. The master in the parable is a symbol of God the Father, who entrusts fathers with the treasure of their family. God trusts you and me to invest in the treasure of our family for the purpose of returning them to Him in a glorified and sanctified form.

Our Lord also discloses that each servant is given the freedom to determine in what manner and to what level he ought to invest. In His parable, some of the servants invest wisely, receiving a return on their investment, while another slothfully squanders his freedom by not investing his talent.

In a similar way, your position of authority comes with the liberty to choose how you will invest in your family's lives. Because of this, you and I can easily misunderstand our liberty as a freedom to serve ourselves, our passions and boyish dreams, while neglecting those we are called to serve. Though you have the freedom to determine the best means to serve your family, it is imperative that you remain faithful to the source of your freedom and authority—God.

You stand before God as His representative of your wife and children. Your role as God the Father's representative is one of the key ways in which you respond to God and His call. Responding to God and claiming as our own what is God's for the purpose of ensuring that they remain God's own is the basis of our relationship with the Father.

The Father entrusts your family to your fatherhood to ensure that they may become aware that God treasures them and in turn that they treasure God.

Several popes and saints proclaimed that "God entrusted to St. Joseph his most sacred treasures"—Jesus and Mary. Joseph, as God the Father's representative, was responsible to God for the Holy Family. Joseph claimed the Holy Family as his own, investing himself in them to ensure that nothing would separate them from God's holy will. Like Joseph, God has granted you the tremendous treasure of your family, and by investing in them you will help them remain God's treasure and also treasure God.

> **TAKE THE LEAD** When encountering a trial, test, suffering, or inconvenience, rather than complaining or drawing attention to yourself, secretly surrender it to God, uniting it to a prayer for the needs of your wife and children. Strive to maintain this spirituality. You will discover that over time your silent example and secret sacrifices will obtain peace in your home.*

* See Examen *Lead by Loving, Love by Leading* on page 448

QUALITIES OF THE MAN OF AUTHORITY

123. THE DUTIES OF A TRUE LEADER

Understanding the goal, having a purpose, and pursuing a singular aim is one of the key attributes of an effective leader. People rarely drive their cars without having a destination in mind. Yet, many fathers "drive" through life as though it is recreation, without a destination. One of the key attributes of an effective father-leader is to clearly understand your goal—what you are saving your children from, but more important what you are saving them for.

3 WAYS TO ASSUME YOUR AUTHORITY

In your pursuit to author the story of God's self-giving love within your family, you will encounter three tenacious, relentless enemies: the world, the flesh, and the devil. These are the enemies from which we want to save our children. But what are we saving our children for? It is not enough to merely lead our children from these threats; rather, we must lead them to the truth.

Your mission as father and leader is to lead your family away from the world toward the reality and destiny of heaven; away from the flesh (concupiscence) toward the Spirit; and away from the devil, the master and slave of rebellion, toward obedience to God—true freedom.

The world is at war with heaven; the flesh is at enmity with the Spirit; and the devil attempts to undermine authentic freedom, which is obtained by obedience to God. Freedom is only free if it is not enslaved to disordered passions. Rebellion, which often poses as radical freedom, is nothing less than slavery to one's pride and passions.

You exercise your charitable authority by standing guard between each of these ideals and their opposing enemy. In other words, if a father is to overcome the world and lead his family to heaven, he must fulfill the responsibility of protecting. If a father is to empower his family to overcome the flesh and live by the Spirit, he must fulfill the responsibility of providing. If a father is to defeat the devil and lead his family away from rebellion, he must instill obedience to God by means of fulfilling the responsibility of teaching.

Freedom (obedience to God) + love (living by the Spirit) = happiness (eternal beatitude in heaven).

We fathers experience true freedom when we obey God's commission to protect, provide, and teach our children. When we are obedient in this way, we overcome the enemy of the devil (rebellion). When our expression of protecting, providing, and teaching is animated by Christ's love and mercy, we live by the Spirit and overcome the flesh, which is ultimately rooted in disordered self-love. By consistently striving to live in freedom that is animated by love, we will experience the ideal of happiness that can only be discovered by living in communion with God—and leaving the false promises of the world behind.

> **TAKE THE LEAD** When encountering a trial, test, suffering, or inconvenience, rather than complaining or drawing attention to yourself, secretly surrender it to God, uniting it to a prayer for your wife's and children's needs. Strive to maintain this spirituality. You will discover that over time your silent example and secret sacrifices will obtain peace in your home.*

---

* See Examen *Lead by Loving, Love by Leading* on page 448

PILLAR 3: ASSUME YOUR AUTHORITY [EMBRACE CHARITABLE AUTHORITY]

PROTECTING

124. A MOST INSIDIOUS ENEMY

Typically, there exist two types of enemies: the enemy who exists "outside" the camp, and the enemy who lives on the "inside" of the camp; the enemy who is easily identifiable, and the enemy who is unidentifiable—who appears to be on "our side."

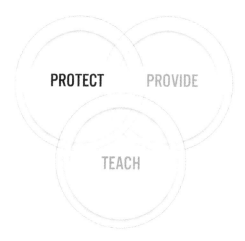

Peppered throughout human history are the painful accounts of the spy, the traitor, the man who appears to be one of the team, an "inside" comrade who sells his soul to obtain his desired pleasure.

Among the most notorious of betrayers is the general, Benedict Arnold, who fought for the Continental Army during the Revolutionary War, leading the Americans to several decisive victories over the British. However, when Arnold didn't receive the recognition and honor that he believed was due to him, he entered secret negotiations with the British to surrender the post at West Point in exchange for money and a commanding position in the British Army.

A more common and perhaps universal symbol of the traitor is Judas Iscariot. Judas, in exchange for thirty silver pieces, sold his three-year friendship with Jesus, disclosed Jesus' and his apostles' secret whereabouts, and led the cohort of temple guards to Jesus, whom he kissed as a signal that Christ was the man that they should apprehend. Truly, the depth of betrayal.

The human father may have one of the most thankless jobs in the world. By the sweat of his brow, by the work of his hands, and by burning up long evening hours, he scrapes out a meager living for the purpose of putting clothes on his family's back, food on the table, paying the mortgage, insurance, college tuition, heating and gas bill, only for his children to come of age and strike out to build a life for themselves—quite often without much of a thank you.

It would make more sense for children to throw parties in honor of their parents' investment in their lives, than parents—who have paid for education, clothing, food, shelter, athletics and hobbies throughout their child's life—paying for graduation parties, wedding receptions. Of course, the provision for such celebrations honor past accomplishments and the hope of a promising future. Yet, in a certain sense, the father and his heroic, consistent, selfless investment in his child is often forgotten, or not acknowledged.

When a father does not receive recognition and acknowledgment, he can more easily be seduced into betraying those for whom he is fighting, defending, and serving in exchange for money, lauds, honor, "a commanding position."

The father who succumbs to such allurements becomes distracted from the ultimate goal of his vocation: to lead his wife and children to heaven. He becomes the "unidentifiable" enemy who lives on the "inside" of the camp, who poses as a Christian, perhaps attends Mass on Sunday, but whose heart is not aflame with the love of God. Thus, the lukewarm father inadvertently teaches his children that a lukewarm faith is acceptable, and that religion and God are banal, boring, tasteless, and not worth sacrificing for.

Our Lord Jesus offers a stern warning to those of us who have fallen—or are falling—into the diabolical trap of becoming a traitor: "Be either hot or cold; but not lukewarm lest I spit you out from my mouth" (see Rev 3:15). When a person vomits, they initially resist the impulse to do so because they want to hold their food inside. The Lord also wants to keep us with Him, inside of Him, and yet, if we become lukewarm fathers who sell off our vocation in exchange for the world, the flesh, and the devil, we will be expelled from Him.

Though we may not receive the recognition we desire, nevertheless we are commissioned with the heroic duty of overcoming the traitor inside and being the man who defends his family and faith unto death.

> **TAKE THE LEAD** Ask yourself: When was the last time I discussed heaven, hell, death, and God's judgment with my children? When was the last time I explained to my family the consequences of sin? If you haven't done so, what is stopping you? Many of us don't feel equipped to discuss such serious matters. Others feel that due to their own sins, they have no right to talk about such things. However, it is our duty to bring the reality of the eternal into our home. This is not your home. Over the next several reflections be intentional about sharing your love for Jesus with you family and share with them the glory that God desires to share with them for all eternity. But, for them to respect the grandeur of heaven, they must understand the loneliness of hell.*

* See Examen *Protect* on page 448

PROTECTING

125. SAVING *FROM* AND SAVING *FOR*

Many of us during our childhood received our fair share of parental warnings expressing the possible negative consequences of our poor decisions. "Don't run in the street—you could get hit by a car." "Don't have sex before you get married—you could contract a sexually transmitted disease." "Don't miss Sunday Mass, lest you find yourself in hell."

Such commands are known as the "thou shalt nots." It is important that we fathers indicate the potentially grave outcomes that are a product of our children's poor decisions—particularly when forming and educating our children in those things that are potentially harmful and damaging. However, it is all too easy to focus repeatedly and consistently on the "thou shalt nots," rather than the "thou shalts."

It is a common parenting practice to teach our children for the purpose of saving them *from* hell and be remiss about teaching them for the purpose of saving them *for* heaven; to focus on saving our children *from* damnation, while forgetting that we are saving them *for* glorification.

To be a staunch defender and shepherd of your family, it is vital to identify the wolves that will attempt, or are attempting, to undermine your authority and steal, kill, and destroy your sheep. But even more essential to raising children to be saints is to identify, understand, and convey to them their eternal destiny.

It is not enough to share the truth with our children of the pain and isolation that exists in hell, and simply state that the goal of their life is to "get to heaven." It is imperative that we reveal to them the glorious nature, ecstatic experience, and infinite joy of heaven; which means that we should understand and experience this reality in our own lives to some degree.

If our children do not understand how powerful, blissful, ecstatic, and fulfilling heaven is, they won't desire it. Desiring *not* to go to hell doesn't create a true desire for heaven—it simply helps a person

PILLAR 3: ASSUME YOUR AUTHORITY [EMBRACE CHARITABLE AUTHORITY]

desire not to desire hell. Fear of punishment can awaken a child to the awareness of sin, but the awareness of sin is only good insofar as it helps a child understand that he needs a savior.

For example, many parents will warn their children that having sexual intercourse before marriage is bad. Yet, so many young people disregard their parents' counsel only to discover that the sexual act is potent with pleasure. Even though having sexual intercourse before marriage is immoral, and nearly always is associated with a painful consequence, nevertheless, God created sexual intercourse to be pleasurable.

But what if parents communicated God's intention behind sexual intercourse, its richness and eternal significance, and also the physical pleasure associated with the act? Perhaps our children would be more likely to reverence and respect such an act and strive to wait to engage in sexual intercourse until the proper time.

It is up to us fathers to develop and perhaps master the art of sharing with our children the glories of sexuality, the glory and identity of God, and the eternal mind-blowing destiny that He has prepared for all of His children. By doing this, we will not have to depend on, or resort to, convincing our children to live a life of holiness by using "fear factors" and "thou shalt nots." Indeed, we will not need to scare them out of hell, but rather we will love them into haven. This may very well be the best way to save your children from the world and for heaven.

TAKE THE LEAD Ask yourself: When was the last time I discussed heaven, hell, death, and God's judgment with my children? When was the last time I explained to my family the consequences of sin? If you haven't done so, what is stopping you? Many of us don't feel equipped to discuss such serious matters. Others feel that due to their own sins, they have no right to talk about such things. However, it is our duty to bring the reality of the eternal into our home. This is not your home. Over the next several reflections be intentional about sharing your love for Jesus with you family and share with them the glory that God desires to share with them for all eternity. But, for them to respect the grandeur of heaven, they must understand the loneliness of hell.*

---

* See Examen *Protect* on page 448

PROTECTING

126. HOW TO OVERCOME THE ENEMY OF THE WORLD

Our eyes are made for gazing upon beauty. Beauty enthralls us and has the power to captivate our attention. The beauty of the creature has been created for the purpose of signifying and leading to the Creator. When the Creator's beauty saturates His creation, we sense a need to praise God and His creativity. However, far too often we become fixated on the creature to the neglect of the Creator of the creature.

God creates beauty with the power to summon us from ourselves and into another, yet without becoming "stuck" in the other, in the creature. God desires that we are summoned through the creature toward the Creator. Often, however, we peer out only to draw creation into ourselves. At this point, we become black holes of self, using beauty for our selfish end and not for its true and noble purpose—to draw us to God.

The enemy—known as the world—opposes the father-protector, attempting to convince men to live for what is seen rather than unseen; to live for the creature rather than the Creator; to fixate upon the temporal rather than the eternal.

The empire of the world's foundation is the shifting sand of human respect, which tempts fathers to succumb to the allures of vainglory, false ambitions, temporary prestige, or man-made self-confidence. These things are of the earth, and "[h]e who is from the earth belongs to the earth, and of the earth he speaks."

The things of the earth can cause a man to become jealous, envious, prideful or bitter about his circumstances; whereas the things that are above afford a deep, inner, lasting peace that is not derived from self-confidence, but the self's confidence in God. Therefore, we are to "[s]eek the things that are above, where Christ is seated at the right hand of God" (Col 3:2–3).

In other words, it is vital that you protect your family from the temptation to desire to be noticed by men, and instead educate them to live to be known by God alone. This temptation comes in the form of the neighbor's success, the latest invention or gadget, what's popular, who's popular, what and who is trending. But notice all that is trending is just that—fleeting; while God is eternal.

This is one of the most important lessons you can teach your child. By doing so, you are protecting your child from slavery to the world and helping them to find freedom in being the person that God has created and destined them to be.

You can accomplish this—by God's grace—by living a life that is "[h]idden with Christ in God" (Col 3:3). This type of hiddenness can only be derived from confidence and trust in the heavenly Father and your belief that He has chosen you, desires you, and has destined you to share in His glory.

If you and I have confidence in the heavenly Father, we will become capable of transmitting this fatherly confidence and trust to our children; and our children who receive the gaze of the Father through their human fathers will be protected from seeking the disordered affirmation of the world.

> **TAKE THE LEAD** Ask yourself: When was the last time I discussed heaven, hell, death, and God's judgment with my children? When was the last time I explained to my family the consequences of sin? If you haven't done so, what is stopping you? Many of us don't feel equipped to discuss such serious matters. Others feel that due to their own sins, they have no right to talk about such things. However, it is our duty to bring the reality of the eternal into our home. This is not your home. Over the next several reflections be intentional about sharing your love for Jesus with you family and share with them the glory that God desires to share with them for all eternity. But, for them to respect the grandeur of heaven, they must understand the loneliness of hell.*

---

* See Examen *Protect* on page 448

INVESTING YOUR TALENT

127. LOSING YOUR TALENT

What is your greatest treasure? For one person, it may be his possessions; for another, his pride of place and prominence in his community; perhaps for another it is his wealth; for still others, their achievements. The list of what man treasures is nearly endless. But how many would respond to the aforementioned question with this response? *My fatherhood—my wife and children—are my most valued treasure.*

Like a man who is unaware that the land he owns has a sizable treasure buried just below the ground's surface, often we fathers forget and neglect the treasure and glory of our fatherhood. What is the consequence of neglecting to discover the treasure of our fatherhood? Perhaps the most painful regret is to finish our life asking, "What if I had done this differently?"

In Jesus' Parable of the Talents, the master departs on an extended journey and entrusts his wealth to three servants. To one, he entrusts five talents; to another he entrusts two talents; and to the third servant he entrusts a single talent—each according to their own ability.

When Jesus lived on earth, a talent was considered a large amount of money, equal to approximately 6,000 drachma, or denarius—Greek or Roman silver coins. One denarius is believed by scholars to have been a Roman soldier's daily pay. In other words, the approximate worth of a single talent was 6,000 days' wages, or nineteen years' worth of salary.

Why is this significant? Because it testifies to the first important truth we can derive from this parable: the master is incredibly generous and entrusts His servants with much. This truth is the foundational premise of Jesus' parable, and it is the foundation of our fatherhood.

God, symbolized by the master, is exceedingly generous, and one of the greatest treasures—talents—that he entrusts to us fathers—besides our faith—is our fatherhood.

The second lesson we obtain from this parable is that our children are an incredible treasure. Many fathers don't see their children this way, but rather view them as a burden, a distraction or nuisance. You and I are to understand, appreciate, and love the treasure of our children.

In this parable, the master returns after his extended departure and settles accounts with his servants. Here we discover the third truth: in the end, we will have to make an account of how we invested in the treasure of our children.

Jesus relates that the first two servants invested and doubled their master's treasure and therefore were rewarded richly. The third servant, however, buried his talent, to which the master responded by taking his talent and giving it to one of the other servants.

Which leads us to the fourth point: if you and I neglect our vocation by avoiding investing in our children, we will lose them. Though we may hope that if we do lose them they would be given to another trusting servant's care, it is more likely that they will be handed over and tortured by the world, the flesh, and the devil.

Let us return to the question: What is your greatest treasure? It has been said, "God entrusted to St. Joseph His greatest treasures—Jesus and Mary." Joseph tirelessly invested himself in Jesus and Mary to ensure that their lives glorified God. May we also invest in the treasure of our fatherhood, glorifying God and by doing so allowing the generous God to share with us His glory.

> **TAKE THE LEAD** Dedicate some time, at the beginning of each day, to thank God for His generosity. Look deep into your past and meditate upon the pivotal events in your life and how God has brought you to your current place. The key is to meditate on those events that seemed unbearable or incomprehensible and ask God to help you understand how He used those situations to save you for Himself—for something greater. Thank him daily for the good and the so-called bad.*

* See Examen *Protect* on page 448

INVESTING YOUR TALENT

128. YOUR VIEW OF THE FATHER DETERMINES YOUR FATHERHOOD

How do you see God? What characteristics do you attribute to Him? Do you view God as cold, hard, insensitive, and distant? Or do you understand God to be a "sugar daddy," a Santa Claus-like figure, with whom we communicate only when we are in want or are in need of something?

Recall that the foundational premise of Jesus' Parable of the Talents is that the master—who is a symbol of God the Father—is exceedingly generous. If a talent is equal to 6,000 days' worth of wages, or nineteen years' worth of salary; and if a man earns approximately $50,000 a year, a talent symbolizes approximately $1 million. This indicates that the master in the parable entrusted the first servant with an amount akin to $5 million, the second servant with $2 million, and the third servant a measly $1 million.

But when the master returns and discovers that the third servant—"the wicked lazy servant"—did not invest the talent, he took it from him and gave it to another. When considering this, we may make the mistake of interpreting the master's action as an expression of his domineering, ruthless, demanding personality. However, there is far more to this account.

Listen to the wicked servant's description of his master: "I know you to be a hard man." "Reaping where you did not sow." "I was afraid." The wicked servant believed his master to be harsh, selfish, cruel—a tyrant who uses people and takes from them what they do not even possess; and this view paralyzed him with fear.

But this characterization of the master was inappropriate. Why did the other servant's double their master's money? Because they trusted the master and believed him to be generous—and He is.

We become who we view God to be. The wicked servant believed his master to be stingy, and therefore he reflected that belief by lacking generosity and trust. Who we believe God to be determines the trajectory of our life. Do we view God as a competitor, or a collaborator; as a pain, or a protector? As a problem, or a pater?

PILLAR 3: ASSUME YOUR AUTHORITY [EMBRACE CHARITABLE AUTHORITY]

If you desire your children to be generous yet responsible, trusting rather than suspicious, compassionate yet firm, caring yet strong, self-giving rather than self-absorbed, it is vital that you embody these characteristics yourself. To be viewed as a generous, powerful, loving father, it is essential that you view the Father in this way.

> **TAKE THE LEAD** Dedicate some time, at the beginning of each day, to thank God for His generosity. Look deep into your past and meditate upon the pivotal events in your life and how God has brought you to your current place. The key is to meditate on those events that seemed unbearable or incomprehensible and ask God to help you understand how He used those situations to save you for Himself—for something greater. Thank him daily for the good and the so-called bad.*

* See Examen *Protect* on page 448

A TRUE SHEPHERD

129. YOUR NOBLE ROLE

What does it mean practically to protect your child? What is the essential reason for protecting your child? And is this reason worthy of your self-sacrifice?

In the scriptural account of Jesus' birth, we find the answers to these questions. Herod—who the Romans hailed as "King of the Jews"—after ascertaining the time of Jesus' birth from the Magi, sent soldiers to find and murder the infant. St. Joseph, as protector of the Christ Child, led his family secretly by night to Egypt, a foreign land, in order to protect and save the child—the true King of the Jews—and His Mother (see Matt 2:13).

This account provides a profound analogy and example for fatherly protection. Herod is a symbol of Satan, whose intent is to destroy the child—that is, our children. Herod is also a symbol of the world and its malignant expression of vainglory, human respect, man-made confidence, and illusive, temporary prestige.

St. Joseph symbolizes all fathers, who are divinely ordained to lead, protect, and ultimately save their families from the devil's destructive designs.

How did St. Joseph protect and save Jesus and Mary? He saved his family while shrouded by the darkness of night. This dark night symbolizes the hidden, secret service of fatherhood.

You and I, rather than living a life like that of Herod, which is aimed at achieving prestige, popularity, pleasure, and power, are to be like St. Joseph who, by embracing the dark, hidden, secret, little-known life of fatherhood, participates in raising children for Christ and thus participates in saving the world.

You, like St. Joseph, are to protect your child from being sacrificed to the world by secretly preparing your child to sacrifice himself on behalf of the world to God. This is your noble role.

TAKE THE LEAD Ask yourself: What activities, obligations, responsibilities, and duties are separating me from spending time with my family? What distractions are keeping me from the ultimate attraction: God in my vocation? Ask God what measures should be taken to remove those hindrances, or at the least minimize them. But more important, after they are removed, with what will you replace the void?*

* See Examen *Protect* on page 448

A TRUE SHEPHERD

130. LEARNING FROM JOSEPH WHAT REALLY MATTERS

What is your ultimate hope for your children? What do you want their life's achievement to be? Often fathers glow and rave about how their sons or daughters became high powered attorneys, college or professional athletes, CEOs of well-known conglomerates. Though our children's achievements affirm us in our parenting and grant us a sense of satisfaction and vicarious success, these accomplishments—as rich and good as they are—are momentary and passing.

While it is necessary and good to have the right kind of pride in our children's achievements, we must be clear as to what the ultimate, lasting, and true achievement is.

Our Lord asked, "What does it profit a man, if he should gain the whole world and suffer the loss of his soul? Or what shall a man give in exchange for his soul?" (Mt 16:26).

After Herod died and the infant Jesus was no longer in danger of being assassinated by the tetrarch, the angel of the Lord commanded Joseph to "[r]ise take the child and his Mother to Israel for those who sought the child's life are dead" (Mt 2:20). The literal meaning of these words in the Greek and Latin is "those who sought the child's *soul* are dead." The point is that Joseph was endowed with the tremendous responsibility of protecting the soul of Jesus.

Financial gain and worldly profit can be highly beneficial, but such profit can also become a great loss if the person's soul is lost in his pursuit to accumulate these things. You and I, as fathers, are called to imitate St. Joseph by intentionally having a singular purpose and ultimate goal for our children: to save their souls.

No ideal, worldly project, or personal achievement can measure up to this holy aspiration. In the end, God will not be concerned with how much money you saved, but whether you participated in saving souls. If we are to be like St. Joseph, a father on earth like the Father in heaven, saving our children's souls for heaven must be our number one goal.

PILLAR 3: ASSUME YOUR AUTHORITY [EMBRACE CHARITABLE AUTHORITY]

TAKE THE LEAD Ask yourself: What activities, obligations, responsibilities, and duties are separating me from spending time with my family? What distractions are keeping me from the ultimate attraction: God in my vocation? Ask God what measures should be taken to remove those hindrances, or at the least minimize them. But more important, after they are removed, with what will you replace the void?*

* See Examen *Protect* on page 448

131. A TRUE SHEPHERD

Have you ever heard someone say in response to the idea that the evils our children encounter daily—peer pressure, the perversion of sexuality, pervasive media, and the like—"Well, we survived, didn't we?" The appropriate response to such a comment is, "I don't want my children merely to survive; I want my children to thrive. I don't want my children to get by, but to get to heaven."

You and I, being endowed with the gift of charitable authority and the divine commission to lead, are called to ensure that our children not only survive their daily battles, but win them. Whether or not we are willing to admit it, our children are at war. Satan is waging a full-scale, multilevel assault aimed at robbing, killing, and destroying our children's innocence and ability to trust in love. The statistics testify to the intensity of the war: teenage pregnancies, abortions, suicide rates, depression, and sexually transmitted diseases are ever increasing.

Remember that our Lord said that the devil is the father of lies who comes to kill, steal, and destroy, and only a good shepherd can shield the sheep from this demonic predator. The human father, like Christ, is called to be a good shepherd who lays down his life for his sheep. Yet, how many fathers have been struck by Satan, and because of this, their children—the sheep—have been scattered?

Today, many fathers neglect to sacrifice themselves on behalf of their children and unwittingly sacrifice their children to the evil one.

Jesus draws a distinction between the shepherd and the hireling. "The hireling, who is not a shepherd, whose own the sheep are not, sees the wolf coming and leaves the sheep and flees. And the wolf snatches and scatters the sheep; but the hireling flees because he is a hireling and has no concern for the sheep (Jn 10:12–13).

Too often, we fathers succumb to the temptation to hire ourselves out to labor for the bread that perishes, that is, to labor for worldly pursuits, ego, human respect, carnal lusts, rather than laboring for the Bread that gives life, that is, laboring for Christ in his children (see Mt 18:13; John 6:27).

When a father submits to this temptation, he can forget that his children are those sheep who have been placed in his care, and that it is his responsibility to shepherd them lest they become scattered. Yet, a good shepherd—a good father—lays down his life for his sheep—his children.

At the end of the day, a shepherd gathered his sheep into a sheepfold, and at the sheepfold gate he laid his body across the threshold to ensure that his flock was protected from predators. The message is clear: if you are coming for my sheep; you must come over my dead body. This is also the attitude of a father who loves his child truly: if the evil one is coming for my children, he must come over my dead body.

St. Joseph surrendered his house in Bethlehem, his stable occupation, to be the shepherd who saved the Good Shepherd, Jesus, from Herod. You, like Joseph, are to lay down your life for your children by surrendering certain aspirations, endeavors, and ambitions to ensure that your children are not scattered by Satan but rather gathered by our Lord.

> **TAKE THE LEAD** Ask yourself: What activities, obligations, responsibilities, and duties are separating me from spending time with my family? What distractions are keeping me from the ultimate attraction: God in my vocation? Ask God what measures should be taken to remove those hindrances, or at the least minimize them. But more important, after they are removed, with what will you replace the void?*

* See Examen *Protect* on page 448

THE SIX ENEMIES

132. YOUR CHILD'S SIX ENEMIES

It may sound odd or melodramatic to say that your child has enemies. Yes, even the youngest of children have enemies. Do you know your child's enemies? Can you identify the major evils that threaten your child's salvation?

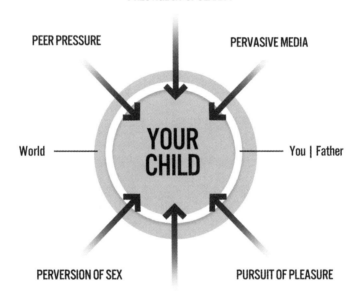

Recently, an ever-growing army of radical, hostile terrorists enlisted children as young as nine years of age into their militia, arming them with automatic weapons. Why? Because most people would rarely identify a child as an enemy or as having the power to wield death.

When we neglect to identify the enemy and its forms we most certainly will lose the battle; for how can one win a war when he doesn't know who he is fighting? One of the key factors in winning

PILLAR 3: ASSUME YOUR AUTHORITY [EMBRACE CHARITABLE AUTHORITY]

a battle is to identify who the enemy is, his many forms, his tactics and methods.

You and I, as fathers, have a sacred responsibility to protect our children, and to accomplish this endeavor it is vital that we understand the enemy of the world and specifically identify its cunning forms.

Before proceeding, it is important to understand that each of these "forms of the world" are intrinsically good in themselves. The evil one, who cannot create anything *ex nihilo*, that is, out of nothing, can only use the goods that God has created and deform them into something evil. In other words, each of the forms of the "enemy of the world" is good in its essential form but has been hijacked by Satan.

The devil offers the perverted form of the good as a supposed means to "happiness." Yet, it is our duty as fathers to explain to our children that only a true form of any good can lead to happiness.

The enemy of the world is expressed in a variety of forms; however, there exist six basic forms of the enemy of the world that are aimed at pervading and invading our children's souls. These are the six *P*s: 1) perversion of sex, 2) peer pressure, 3) prestige and popularity, 4) pervasiveness of media and technology, 5) pursuit of pleasure, and 6) poor parenting. Over the next several reflections we will discuss each of these specifically.

> **TAKE THE LEAD** Over the next several reflections, the enemy will be exposed, but more important, the need for your and your child's participation will also be revealed. This will be most challenging. There exists a tendency among men to have a knee-jerk reaction to such truths and force their families to go cold turkey, demanding that all technological devices be burned at the stake. This will certainly drive your children away from Christ. On the other hand, you will be tempted to disregard these enemies as not being real, and to believe that your pure, innocent child is above such temptations. Don't let the devil fool you. Discuss with your wife tactics and strategies to gradually reclaim your home as a kingdom of God. Remember, this will not be a quick fix, but rather an ongoing project.*

---

* See Examen *Protect* on page 448

THE SIX ENEMIES

133. PERVERSION OF SEX: ENEMY 1

Sex. The word alone has the power to halt us in our tracks, evoke imagery in our minds, and make our heart race. The power of sex is akin to nuclear energy: if harnessed it can provide fuel, power, heat, electricity for large subsets of cities and nations that span thousands of miles. Nuclear energy is good. However, if it is gathered into a bomb and placed in the wrong hands, it can be the cause of destruction of countless human lives.

Much like nuclear energy, sex has the power to unite spouses, bond couples to one another, and launch man and woman into the eternal communion of God who invented both sex and marriage.

Sex is good. Not just good, but very good. Yet sex can also be misused, abused, and separated from God's purpose and intention for it. When this occurs, the human heart reaps the miserable consequences of such misuse.

The one-flesh union in marriage was created by God to symbolize Christ's desire for union with His Church, and the fruitfulness of that communion. The evil one, however, maligns and distorts the true meaning of sex, offering it in ways that pervert and distort the divine intention.

Perverted sexuality becomes more powerful when a father makes several basic mistakes: first, he neglects or avoids discussing sex with his children; second, he does discuss it with his children, but merely focuses on the biological mechanics of the act; third, he relates sexual sins from his own past.

When a child hears his father recount those mistakes, his sins of the past, the child concludes that his father survived and therefore he or she will survive even if they commit the same sins. The child, however, has little or no awareness of the deep-seated wounds these sexual acts have inflicted on the father.

The fourth mistake is when a father allows illicit sexual content to enter the home via the computer, internet, television programming, magazines, smartphones, and print materials. The fifth, when

PILLAR 3: ASSUME YOUR AUTHORITY [EMBRACE CHARITABLE AUTHORITY]

a father demeans authentic sexuality, the one-flesh union, and the marital act by means of vile jokes and rude comments. Sixth, when a father convinces his child that the sexual act and the human body are dirty, or impure, transmitting the idea that sex is sinful.

There are three ways that a father can overcome these mistakes: first, by understanding the divine purpose and design behind the body and the sexual act (and seeking out those resources that explain God's glorious plan for sex); second, by communicating that divine purpose to your children in a way that upholds the glory, beauty, and sacredness of the sexual act; third, by striving to be a man who is chaste, pure, and loves his wife as Christ loves the Church.

We ought to become the man we desire our sons to become, and the type of man we desire our daughters to marry.

> **TAKE THE LEAD** Allocate time to analyzing your interpretation and understanding of "sex." Ask yourself: do I understand God's intention for creating sexual union? Am I bound by the world's perception of "sex"? Can I discern the counterfeit from the true good of sexual union? Can I articulate the beauty, glory, and goodness of sexual union without being ashamed of a personal disordered view of sex? If you are like most men, you struggle with viewing sex as dirty, shameful, or a means to gratify disordered urges. Make it a point to find and use resources such as Christopher West's *Naked Without Shame* series, or his book *Good News about Sex and Marriage*. There exist numerous excellent resources under the topic Theology of the Body.

* See Examen *Protect* on page 448

THE SIX ENEMIES

134. PEER PRESSURE: ENEMY 2

Friendship is an essential aspect of human existence. Without friendship we can become isolated, lack personal growth, and lack in social development. Friendship in its authentic form does three things: first, it harmonizes two people by means of trust and relationship; second, it affords a context in which friends can learn how to express disinterested, self-giving love; and third, friends ultimately lead each other toward union, harmony, and friendship with God.

There may be very few things as painful as witnessing one's own child living in isolation; watching them endure their young life without experiencing authentic friendship. Even more unsettling is seeing your child latch on to a friend only to have that friend ignore, marginalize, or betray your child.

Friendship is the context in which our children learn how to live in relationship and strengthen their ability to trust, while also learning how to overcome significant personal loss.

Parents, in the context of their children's social life, can often default to one of two extremes: either overprotection or premature injection. Parents can become so fearful of school system's agendas and peer influence that they overprotect their children by isolating them from society. This type of parenting often causes a child to rebel or become antisocial.

On the other hand, some parents inject their children into the many and varied social, academic, and athletic activities in hopes that their children will be accepted by their peers. This can place unhealthy expectations on a child to "fit in," or inordinately desire to be a part of the "in crowd." Many parents attempt—usually subconsciously—to live vicariously through their children in hopes of receiving the satisfaction of being accepted, included, liked, and popular.

Though certain types of schooling are better equipped to form and educate children without "social drama," they cannot avoid the reality of peer pressure and a child's longing to be included.

PILLAR 3: ASSUME YOUR AUTHORITY [EMBRACE CHARITABLE AUTHORITY]

Our children's friends, schoolmates, and peers have tremendous influence on them. The social pressures our children encounter daily are very intense and can almost always lead to a questioning of their personal identity. Often kids believe that high school is life, is the only world that exists, and that tumultuous period represents the best years of their life.

Sometimes it takes the child's entire will to persevere through what can be some of the most hellish years of their lives—and sometimes they don't make it.

How is a father supposed to navigate the difficulties of his child's social life? A father does not neglect protecting and focus exclusively on injecting. Nor does a father overprotect and neglect to eventually inject his child in society. The two are not mutually exclusive. A father is called to protect in order to inject. We protect our children for the purpose of preparing them to eventually be injected into the world, that they may lead their peers from the world to Christ and not be led from Christ to the world.

This indicates that if you desire your child to have healthy friendships, it is important to intentionally work at developing an intimate relationship with your child. An overwhelming amount of evidence validates that those children who have an intimate, trusting relationship with their father are more capable of selecting friends who edify them.

> **TAKE THE LEAD** Few children desire to merely be accepted, but rather chosen. During the next couple of reflections try to identify ways that you can "go out of your way" to choose your child. This could be as simple as engaging your child in a meaningful conversation that lasts more than two minutes; looking your child in the eyes when they are talking; asking your child to tag along with you during your next errand; blessing your child with a treat unexpectedly. All of this subconsciously says: I desire to be with you. By making this a habit, your child will become more confident that they are worthy of being chosen, and begin to stop looking for acceptance among peers.

* See Examen *Protect* on page 448

THE SIX ENEMIES

135. PROTECT TO INJECT: PEER PRESSURE, PART 2

How is a father to protect his child for the purpose of injecting them into the world? Though there exist a variety of ways to protect our children in order to prepare them to be the person God created them to be, there are several fundamental counsels that are critical to our children's formation.

First, it is highly beneficial to refrain from indoctrination, but rather focus on salvation. When a father indoctrinates his child, he imparts his beliefs to his child without teaching his child to think critically, and almost always at the expense of teaching the child to live in authentic relationship with God. In this case, religion loses its purpose and becomes an end in itself. Religion, however, is at the service of leading a child into relationship with God. To lead your child into a relationship with Christ is to live your religion in a way that conveys your own relationship with God.

When your child sees you "practicing" your religion in a way that demonstrates that you have an intimate relationship with the Father and His Son, your child is more likely to become attracted to faith in God.

After your child experiences an intimate relationship with Jesus, it is important to reinforce that there exist two types of people: those who receive the glory that God imparts to them (talents, gifts, abilities) to glorify themselves; and those who use the glory that they have received from God to glorify God.

If a child has an intimate relationship with Jesus, and realizes that their gifts and glory are at the service of glorifying God, the child will begin to experience freedom from "trying to fit in" and won't succumb to the pressure applied by their peers.

Third, if a child does not sense that he is valued by his father he will mistakenly intuit that he is not loved by the Father. If a child does not feel affirmed at home, they will seek affirmation from their peers in unhealthy ways. To ensure that a child becomes the person God is calling them to be, we must intentionally engage them; give them specific, individual attention; and point out their strengths, beauty, goodness, dignity, talents, and gifts.

Overall, it is essential that you communicate to your child—often—that peers don't determine your child's value. God alone determines a child's value and God doesn't make junk. It is up to you to be the human expression of God's love for your child.

> **TAKE THE LEAD** Few children desire to merely be accepted, but rather chosen. During the next couple of reflections try to identify ways that you can "go out of your way" to choose your child. This could be as simple as engaging your child in a meaningful conversation that lasts more than two minutes; looking your child in the eyes when they are talking; asking your child to tag along with you during your next errand; blessing your child with a treat unexpectedly. All of this subconsciously says: I desire to be with you. By making this a habit, your child will become more confident that they are worthy of being chosen, and begin to stop looking for acceptance among peers.

* See Examen *Protect* on page 448

THE SIX ENEMIES

136. PRESTIGE AND POPULARITY: ENEMY 3

The desire to be glorified is an innate and intrinsic human longing. But what is true glory? How is it attained? If our children misunderstand what true glory is and are deceived into pursuing a counterfeit form of glory, they will eventually experience personal emptiness, depression, and perhaps even despair.

Children are often and easily convinced that to be happy they need to be famous musicians, celebrities, sports heroes, and the like. The enemy of the world convinces them that prestige and popularity are the means to fulfillment, satisfaction, and happiness. In other words, children are easily convinced that the road to glory is to be noticed by men; and often, we fathers reinforce this misconceived notion.

Sports activities, music performances, show choir, and the performing arts are good. Acting school is good. But when these activities become the priority, these goods can become gods.

At the heart of this cultural phenomenon is the temptation for parents to live vicariously through their children. Often, parents seek value and satisfaction in their children being popular, liked, and receiving the lauds and accolades of their peers.

It is easy to fall into this trap. What begins as toddler T-ball inadvertently evolves into the child being on the traveling team in three different sports, or being on three different teams in the same sport. And when the children multiply, so also does the time commitment.

Too often these activities can entice us to neglect family dinner, evening family time, prayer as a family, or even Sunday Mass. When these things are consistently neglected, or become secondary to our children's activities, we have made the good a god. When a father allows this, he transmits to his child the idea that the essence and meaning of life is to have prestige, be popular, and gain the recognition of men.

You and I are given the responsibility to raise our children to holiness, to defend them from the ever-invasive world and lead them to communion with God. Are you succeeding in this endeavor?

Ask yourself: Are my child's activities at the service of my family, or is my family at the service of our children's activities? Is our family being sacrificed on the altar of activities, and if so, what activities should be sacrificed for the sake of our family?

Such sacrifices initially do not make a father popular with his children. However, the child of a father who is willing to sacrifice the world for his child, rather than sacrificing his child to the world, will eventually understand that he is loved, not only by his earthly father, but also and more importantly by his heavenly Father.

> **TAKE THE LEAD** Ask yourself: Are my children's athletic, social, and even academic activities straining my family's ability to simply be together? Are we able to eat dinner together as a family consistently? These are difficult questions because usually the answer to such questions is that we have allowed activities to dominate our family culture. Perhaps it's time to "take back" your family. Begin by taking small steps. With your wife, identify those activities which are most superfluous and perhaps burdensome to your family culture. Then discuss ways to approach your children with the idea of removing those activities in a positive manner. For example, "Your mom and I would like you to consider not attending this activity, because we want to have dinner with you on that night." By doing this, you are not simply relating to the child: "You are way too busy," but rather, "We desire to be with you."

* See Examen *Protect* on page 448

THE SIX ENEMIES

137. PURSUIT OF PLEASURE: ENEMY 4

Why do we desire dessert after dinner—or before dinner? Why do so many people drink soda instead of water? Or sleep on a comfortable mattress instead of on the floor? Why is it becoming standard for vehicles to have heated seats?

Human beings are creatures of comfort. In making decisions regarding food, climate, vacations, clothing, music, entertainment, or housing, we instinctively gravitate toward those things from which we may derive the most pleasure.

God created pleasure. Understanding this truth is essential to living a fully human life. All of creation in its essential form God has deemed good (see Gen 2), and for the most part pleasurable. The word "Eden," the name of the Garden that God initially created, literally means "pleasure park."

The purpose of pleasure is to remind us of the One who created it. God grants pleasure to man that man may be reminded that only in God will man find ultimate pleasure. Yet, our existence is not one perpetual experience of pleasure; only in heaven can we achieve such a state. When we forget that earth is not heaven and attempt to create a life that consists of perpetual pleasure, we become discouraged, and depressed. Why? Because inevitably sufferings, trials, misfortunes, challenges, and conflicts will occur.

Our disdain for challenge and trials can indicate that we have reduced pleasure to being synonymous with comfort. We often believe that comfort affords pleasure; yet pleasure cannot be reduced to being comfortable. When we become too comfortable, we become lazy, slothful, unfulfilled, unsatisfied; in other words, we derive very little pleasure when we become too comfortable. This is one of the reasons children become depressed, lifeless, and lack hope. Comfort bores them, and yet they believe that comfort is the path to pleasure and pleasure, the ultimate goal.

Consider that a man can derive great pleasure from a full day of manual labor. Serving someone less fortunate can afford a person tremendous pleasure. Giving food to the poor or sharing his possessions with those who are impoverished can grant a man significant pleasure. Often the greatest pleasures are derived from self-sacrifice, serving others, and sharing ourselves and our goods with others. Why? Because these actions lead us toward the greatest pleasure—communion with others, and ultimately communion with God.

Communion with others helps us come to the full realization of ourselves, our identity and our destiny. Becoming who we really are—who God has destined us to be—affords the greatest sense of fulfillment. We can only arrive at this type of self-knowledge by living in relationship with others. "Man cannot discover himself except by becoming a sincere gift" (see GS 24).

One of the greatest lessons that a father can teach his child is to use his skills, talents, and abilities for the purpose of being a gift to another. When our children begin to apply this lesson to their own lives, they discover that work, sacrifice, and self-giving can afford the greatest pleasures. When our children make this discovery, they are empowered and become more capable of overcoming the enemy in the form of the pursuit of comfort and pleasure.

You and I, as fathers, are to lead our children in thanksgiving to God for all the many and varied pleasures of life, while also teaching them, through our word and example, that life's greatest pleasures can only be derived from self-giving that affords true communion with God and others.

> **TAKE THE LEAD** Identify ways that you could introduce your child to the idea of being a sincere gift to others. For example, visit the elderly in a local nursing home, or serve at the local soup kitchen. Your local church should have plenty of options for helping those who are in need. This may also help you be more intentional in loving your neighbor as yourself. Nevertheless, the key is to draw your child into such experiences, which will not only penetrate your child's heart, create powerful memories, and give the child a deep respect for human beings, but also will solidify your relationship with your child.

* See Examen *Protect* on page 448
THE SIX ENEMIES

138. PERVASIVE MEDIA: ENEMY 5

Can you deny yourself watching television or movies for a week? Are you willing to shut down your smartphone for two full days? Are you capable of unplugging from blogs, news sites, and other forms of entertainment for a month? Any of these would pose a great challenge to most men. If we fathers cannot master or mitigate our dependence on media, how can we expect our children to do it?

How does a father regulate his child's time viewing television, using a smartphone, logging on to YouTube, Instagram, Facebook, and other forms of social media, playing video games, or listening to streaming music?

This is one of the hot-button issues. With the advent of mobile technology and social media it has become extremely difficult, really nearly impossible, to defend one's child from the enemy of the world. In fact, the enemy of pervasive media is the context in which your child's other enemies of perversion of sex, peer pressure, prestige and popularity, and pursuing pleasure all converge. Technological mediums provide all things to all people at all times in an unrestricted, unfiltered, unlimited manner.

It has been said that sixty seconds of television could undermine, if not destroy, fifteen years of parenting. Technology is good when it transmits good things; but technology can be an insidious evil that undermines your fatherly authority and ability to lead your family to God when it transmits morally evil things.

A gun is good for defense and putting dinner on the table. Yet, would you be wiling to place a fully-loaded automatic weapon in a nine-year-old boy's possession? Without realizing it, that is what we do when we give our children smartphones during their adolescence. We give our children the ability to "surf" unrestricted, unfiltered, unregulated content without any supervision. Studies demonstrate that when young boys (and often young girls) encounter pornography accidently, they become attracted and eventually addicted. From this point on, their entire worldview changes from giving to using.

How is a father, who is endowed with the responsibility to lead, to protect his child without making his child feel restricted?

We will discuss ways that we can approach this delicate issue in the next reflection. For now, it is imperative that you believe "as for me and my house we will serve the Lord." This is your banner, your mantra, your call to duty.

> **TAKE THE LEAD** During the next three reflections, seriously consider if your family's consumption of social media, the internet, web apps, video games and the like are consuming your family. Identify ways to help minimize the time spent on mobile devices and the computer, while also purchasing effective internet filtration software that will protect you, your wife, and your children from predatory infiltration. Make every attempt to avoid communicating that you are attempting to "restrict" the use of pervasive media, but rather that your hope is to build an incredible family culture and those mobile devices and social apps sometimes inhibit that goal.

* See Examen *Protect* on page 448

THE SIX ENEMIES

139. PERVASIVE MEDIA, PART 2

In times of antiquity, cities were surrounded by walls of defense. When a city wall had been penetrated or breached by an enemy, it was highly probable that the city and its inhabitants would be overtaken. Analogously, it is very difficult for a family that has been invaded by, and has become addicted to, the use of technological mediums to overcome this insidious enemy.

Allowing our children access to mobile devices, ownership of smartphones, or their own social media accounts at an early age, and then attempting to regulate their usage of these mediums is like trying to put toothpaste back in the tube after it has been squeezed out. In other words, if you have already introduced your children to the use of these technological mediums, it may be more damaging and traumatic to remove them, than to allow your child to continue using them.

What can a father do to protect his child from the enemy of pervasive media if this enemy has already infiltrated his family?

The following suggestions are not foolproof measures, nor a certain guide to winning the battle over technology, but this counsel can aid a father in taking back his authority from these worldly voices.

Remember that your children are not the enemy—the devil is. It is easy to believe that our children, especially after falling prey to sin and disobedience, lack the ability to be trusted. The truth is that they have been ambushed by the evil one and are often overrun by temptations that are beyond their experience and ability to defend against. Considering this, it is essential that you intentionally and consistently determine ways to win your child's trust. By winning your child's trust, your child will desire to be trustworthy.

Trust is the basis of every real relationship. Without trust there is no relationship. Without trust, a father generally resorts to parenting with rules, threats of punishment, and fear tactics as ways to regulate his child's behavior. Rules are only at the service of fostering a relationship and can never substitute for it. Rules are the necessary testing ground for a child to express trust.

PILLAR 3: ASSUME YOUR AUTHORITY [EMBRACE CHARITABLE AUTHORITY]

It is important to discuss with your child that trust is the foundation of successful relationships. After you sense that your child understands the concept of trust, it is important to afford your child the space and freedom to prove that trust.

It is also important to discuss your expectations, express what would constitute a breach of trust, and repeatedly give your child opportunities to prove that they are trustworthy.

The best strategy and the most successful parenting technique is to build lasting trust in your relationship with your child. When a child trusts you and believes that he is trusted, your child will desire all the more to be trustworthy. There may be nothing that brings as much peace to a father than when his child is trustworthy.

> **TAKE THE LEAD** During the next three reflections, seriously consider if your family's consumption of social media, the internet, web apps, video games and the like are consuming your family. Identify ways to help minimize the time spent on mobile devices and the computer, while also purchasing effective internet filtration software that will protect you, your wife, and your children from predatory infiltration. Make every attempt to avoid communicating that you are attempting to "restrict" the use of pervasive media, but rather that your hope is to build an incredible family culture and those mobile devices and social apps sometimes inhibit that goal.

* See Examen *Protect* on page 448

THE SIX ENEMIES

140. PERVASIVE MEDIA, PART 3

In addition to building a relationship of trust with your child, there are four other ways to help your child navigate the techno-media minefield.

First, refrain from attempting to be your child's friend, but rather be your child's father. Friendship is born from fatherhood, rather than fatherhood being born from friendship. If you attempt to be your child's friend first, you will lose the opportunity to be your child's father. However, if you lead as a father, your child will most likely follow you into friendship. To be your child's friend first is to undermine your power to lead.

Second, take measures that are reasonable. Make every attempt to wait as long as possible before introducing consistent computer use to your child, purchasing a smartphone for your child, or allowing them to surf the net unsupervised. If your child needs to use a computer, make every attempt to have them use the family's computer.

Install filtration and protection software that helps prevent useless temptations. If your child has his own smartphone or mobile device, make every effort not to allow them to use the device in their bedrooms privately, or after bedtime.

It may be necessary to remove your cable service, disconnect regular television programming, begin watching movies as a family, not allow access to social media, or allow limited access, while always having access to their accounts. Regardless, don't throw the baby out with the bathwater. Make every attempt to redeem the use of technological mediums for God, education, and developing your children's talents.

Third, when placing restrictions on devices ask your child, "Do you think that I want to make your life miserable?" Afterward, reassure your children that you love them and simply want the best for them.

Fourth, be prepared to deal with casualties, misuse, and disobedience. You are not perfect, and neither are you children.

Imperfect fathers cannot raise perfect children. The key is to be patient, compassionate, forgiving, yet firm and uncompromising in your principles.

Remember, if a father is not protecting, he is not loving.

> **TAKE THE LEAD** During the next three reflections, seriously consider if your family's consumption of social media, the internet, web apps, video games and the like are consuming your family. Identify ways to help minimize the time spent on mobile devices and the computer, while also purchasing effective internet filtration software that will protect you, your wife, and your children from predatory infiltration. Make every attempt to avoid communicating that you are attempting to "restrict" the use of pervasive media, but rather that your hope is to build an incredible family culture and those mobile devices and social apps sometimes inhibit that goal.

* See Examen *Protect* on page 448

THE SIX ENEMIES

141. POOR PARENTING: ENEMY 6

Have you ever heard a parent say that they would never impose their own religious beliefs upon their child, that they will allow their child to come to their own conclusions and make their own decision regarding God, faith, morals and the Church?

This logic is absurd. No parent says, "I'm not going to impose any dietary restrictions or regulations on my child. I'll simply allow him to discover which foods he determines to be best for his well-being." Or, "I'm not going to educate my child in the sciences, arts, or trades. I'll let her decide what she thinks is important to know." This may appear to be affirming a child's liberty, but a child needs to develop adequate knowledge, experience, and wisdom to make such decisions. If a father allows his children unbridled freedom to make their own decision, he is actually imprisoning his children in their ignorance.

In the context of parenting, a father often toggles between two extremes: he either neglects to protect—he allows his child unregulated liberty; or he overprotects—he locks the child up. When we neglect to protect, believing that we are offering our children freedom, they become enslaved to their passions. Children who are not protected by their fathers eventually feel unloved and uncared for.

Discipline in the form of protection is essential for a child to experience a father's love. "For those whom the Lord loves He disciplines, and He punishes every son He receives" (Heb 12:6). Discipline as a form of protection is a divine expression of love. Why? Because when you protect your child from something, you are actually preparing them for something greater.

The other parenting disorder is overprotecting. When a father overprotects, he suffocates his children's hopes, dreams, and aspirations. He locks them up in his rigid world of rules, using religion as a means to keep his child in check and modify his behavior.

A father who overprotects resorts to using scare tactics to control his child. The overprotective father conditions his child to believe that everything is bad. Television is bad, sex is bad, friends

PILLAR 3: ASSUME YOUR AUTHORITY [EMBRACE CHARITABLE AUTHORITY]

are bad. This type of repression will only cause the child to despise God's goodness in creation, or to overindulge in it.

The golden mean between neglecting and overprotecting is to "protect for the purpose of injecting." During a child's early years of formation, a father is more protective to ensure that a strong moral foundation is established in his child. As the child demonstrates that he is building upon that foundation—being trustworthy with the freedom given to him—a father can begin to trust more and protect less.

A father of a five-year-old boy who desires to be a fireman doesn't give him an ax and a fireman's hat, and throw him into an inferno. A father who is a protector trains his child for years about fire, its goodness, its power, and its ability to destroy. He teaches his child to respect and master fire.

You and I will become true protectors when we train our children—for years—to see goodness in everything, while also teaching them the art of identifying the counterfeits.

> **TAKE THE LEAD** Determine if you neglect to protect, or overprotect your children? If you discover that you are leaning in one direction more than the other, identify ways to find the golden mean, which is to develop a relationship with your child based on trust. Consider situations in which you can give your child the opportunity to build trust. If your children prove to be trustworthy, affirm them in what they have done. If they have broken your trust, try not to immediately blame your child, but rather examine why your child may not trust you. Rather than blaming your child for breaking your trust, ask yourself where you have undermined your child's trust in you. Perhaps with this in mind, you can discuss rebuilding trust in your relationship with your child.

* See Examen *Protect* on page 448

THE SIX ENEMIES

142. YOUR POWERHOUSE

Do you desire to have a family that merely survives the world's assaults or a family that changes the world, winning it for Christ? Do you desire that your family become a powerhouse that gives power to the house of God, the Church?

The family is the fundamental cell of society. As the family goes, so goes the world. This is the power and influence of the family. But what is the power behind this "cell" of the family?

You—the human father.

In the human body, mitochondria are organelles that exist within a cell that make it a "powerhouse." By converting nutrients and oxygen through a process called aerobic respiration, mitochondria enable the cell to breathe and generate ATP (energy needed for the cell to metabolize). Mitochondria provide 90 percent of the energy needed to sustain life and organ function. Without it, most animals, including humans, could not exist, because oxygen would not be transferred into the cell to create energy.

What mitochondria is to the cell, a father is to his family. If the cell of the family is to breathe with the Holy Spirit, a father must convert the information from the foreign, outside world into safe material for his family to ensure that his family thrive.

Mitochondria is comprised of membranes that filter out particles that bombard the organelle. The innermost fine-tuned membranes of the mitochondria are called the cristae. The folds in the cristae membrane ensure that the best molecules are used to make energy and increase cell respiration.

The human father is like cristae, or Christ, in that he filters out the junk of the world, while ensuring that only what is good will be accepted into the "cell" of his family. Like the cristae, a father is called to maximize the "energy" of the family by serving his family as Christ serves the Church.

There is a tendency among some fathers to fearfully reject all that the world offers, believing it to be malicious in nature. This rejection is often a rejection of God's gifts and resources given to man. It is a father's duty to discern which resources are good, useful, and beneficial to his family, while keeping what has potential to harm his family out.

You can help make your family into a powerhouse by converting the elements of the outside world into what will help your family change the world.

> **TAKE THE LEAD** Over the course of the last several reflections, the enemy has been exposed. Remember, there exists a tendency among men to have a knee-jerk reaction to such truths and force their families to go cold turkey, demanding that all technological devices be burned at the stake. This will certainly drive your children away from Christ. On the other hand, you will be tempted to disregard these enemies as not being real, and to believe that your pure, innocent child is above such temptations. Don't let the devil fool you. Again, discuss with your wife tactics and strategies to gradually reclaim your home as a kingdom of God. Remember, this will not be a quick fix, but rather an ongoing project.*

* See Examen *Protect* on page 448

PROVIDING

143. DOMINION OVER WORK—OR DOES WORK DOMINATE YOU?

Are you tired, emotionally exhausted, overwhelmed, stressed, and burdened? Are obligations, duties, and responsibilities bearing down upon you? Is the weight of financial duress, home repairs, or the desire to keep up with your neighbors and friends causing you to be anxious? If you answered yes to any of these questions, consider yourself normal. The aforementioned stressors are indications that you are living in the tenacious battle of fatherhood.

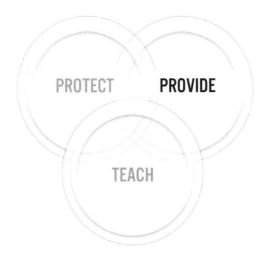

The evil one knows that the human father is the key to the renewal of the Church and the conversion of the world. His objective is to take you down, to remove your ability to be intentional, to distract your attention from your vocation, from your family. His goal is to rob you of your physical, emotional, and spiritual fervor. Work and finances are the key fronts upon which the evil one will engage you and attempt to distract and destroy your ability to lead. Why? Because inherent in your being is an authentic desire to be a provider. Yet, the devil uses this desire against us, to betray us, so that in our effort to provide materially, we neglect to provide spiritually. We neglect to lead our children to heaven.

A father's life is comprised of multiple ongoing responsibilities that pertain to three categories: God, family, and work. In the beginning, God gave Adam two fundamental commands: first, "Be fruitful and multiply; fill the earth and subdue it." Second, "Dress and keep the garden." In other words, work at raising a family, and raise a family by working.

These two commands and our efforts to integrate the two worlds of work and family can often bite at each other and torment the human father if they are not integrated by the One who issued the commands. You and I live in continual tension between the two spheres of family and work. Work is a tremendous gift from God. It affords opportunities to unlock our creativity, passions, to express and use our talents, to collaborate, to exercise the mind and body; and it enables us to provide for our families. Work is good.

However, excessive focus on work can cause us to neglect our vocation of fatherhood; on the other hand, if we focus too little on work, we become slothful, and by our erroneous example teach our children to do the same.

Our challenge as fathers is to have dominion over our work without work dominating us. Work is to be the servant of our vocation, rather than our vocation being at the service of our work.

Let us ask St. Joseph, the model of all workers, who used his work as a means to build the temple of his domestic church, his family, to aid us in placing our occupation at the service of our vocation.

> **TAKE THE LEAD** Has your occupation mastered you, or are you the master of your occupation? Are you able to say no to the boss for the purpose of saying yes to your family? Are you able to shut down the smartphone while at home with the family, or do you shut down in front of the family while using your smartphone? During your fifteen-minute prayer time with God, ask Him if your occupation is truly at the service of your vocation. Ask Him what tactics should be implemented to regain and maintain a proper balance between your occupation and your vocation.*

---

* See Examen *Provide* on page 449

PROVIDING

144. THE DIVINE PURPOSE OF WORK

What is the divine purpose of your work? Why did God create work? Why do we labor? Obviously, we labor for the purpose of earning a wage. But is money the ultimate reason why we work? Christ gives us the answer to this perplexing question in the account of His feeding the multitudes with the loaves and fishes.

After Jesus multiplied the loaves and fishes, feeding approximately five thousand men—not including the women and children—the crowds followed Jesus in hopes of discovering and obtaining the power to do what Jesus did—multiply food without labor. It is in this context that Jesus gives the definitive statement regarding work: "Do not labor for the food that perishes, but labor for that which the Son of Man will give you" (Jn 6:27).

Our Lord discloses the ultimate reason and purpose for our work: We are to labor in order to provide materially for ourselves and our children. And yet, Jesus conveys a greater purpose: labor for the Bread of Life—for Jesus Himself.

Which raises the question: How do we work for Jesus? First, we orient our day, our labor schedule—as much as reasonably possible—around Jesus and our scheduled prayer times. We schedule our work around Jesus, rather than scheduling Jesus around our work.

Second, we make receiving the Bread of Life the priority of our labors. By doing so, Jesus will empower, inspire, and guide our efforts at work. He promises: "He who abides in Me, I will abide in Him" (Jn 15:4). With Jesus, His wisdom, charity, perseverance, and humility in us, we cannot help but labor more effectively.

Third, we labor for Jesus in our children. Our Lord said, "Whoever receives one such child in my name receives not only Me, but the One who sent me" (Mt 18:5). We receive Jesus in the Eucharist, and in a unique way, we receive Jesus in our children. Considering this, the ultimate purpose of work is to achieve communion with God personally, and to lead our family to communion with God.

PILLAR 3: ASSUME YOUR AUTHORITY [EMBRACE CHARITABLE AUTHORITY]

St. Joseph literally labored for Jesus, the Bread of Life, his son. For Joseph, work was not an end in itself, but was for the purpose of entering into communion with Jesus.

Similarly, your work is at the service of entering and achieving communion with Jesus, who lives in your child. When your labors are oriented in this manner, and work is understood in this way, the burden of work tends to diminish and is eventually replaced—though never completely—with satisfaction and delight.

> **TAKE THE LEAD** Has your occupation mastered you, or are you the master of your occupation? Are you able to say no to the boss for the purpose of saying yes to your family? Are you able to shut down the smartphone while at home with the family, or do you shut down in front of the family while using your smartphone? During your fifteen-minute prayer time with God, ask Him if your occupation is truly at the service of your vocation. Ask Him what tactics should be implemented to regain and maintain a proper balance between your occupation and your vocation.*

* See Examen *Provide* on page 449

PROVIDING

145. THE ENEMIES OF PROVIDING

If the purpose of your work is to aid you and your family in achieving communion with God—which is the highest spiritual goal—it is important that we identify the enemy of an authentic work ethos: the flesh.

The flesh tirelessly bombards us fathers and tempts us to fixate upon the material instead of using the material as a means to focus on the spiritual. Our Lord said, "That which is from flesh is flesh; and that which is born of the Spirit is spirit (Jn 3:6); and it is the "Spirit that gives life, for the flesh is of no avail" (Jn 6:63).

Indeed, "They who are according to the flesh mind the things of the flesh, but they who are according to the spirit mind the things of the spirit. For the inclination of the flesh is death, but the inclination of the spirit is life and peace. For the wisdom of the flesh is hostile to God, for it is not subject to the law of God, nor can it be. And they who are carnal cannot please God" (Rom 8:5–8).

"Therefore, brethren, we are debtors, not to the flesh, that we should live according to the flesh, for if you live according to the flesh you will die; but if by the spirit you put to death the deeds of the flesh you will live" (Rom 8:12–13).

These words sting and can perplex a father who "lives in the world" and confound those of us who interpret the flesh as being the human body. However, the flesh, as used in these citations, is not to be confused with the human body. The body itself is good. When the appetites of body become disordered, those appetites become fleshly. As St. Paul says: the "works of the flesh are manifest, which are immorality, uncleanness, licentiousness, idolatry, witchcrafts, enmities, contentions, jealousies, anger, quarrels, factions, parties, envies, murders, drunkenness, carousing and suchlike" (Gal 5:19–21).

When we live according to the flesh we use work as a means to attain things that feed our disordered passions.

The six enemies of spiritually oriented labor are: 1) debt (financial worries and instability, which is caused by living beyond our means); 2) ego (using our labor to "keep up with the neighbors," to maintain an "image"; 3) need to be needed (a disordered desire to be wanted and noticed for our work and contribution, subconsciously believing that we have to be continually producing to have value); 4) avoiding investing time in the family (immersing ourselves in work to avoid what may be considered as the "trivialities" of life); 5) avoiding spending time with God (maintaining busyness while neglecting prayer time); and 6) the belief that there is not enough time (work receives the first and best of our time).

Let us ask St. Joseph to obtain for us the grace from God to examine honestly the motivations behind our labors, while also asking him to help us labor for what is eternal—our family's salvation.

> **TAKE THE LEAD** Has your occupation mastered you, or are you the master of your occupation? Are you able to say no to the boss for the purpose of saying yes to your family? Are you able to shut down the smartphone while at home with the family, or do you shut down in front of the family while using your smartphone? During your fifteen-minute prayer time with God, ask Him if your occupation is truly at the service of your vocation. Ask Him what tactics should be implemented to regain and maintain a proper balance between your occupation and your vocation.*

* See Examen *Provide* on page 449

PROVIDING

146. IS IT GOOD ENOUGH?

A father is responsible for using his talents, energies, skills, intellect, will, and passions to provide food, shelter, and clothing for his family. And yet there is a grave temptation to believe that by providing material goods for our family it is "good enough." However, Jesus asks us, "Is not life more than eating and clothing (see Lk 12:23; Mt 6:25–34). What is this "more" that Jesus speaks of?

A shortsighted, temporal vision of providing material goods prevents a father from using those material goods to direct his family to greater spiritual realities—to the "more" that God desires us to have. In other words, if a father does not recognize that God the Father has provided for his fatherhood in order that he may provide for his children—to ensure that they come to believe in the heavenly Father's provision and generosity—he can easily slip into a disordered enslavement to the flesh, with its heavy yoke of concupiscence. When we cut ourselves off from our ultimate spiritual end, we are left with the task of expecting the infinite, the glorious, from material, temporal things that cannot satisfy the human hearts longing for love.

To provide for the flesh in this way ultimately leads to the death of a child's soul. Why? Because when a child witnesses his father providing primarily for the flesh, the child begins to believe that the meaning of life is to acquire goods rather than to use goods to acquire the Spirit.

What is the purpose of providing shelter, clothing, or food? Too often we can hyperfocus on temporal realities rather than the spiritual goal. A father provides shelter to ensure that his home not only protects his family from the elements, but also so that his home becomes a domestic church. A father provides food not only to nourish his child's body, but also as a symbol and reminder of the heavenly Father's provision and generosity. A father provides clothing to ensure that his child not only be protected from physical exposure, but also that the child begin to comprehend God the Father's desire

PILLAR 3: ASSUME YOUR AUTHORITY [EMBRACE CHARITABLE AUTHORITY]

to clothe the child in Christ, with the dignity and power of salvation, and that the child's soul may not be exposed to evil.

Providing temporally is essential to understanding how to provide spiritually. When a father enters the practicality of providing temporally, he can deduce spiritual conclusions, which help him move beyond an "it's good enough" attitude.

To provide temporally without a spiritual motivation is not "good enough." But to provide temporally while striving to maintain a spiritual outlook will draw you into the reality of God the Father's continual, benevolent giving and provision for you. When you begin to comprehend the generosity of the Father, you will become a most generous father.

> **TAKE THE LEAD** Has your occupation mastered you, or are you the master of your occupation? Are you able to say no to the boss for the purpose of saying yes to your family? Are you able to shut down the smartphone while at home with the family, or do you shut down in front of the family while using your smartphone? During your fifteen-minute prayer time with God, ask Him if your occupation is truly at the service of your vocation. Ask Him what tactics should be implemented to regain and maintain a proper balance between your occupation and your vocation.*

* See Examen *Provide* on page 449

PROVIDING

147. YOU ARE IRREPLACEABLE

Do you sense that you could be trudging through a series of cycles of days, months, and years, which involve working, eating, sleeping, and beginning this process again, for the sole purpose of providing for the flesh? When this occurs, a father's vitality and vibrancy of life, which is afforded by the Holy Spirit, is stolen by the evil one.

When a father is robbed of such vitality, his children are also robbed of the life that was originally intended to be transmitted through his example to his family.

To maintain and increase this vibrancy and vitality that the Holy Spirit offers to us through our work, our work must have an eternal perspective.

To overcome the flesh and live in the vibrancy of the Spirit, it is imperative that we place our occupation at the service of our vocation. Keep in mind that your identity is not derived as much from your occupation as from your vocation. At work you are replaceable; but at home you are irreplaceable. Your identity is not founded upon what you "do for a living," but rather upon those for whom you are living.

By means of your occupation, you are fund-raising for your ministry—your family. Your family is not at the service of work and goods; but goods and work are at the service of your family. Grace builds upon nature, and therefore it is important that we fathers utilize the goods that God provides in order to provide our family a path to the ultimate goal.

One of the key ways by which you can use the goods that God has provided for the purpose of leading your children to the ultimate Good, is by thanking God—in the presence of your family—for God's provision. Often, we believe that God only desires us to sacrifice, that is, to give up a good. At times, this is true. However, God discloses to us emphatically throughout the Scriptures that the sacrifice He most desires is the sacrifice of thanksgiving and praise.

When we offer this type of praise to God, the vibrancy of the Spirit returns and we begin to see all of life as a gift. This joyful receptivity to God's goodness cannot help but "infect" our children.

You are the guide who leads your family in this ode of thanks and praise, and this is why you are irreplaceable.

> **TAKE THE LEAD** Has your occupation mastered you, or are you the master of your occupation? Are you able to say no to the boss for the purpose of saying yes to your family? Are you able to shut down the smartphone while at home with the family, or do you shut down in front of the family while using your smartphone? During your fifteen-minute prayer time with God, ask Him if your occupation is truly at the service of your vocation. Ask Him what tactics should be implemented to regain and maintain a proper balance between your occupation and your vocation.*

* See Examen *Provide* on page 449

PROVIDING

148. WORKING FOR RESPECT

If a man's foundational, innate need is to be respected, work can often become the vehicle by which he attempts to obtain praise, validity, and the respect and admiration of his peers.

"Work can often be the mistress that steals time and attention from our wives and children" (Matthew Pinto, author and speaker). Why do so many men rob their families of their presence and instead "burn the midnight oil," working countless hours of overtime, often missing family dinner, children's activities, and family time?

One reason for this dynamic is that often at home a father doesn't receive the accolades, honors, and affirmation that he desires and may authentically need. Consequently, we fathers can often surrender to the temptation to be noticed by men; we may place ourselves and our work on stage in the public sphere, with the underlying motivation for human respect rather than being known by God. The respect of men, however, is shifting sand upon which we should not build our kingdom.

The reason that we should not attempt to base our life on winning human respect is because our identity leads to our destiny. Attempting to win and maintain human respect will eventually push us away from our true identity—who God has created us to be. Why? Today, we may have the admiration of those around us; but tomorrow, we may fall into disgrace. The man who chooses to be noticed by men changes his behaviors, personality, clothing, friends, and pursuits in his desire to win the praise of others. He eventually becomes enslaved to their perception of him. When this occurs, he distances himself from his true identity and becomes incapable of discovering his true, God-given destiny.

We do not remember St. Joseph for any of his works of carpentry, yet today he is the most known and lauded father of all time—precisely because of his fatherhood.

God is a hidden God, a hidden Father, and we are called to be like St. Joseph, to be icons of God the Father, "Who is in secret" (Mt 6:1).

Rather than avoiding the reality and perhaps pain of not receiving the affirmation we desire at home, and attempting to overcome this deficit by working more hours, let us strive to embrace our vocation with greater intention, working to win our children's hearts for God. Perhaps then we will begin to experience the true affirmation and respect that is founded upon love.

> **TAKE THE LEAD** Has your occupation mastered you, or are you the master of your occupation? Are you able to say no to the boss for the purpose of saying yes to your family? Are you able to shut down the smartphone while at home with the family, or do you shut down in front of the family while using your smartphone? During your fifteen-minute prayer time with God, ask Him if your occupation is truly at the service of your vocation. Ask Him what tactics should be implemented to regain and maintain a proper balance between your occupation and your vocation.*

* See Examen *Provide* on page 449

THE SIGN OF A TRUSTING SON

149: THE RISK OF PLAYING CATCH-UP

Have you ever felt as though there is not enough time to meet the ever-pressing demands of life? Whether we are attempting to dig ourselves out of a despairing financial situation, trying to complete several fixer-upper projects around the house, meeting pressing deadlines at work, attempting to put more money in the bank, or trying to obtain that long-desired promotion, there never seems to be enough time in which to achieve these ideals.

Where can a father find the time needed to catch up? After exhausting the hours of a typical work week, and working late nights, many men consider Sunday as a viable time to "get ahead." And why not? Sunday appears to be a day in which most of the world sleeps in, and the phone rarely rings.

Yet, employers have realized that men have difficulty restraining themselves from working on Sunday. Businesses remain open, buying, selling, and trading on the Day of the Lord for the purpose of increasing revenue. Many men understand Sunday as a day to make more money, or increase the value of their home, or get ahead on work. And yet, quite often, many men who work on Sunday remain in their pitiful situation. Why? Because when a man works on the Lord's Day, he is choosing to do it his way and not God's way. To an overconfident, self-reliant, independent man, this may not sound too bad. Most of us think that we can accomplish great good on our own. Perhaps we ought to examine more carefully Jesus' admonition: "Apart from Me you can do nothing" (Jn 15:5). Truth does not lie.

If a man is a Christian and is decidedly disobedient to God's commands, he denies the very source of his own authority. When a man uses, or rather misuses, his own authority to deny the One who has authority over him, he disobediently steps outside the realm of grace, becomes highly vulnerable, and is left to deal with the devil on his own—without God's divine protection.

PILLAR 3: ASSUME YOUR AUTHORITY [EMBRACE CHARITABLE AUTHORITY]

This is precisely why many men who labor for gain on Sunday lack interior peace, are continually overwhelmed with anxiety, and suffer from mental and emotional fatigue.

St. Joseph was a just man, which means that he was a righteous man who devoutly submitted to and fulfilled God's law. St. Joseph, being just, did not waver from obediently fulfilling the Lord's command to "Keep holy the Sabbath." Joseph's example reminds fathers that it is not enough to abstain from servile labor on Sunday, but to make every attempt to "keep it holy."

A just man understands that it is just to give to the giving God His due. And yet, God asks so little, only for us to obey, that we may have much.

> **TAKE THE LEAD** How do you spend your Sundays? Most of the Ten Commandments are negative; that is, they are composed of "Thou shall nots." However, the command regarding the Sabbath is positive in character: Keep holy the Sabbath. What does it mean to make something holy? It simply means to set it aside for God, and to do with it as God desires. Take some time over the next several reflections to identify ways to reclaim Sunday for God. Remember, the command is not negative—it's not "Don't miss Mass or you'll burn in Hell." The command is positive: How can I rejoice with my family in a spirit of gratitude and joy? Attending Holy Mass is certainly a part of that gratitude. Now it is up to you to take the joy that is derived from the Mass and carry it out during the rest of the day.*

* See Examen *Provide* on page 449

LEAD | THE FOUR MARKS OF FATHERLY GREATNESS

THE SIGN OF A TRUSTING SON

150. SLAVE OR SON?

What is the point of keeping holy the Lord's Day? What real significance does it have on your life? We find an answer to these questions in the creation account.

THE HUMAN FATHER'S 3 WORLDS

Excessive focus on material goods, ego (success), getting ahead, causes a father to neglect the spiritual responsibilities of fatherhood and become preoccupied with work

Excessive preoccupation on family, marital problems, hobbies, or a consequence of laziness, lack of motivation, depression diminish a man's motivation to work

Till and keep the garden.   **GOD'S COMMANDS**   Increase and multiply.

Spirit of the Lord's Day
1) Thanksgiving that God has provided
2) Trust that God will provide

Man uses work to glorify God by working for Jesus -
the food that will not perish

Recall that man was created on the sixth day along with the animals. This indicates that man is like the animals and has roots in the animal kingdom. However, man is different than the animals in that he was created with a soul, an intellect, an ability to meditate, order his passions, and commune with God.

God created man on the sixth day but has made him for the seventh day. In the creation account, the seventh day was the day that God "rested" from creating the heavens and the earth. God commands every man to imitate His divine example by resting on the seventh day.

The seventh day rest was established by God to provide a time in which God could rest in man and man could rest in God. Other days may pass by without a specific marked time for communion with God; however, the seventh-day rest is ordained by God as a way for us to abide in Him and Him in us.

The sixth day is a symbol of the beast. The intention of the ultimate beast, the devil, is to make us like animals, who are burdened and enslaved, who spend their lives consuming and being consumed by the world. God commands the seventh day to be a day when man can cease being like a beast and become a son.

The seventh-day rest is a sign of the covenant between God and man. Instead of a contract—man exchanging goods with man—God and man enter a covenant—an exchange between God with man.

Prior to becoming a great father, you and I must become faithful sons; and to be faithful sons we must learn to trust in the Father. Jesus warned, "Unless you become like a little child you will not inherit the Kingdom of God" (Mt 18:3). Our eternal salvation depends upon us becoming childlike sons. To be a childlike son demands that we relax from the burden of the beast, consuming things and being consumed by things, and trust that God will provide. God wills to free us from enslavement to the sixth day. This demands that we demonstrate our faith in Him by resting with God on the seventh day.

If we choose to neglect His command to rest and focus on attaining wealth, "We become like the rich who lack understanding, and are like the beasts that are destroyed" (see Ps 42:9).

If you desire to be a father who is trusted with God's favor, it is vital that first you become a trustworthy son, who expresses his trust in the Father by resting in God on the Lord's Day.

TAKE THE LEAD How do you spend your Sundays? Most of the Ten Commandments are negative; that is, they are composed of "Thou shall nots." However, the command regarding the Sabbath is positive in character: Keep holy the Sabbath. What does it mean to make something holy? It simply means to set it aside for God, and to do with it as God desires. Take some time over the next several reflections to identify ways to reclaim Sunday for God. Remember, the command is not negative—it's not "Don't miss Mass or you'll burn in Hell." The command is positive: How can I rejoice with my family in a spirit of gratitude and joy? Attending Holy Mass is certainly a part of that gratitude. Now it is up to you to take the joy that is derived from the Mass and carry it out during the rest of the day.*

---

* See Examen *Provide* on page 449

THE SIGN OF A TRUSTING SON

151. THE SIGN OF THE COVENANT

Why can it be so challenging to restrain oneself from working on the Lord's Day? Recall that to be a true son demands trust. Trust is the foundation of every true relationship. Keeping the Lord's Day offers man the opportunity to express two things: first, his thanks and gratitude for God's provision during the previous week; second, his faith and trust that God will continue to provide during the following week.

The law of the Sabbath rest, what Christians call the Lord's Day, is a sign of God's covenant with His people. (The ultimate sign of the covenant is the Eucharist, which is offered primarily in the context of the Lord's Day.) A contract is a commitment to an exchange of goods between persons, whereas a covenant is an exchange of persons—for good.

The Lord's Day is a covenant comprised of an exchange of oaths between God and man. God promises that He will provide for man, and man promises to be thankful for what has been given, while also trusting that God will continue to provide.

Obedience to this covenant is an expression of a childlike trust in and dependence on the Father's generosity. When we labor for wages, carry out our own pursuits, and neglect to commune with God on the Lord's Day, we become slaves to Satan, beasts who break faith; we negate the covenant and rather than inheriting God's blessing we incur a curse.

In the Exodus account, God commanded the Israelites to gather manna for six days, on the sixth day gathering double the amount, for on the seventh day they were to rest from gathering. However, some of the Israelites mistrusted, and either hoarded too much manna, or set out to gather it on the Sabbath. Because of this, the manna bred worms and some of the people perished.

The Israelites were commanded to give rest to the land every seventh year, which meant no planting or harvesting of crops. Yet, the Israelites failed to fulfill seventy Sabbath years, and therefore received the punishment of being deported to Babylon for seventy Sabbath years (490) in order to give rest to the land.

How do these accounts relate to us?

Those who attempt to achieve success by working on the Lord's Day may initially experience some success; however, their work will eventually betray them, come to ruin, or cause them to lose much, if not all, of what they have gained. Often, we sense that we are spinning our wheels, taking two steps forward and two steps back. We must ask ourselves: do I regard the Lord's Day as a delight?

The Israelites always had enough. They were given the promised land, which contained cities, crops, farms, and produce of the former inhabitants of that land—and yet they wanted more.

As Isaiah said, "If you refrain from trampling the Sabbath, from *following your own pursuits* on my holy day; if you call the Sabbath a delight; the Lord's holy day glorious; If you glorify *it by not following your ways, seeking your own interests, or pursuing your own affairs*—Then you shall delight in the Lord, and I will make you ride upon the heights of the earth; I will nourish you with the heritage of Jacob, your father, for the mouth of the Lord has spoken."

God will not be outdone in generosity.

> **TAKE THE LEAD** How do you spend your Sundays? Most of the Ten Commandments are negative; that is, they are composed of "Thou shall nots." However, the command regarding the Sabbath is positive in character: Keep holy the Sabbath. What does it mean to make something holy? It simply means to set it aside for God, and to do with it as God desires. Take some time over the next several reflections to identify ways to reclaim Sunday for God. Remember, the command is not negative—it's not "Don't miss Mass or you'll burn in Hell." The command is positive: How can I rejoice with my family in a spirit of gratitude and joy? Attending Holy Mass is certainly a part of that gratitude. Now it is up to you to take the joy that is derived from the Mass and carry it out during the rest of the day.*

---

* See Examen *Provide* on page 449

GIVING GOD YOUR WORK

152. WHY ARE YOU DISTRACTED?

Have you ever had the experience of hearing your child carry on for minutes describing something, and realizing afterward that you didn't actually listen to what was said? Very often, our bodies are present to our children, while our minds are elsewhere. Where does your mind go? What are you thinking about when you "check out"?

If we examine our thoughts on such occasions, we usually come to the conclusion that we are preoccupied with a current dilemma, challenge, conflict, deadline, or aspiration. A father's soul is continually burdened with to-do lists and problem solving. When a particular conversation isn't related to one of the problems we need to solve, or tasks on our to-do list, or if we lack a personal interest in it, we default to being mentally preoccupied with our burdens.

If we probe further into this experience, we may realize that we continually mull over these distractions because fundamentally we lack trust in God. When we lack trust in God, we are burdened with the incredible pressure of solving our difficulties ourselves. In a sense, we forget to believe that God will help solve that problem when the time comes. When we forget that God is with us, we misuse the present moment, in which we are to be available to those around us, and instead become distracted with what burdens us. This is a very common experience for every father.

Blessed is the father who can trust God the Father enough to momentarily set aside his worries, angsts, anxieties, and doubts for the purpose of entering into communion with his loved ones.

Work will take as much as you give it. And if you give it your attention when you are supposed to be giving your child your attention, you have allowed your work and worries to dominate you. This only multiplies your anxieties.

"Anxiety is the soul's greatest enemy except for sin . . . . When the heart is anxious and disquieted within itself, it loses the power to preserve those virtues already acquired . . . and the means of resisting the temptations of Satan, who never fails to fish in such troubled waters" (St. Francis de Sales).

Our Lord advises us, "Do not be anxious about your life, for your Father knows that you need all things. But seek first the kingdom of God and His justice, and all these things will be given you besides" (Mt 6:33). You and I, as fathers, are to seek the Kingdom of God, which is the communion of the Trinity, in our children, in our family. You owe God, your wife, and children this justice: to be present to them in the present moment. To commune with them.

Give your doubts, mistrust, and anxiety to God, enter into the present moment with your wife or with your child, and "do not be anxious about tomorrow; for tomorrow will have anxieties of its own." Simply remind yourself, "I am provided for in this moment—and that is good enough."

> **TAKE THE LEAD** Make family dinner a constant staple in your family's life. Identify those things that prove to be obstacles to family dinner and be intentional about removing them as much as possible. As leader of your family, make every effort to gather the family around the food, and while doing so, lead your family in giving thanks to God for His protection, provision and love given that day.*

* See Examen *Provide* on page 449

GIVING GOD YOUR WORK

153. GOD'S SUPERNATURAL LAW OF GLORY

Recall that there are basically two types of people: those who use the glory bestowed upon them to draw people to themselves; and those who use themselves to draw people to God's glory. When we analyze the varied and multiple motivations behind our labors and works, these two fundamental reasons are the motivation behind all the others: to give glory to God by your work, or to work to bring glory to yourself.

You and I continually live in the tension between the old Adam and the New Adam. The old, original Adam caved in to the temptation of mistrusting God's benevolence, believing that God did not want to share His glory. But Jesus, the New Adam, proclaimed, "The glory that You [the Father] have given Me, I have given to them [us] that they may be one, even as we are one" (Jn 17:22).

The Father shares His glory unreservedly with the Son, and the Son shares His glory unreservedly with us; and we are to use this glory to draw people together, particularly our family, "that they may be one"—in God.

Is your work at the service of glorifying God? Ask yourself, "Do I use my work to draw attention to my individual abilities, talents, and gifts, my personal, individual glory; or do I use the glory God has imparted to me for the purpose of sharing with others the glory of God, that they may also rejoice in God's glory?

"St. Joseph, a 'righteous man' whom Divine Providence placed alongside Jesus and Mary to provide the Holy Family with his daily labor, reminds us that the ways of salvation also pass through human work and invite us to seize the opportunities it offers. In performing his duty, St. Joseph presents himself as a man capable of affecting synthesis between faith and life, between the demands of God and those of man, between personal needs and the good of others" (Pope St. John Paul II).

St. Joseph simply performed his duty for the glory of God, and God glorified St. Joseph. This is God's supernatural law of glory:

glorify God in your work, and God cannot help but work to glorify you.

> **TAKE THE LEAD** Make family dinner a constant staple in your family's life. Identify those things that prove to be obstacles to family dinner and be intentional about removing them as much as possible. As leader of your family, make every effort to gather the family around the food, and while doing so, lead your family in giving thanks to God for His protection, provision and love given that day.*

* See Examen *Provide* on page 449

GIVING GOD YOUR WORK

154. EATING TO GLORIFY GOD

Let's return to St. Paul's admonition: "Whether you eat or drink, or do anything else, do all for the glory of God" (1 Cor 10:31). Which raises a question: How can we eat and drink in a manner that brings glory to God? The answer to this question is fundamental to becoming a father of glory.

God, through the psalmist, declares, "He who offers the sacrifice of praise [thanksgiving], honors me." (Ps 49:23).

One of the purposes behind our work—perhaps one of the most important—is to work in order to gather food, and to gather the family around that food in a spirit of thanksgiving and praise to God.

Meals with the family, especially family dinner, afford us fathers the opportunity to "eat and drink for the glory of God" by "offering the sacrifice of thanksgiving" to God for all that He has given. This is one of the most effective ways to honor God and to develop a spirit of thanksgiving in your children.

When a child witnesses his father's thanksgiving for the food gathered and the family gathered around that food, the child learns that the heart of a relationship with the Father is thanksgiving.

Family dinner, approached in this way, becomes a symbol of the Mass. In the Mass, our heavenly Father gives us "His food—His Bread—His Son's Body and Blood." God the Father gathers us—His children—around His Son in the Eucharist, which is the Greek word for thanksgiving. As God's children, we enter Jesus' thanksgiving sacrifice and gather this "Bread" into ourselves, and by doing so, the Father gathers us to Himself.

You as a father, also gather your children in thanksgiving around your table. Your table, then, becomes a type of the altar, upon which a father's sacrifice of thanksgiving is offered. You, as the father, become a symbol of the priest, who gathers his family, his congregation, to God. God designed family dinner to draw us into His Family.

St. Joseph gathered food by means of his work, and by doing so, he gathered his family around that food; and consequently, Joseph's family was gathered to God in an ode of thanksgiving and praise. Joseph literally fed bread to the Bread of Life, and from this "Bread" we all receive life.

In a similar manner, if you gather your children around your thanksgiving sacrifice, you will be planting within them the desire to offer their own thanksgiving sacrifice, which glorifies God. Indeed, "[t]he one who offers thanksgiving as his sacrifice glorifies Me" (Ps 49:23).

> **TAKE THE LEAD** Make family dinner a constant staple in your family's life. Identify those things that prove to be obstacles to family dinner and be intentional about removing them as much as possible. As leader of your family, make every effort to gather the family around the food, and while doing so, lead your family in giving thanks to God for His protection, provision and love given that day.*

* See Examen *Provide* on page 449

TEACHING

155. THE FUNDAMENTAL LESSON OF FREEDOM

The very essence of fatherly leadership is to be a teacher, and at the heart and core of a father's teaching is the lesson of freedom. But what is true freedom? Modern man believes freedom is the ability to do what I want, when I want, how I want. This is not freedom, but slavery. For example, if an alcoholic cannot deny himself a beer, is he truly free while drinking that beer? He believes that he can do as he pleases—that he is free. Yet, in reality, he cannot overcome his disordered passions, and therefore cannot do what would truly please him.

"To teach in order to lead others to faith is the task of every preacher and believer" (St. Thomas Aquinas). A father is one who teaches by word and example in order to lead his child to faith in God, which affords true freedom.

Freedom + love = happiness. Heaven and communion with God is the "place" of ultimate happiness. Freedom, which is derived from obedience to God + love, and which is living in the Spirit (rather than the flesh), affords true, enduring happiness that the world cannot offer.

If a father neglects his responsibility to protect and provide, he will eventually encounter the relentless and ruthless enemy, the devil, who will induce a father's child to rebel against his fatherly authority. To avoid the rebellion that is of the devil, it is imperative that a father teach his child that the fruit of lived obedience to God is the ultimate, authentic liberation for which Christ has set us free (Gal 5:1).

Only by believing and living the Lord's Word can a person attain true freedom, as Christ Himself attests:

Everyone therefore who hears these words and acts upon them, shall be likened to a wise man who built his house on rock. And everyone who hears these words and does not act upon them, shall be likened to a foolish man who built his house on sand. And the rain fell, and the floods came, and the winds blew and beat against that house, and it fell and was utterly ruined" (Mt 7:24–27).

The father who hears the words of Christ and acts upon them experiences the freedom of a life that cannot be destroyed by the devil, whereas a man who believes himself to be "free" from the words of Christ is enslaved to pride, and the "life" that he builds will eventually fall into ruin.

"The truth shall set you free" (Gal 5:1). Considering this, it is imperative that you, as a father, understand, live, and embody the truth of Christ's teachings in order to transmit to your children the knowledge that obedience to Jesus' truth is true freedom—a freedom that leads to true happiness.

> **TAKE THE LEAD** Over the course of the following reflections, make it your aim to study your children's behavior. Identify those behaviors and actions that are agreeable to you, and those that you resent. Now, evaluate your behaviors and actions and honestly discern similarities between you and your child. At this point, if you're honest, you will arrive at a deeper awareness of why your example is the most effective form of teaching. Don't despair. If something in your behavior needs changing, simply ask God for the grace and resolve to do it.*

---

* See Examen *Teach* on page 450

PILLAR 3: ASSUME YOUR AUTHORITY [EMBRACE CHARITABLE AUTHORITY]

TEACHING

156. THE MOST EFFECTIVE TEACHER

Perhaps you've heard someone say, "Do as I say—not as I do." This is perhaps one of the most ineffective forms of teaching because it expresses the height of arrogant hypocrisy: to expect others to submit to rules, while believing yourself exempt from those rules. Initially, a child may obey the words and commands of their parents out of reverence, or fear; but if the parents do not "do as they say," eventually a child will do the same.

Our children will more often follow and imitate our example rather than our words. As one son said to his father, "I listen to fifty percent of what you say and one hundred percent of what you do."

The most effective teacher is Jesus Christ. How can it be that after two thousand years of Jesus' brief life on earth, His teachings are not only taken seriously, but embodied by so many? The answer is simple: Jesus lived what He taught and taught what He lived.

The prophet Isaiah indicated that the father has been divinely endowed with the powerful role of teaching: "Fathers shall make [God's] truth known to [His] children" (Isaiah 38:19). Our duty as fathers is to make God's truth known to our children, and we do this by example and word—but primarily by our example. In other words, like Christ, we live what we teach and teach what we live.

A father's words must be informed by the Father's Word, and his example must imitate Christ's example. Indeed, a father's word ought to reflect his example, and his example should reflect the Word. Your example is primary, while your words are secondary. Your example makes your words worthy of belief.

If you desire your child to be obedient to your word, it is essential that you be obedient to the Father's Word. Then you will be like Christ: a most effective teacher.

> **TAKE THE LEAD** Over the course of the following reflections, make it your aim to study your children's behavior. Identify those behaviors and actions that are agreeable

> to you, and those that you resent. Now, evaluate your behaviors and actions and honestly discern similarities between you and your child. At this point, if you're honest, you will arrive at a deeper awareness of why your example is the most effective form of teaching. Don't despair. If something in your behavior needs changing, simply ask God for the grace and resolve to do it.*

* See Examen *Teach* on page 450

PILLAR 3: ASSUME YOUR AUTHORITY [EMBRACE CHARITABLE AUTHORITY]

TEACHING

157. THE MOST VALUABLE LESSON

If you could teach your child only one lesson, what would that lesson be? There are countless essential life lessons, but there does appear to be an eternal lesson upon which all other lessons are built.

The human father teaches his children by authoring the story of God's glory in his children's and wife's life. The greatest lesson a father can teach is the lesson of God's glory—what it is, and how to experience it.

The glory of God is eternal, perpetual self-donation, and being made in God's image and likeness, our glory is to have and experience God's glory. Our glory as father-leaders is discovered by giving ourselves away in service to others. This self-giving is not to be confused with self-exploitation, that is, allowing oneself to be abused or misused by another. In its proper form, this being *for* the other is the most effective form of leadership.

A successful leader is characterized by his silent sacrifice freely given on behalf of his subjects—a sacrifice offered without boastfulness on one hand, or complaint on the other.

Jesus, the most effective and successful leader in human history (this is evident by the enduring character of the Church and the response of His faithful followers throughout the centuries), is the most self-sacrificial man who has ever existed.

Referring to Christ's words during the Last Supper, Pope Benedict XVI speaks of the self-sacrificial character of Christ: "Recent theology has rightly underlined the use of the word 'for' in all four [Gospel] accounts, a word that may be considered key not only to the Last Supper accounts, but to the figure of Jesus overall. His entire being is expressed by the word 'pro-existence'—he is there, not for himself, but for others. This is not merely a dimension of his existence, but its *innermost essence* and its entirety. His very being is a 'being-for.' If we are able to grasp this, then we have truly come close to the mystery of Jesus, and we have understood what discipleship is" (Pope Benedict XVI, *Jesus of Nazareth,* Part II).

These words indicate that a father's offering is an "of-for-ring," that is, a self-sacrifice—a living for the other members of his family. This is the most effective way to raise a child to glory, the most effective way to teach, and the most valuable lesson your child may ever learn.

God's glory is expressed in giving Himself to you. Your glory is discovered in giving yourself to God by giving yourself to others—particularly your family.

> **TAKE THE LEAD** Over the course of the following reflections, make it your aim to study your children's behavior. Identify those behaviors and actions that are agreeable to you, and those that you resent. Now, evaluate your behaviors and actions and honestly discern similarities between you and your child. At this point, if you're honest, you will arrive at a deeper awareness of why your example is the most effective form of teaching. Don't despair. If something in your behavior needs changing, simply ask God for the grace and resolve to do it.*

* See Examen *Teach* on page 450

TEACHING

158. TEACH WHAT YOU LIVE; LIVE WHAT YOU TEACH

Often, a young father experiences that confounding moment when the child, who up to this point has been obedient, suddenly rebels, exercises his own will, and acts disobediently. Why are some fathers surprised when their child acts defiantly for the first time? Children generally obey their parents during their early years because of fear and reverence. However, when a child begins to intuit that his or her father does not live what he teaches, the child believes that his father's command is negotiable. The truth is that children emulate and imitate their father's example more so than their words.

Though a father may have relied on the fear factor to ensure his child submits to his authority, the effectiveness of this type of child-rearing won't endure. It is vital that we fathers understand that after the fear and reverence stage "wears off," another form of child-rearing is needed.

If a father desires that his words have lasting impact on his child's life, it is imperative that his example of "being for the other" is intentional, willingly given, and relatively consistent.

Our words must be infused, animated, and supported by the Word. When a child asks questions, is in need of guidance, or is in need of edification, admonition, or encouragement, his father can use examples from everyday life and from his own experience to teach his child life's most valuable lessons.

If your word is to be effective it should never contradict the Word. Therefore, it is essential that you become a man of the Word who reflects upon Scripture. By reflecting on the word, your life will reflect the Word.

There are many men who teach the Word of God but far fewer who live it. To live the Word, the Word must live in you. Our Lord said, "Abide in Me, and I will abide in you" (Jn 15:4). When we abide in Jesus by reflecting and meditating upon His Word daily—particularly the Gospels—the Word will abide in us; and when the Word abides in us, we cannot help but to communicate its truth to our children.

St. Joseph shared the glory that he had received from the Father with God the Son. Indeed, Joseph taught God's word to the Word, primarily by means of his silent example. Joseph lived what Jesus taught, and Jesus taught what Joseph lived. Your children will live what you teach and teach what you live.

> **TAKE THE LEAD** Over the course of the following reflections, make it your aim to study your children's behavior. Identify those behaviors and actions that are agreeable to you, and those that you resent. Now, evaluate your behaviors and actions and honestly discern similarities between you and your child. At this point, if you're honest, you will arrive at a deeper awareness of why your example is the most effective form of teaching. Don't despair. If something in your behavior needs changing, simply ask God for the grace and resolve to do it.*

* See Examen *Teach* on page 450

PILLAR 4

DISCOVER THE DISCIPLE

[Embracing the Child]

GOD ASKS EACH OF US "WHERE ARE YOU?" THIS IS THE PERENNIAL QUESTION THAT HAUNTS THE DEEP SUBCONSCIOUS RECESSES OF MAN'S HEART. THE ANSWER TO THIS QUESTION DETERMINES EACH MAN'S LOCATION IN GOD'S PLAN OF SALVATION, HIS VOCATIONAL MISSION—THE VERY FOUNDATION OF THE SPIRITUALITY OF FATHERHOOD.

A LINK BETWEEN HEAVEN AND EARTH

159. THE GAZE OF THE FATHER

Why is it that many a man, after purchasing a vehicle, catching the big fish, landing the dream job, or finding the dream woman, wants to share his good news with his father first? Is it that we fathers want to make dad proud? It could be. But what lies at the foundation of desiring to make dad proud?

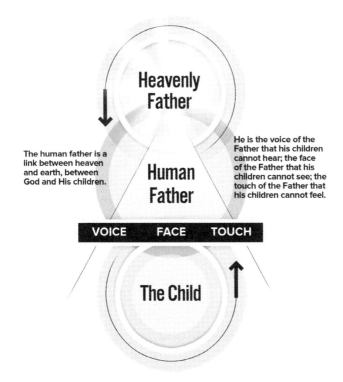

Subconsciously, we look for our human father's gaze because we long for our heavenly Father's gaze. We all desire to be chosen, delighted in, and desired by our earthly father, which indicates a more fundamental desire—to be chosen by our heavenly Father.

But many children as they grow up, rather than feeling chosen and delighted in by their father, feel rejected and unwanted. Such wounds demand a lifetime of healing. The father wound lives on in children who become adults attempting to raise other children. Wounded people often wound people.

When a persistent wound causes a father to doubt the Father's delight in him, he will struggle to delight in his own children. When this happens, the wound is transferred to yet another generation of children who will not feel chosen.

The future of the world, the Church, the family, and our children depends to a great extent on the identity of the human father. What can the human father offer that has the ability to change the world?

The human father's essence, his very identity and mission, is to be an icon of the heavenly Father. An icon is a piece of religious art that is created for the purpose of transmitting a divine message to one who gazes upon it. You transmit God the Father's gaze to your child, as you gaze upon your child and your child gazes upon you.

This is not wishful thinking or pious idealism, but rather the very plan of God. As St. Paul says, "I bow my knees before the Father of our Lord Jesus Christ from whom all fatherhood derives its name" (Eph 3:15). You and I, the human father, are named and claimed by God to bear His image to this world.

St. Joseph was the human face of the Father to God the Son. You also are called to be the human face of God the Father to your child. By becoming this iconic image of God the Father, you will help in the transformation and conversion of this world.

> **TAKE THE LEAD** Evaluate the last five conversations you have had with each of your children. Determine if you actually stopped, looked into your child's eyes, and intentionally listened. Now ask yourself, when was the last time I set out to choose to spend time with my child—to seek my child out? Make it your aim and purpose to choose your child above all those things you think cannot wait until tomorrow. Stop and gaze into your child's eyes and strive to see a heart that longs to be chosen, desired, and delighted in.*

---

* See Examen *Identify the Temple* on page 451

A LINK BETWEEN HEAVEN AND EARTH

160. A LINK BETWEEN HEAVEN AND EARTH

How does a man become a man truly? The world continually bombards men with the insidious message that a real man is determined by the number and frequency of his sexual conquests, the number of digits in his salary, how many friends he has, the type of car he drives, the size of his biceps, the size of his portfolio, how many marathons he has completed, or how many fights he has won.

Yet, all of these examples by which a man judges himself—and others—signify what he gains for himself and not what he contributes to others. A boy is selfish. A man is selfless. A boy takes, a man gives. Authentic manhood can only find its fulfillment in fatherhood; the pinnacle of true masculinity is spiritual paternity—begetting spiritual life in another. In other words: raising a child raises a man.

To be raised up, one must first lower himself. When you lower yourself to your child's level—entering their world of hope, imagination, innocence, their need for affirmation, attention, and love—you become capable of lifting your child to Heaven.

This is precisely what the Word did: He came down to our level, embraced our limited, fallen, broken, tired nature, and bearing all of us on His broad shoulders, that is, in His very self, He has lifted us up to His Father.

The way to raise your children up is by lowering yourself to their level—by serving and loving them. The human father has been established by God as a bridge between heaven and earth, between God and His children. He is the voice of the Father that his children cannot hear; the face of the Father that his children cannot see; the touch of the Father that his children cannot feel.

"Stooping down" to our children's level means that we stop (what we are doing), look (into their eyes), and listen (to what they are really saying). Often a child is simply saying, "Dad, I want you to notice me."

The most effective way that we can transmit the Father's love to our children is to become like St. Joseph, who raised the "[h]uman face of God and the divine face of man" (Pope St. John Paul II), and to become the voice, face, and touch of the Father to our children.

TAKE THE LEAD Evaluate the last five conversations you have had with each of your children. Determine if you actually stopped, looked into your child's eyes, and intentionally listened. Now ask yourself, when was the last time I set out to choose to spend time with my child—to seek my child out? Make it your aim and purpose to choose your child above all those things you think cannot wait until tomorrow. Stop and gaze into your child's eyes and strive to see a heart that longs to be chosen, desired, and delighted in.*

* See Examen *Identify the Temple* on page 451

PILLAR 4: DISCOVER THE DISCIPLE [EMBRACE THE CHILD]

A LINK BETWEEN HEAVEN AND EARTH

161. SHOW US THE FATHER

What satisfies you? Maybe chocolate? But if chocolate satisfies us, why after eating a piece of chocolate do we instantly crave more? We crave more because the satisfaction that food, sex, depressants, stimulants, narcotics, money, honor, prestige, fame, success, victory, fans, and lauds offer is momentary, fleeting, and illusive. It seems that one Super Bowl championship ring isn't enough, but two might satisfy. One million, three hundred and forty-eight thousand, two hundred and fifty-four hits on a YouTube video is good, but two million would be better.

Years ago, a man in his mid-seventies—a very, very wealthy man—and I were discussing his latest project: the development of a resort on an obscure island in the Caribbean. I asked what drove him, at his age, to embark on such a project. His answer: "My friend is wealthier than I am. It burns me. I am trying to find ways to surpass him." Regardless of how much we have or how old we are, we always want more. This craving for more is not completely disordered. At the foundational core of that desire for more is an indication that we are made for more—the More that alone can satisfy the human heart.

The apostle Philip, on the night before Jesus' ultimate act of sacrificial love, pleaded with his Lord, "Show us the Father and we shall be satisfied" (John 14:8). Indeed, whether or not we acknowledge it, the longing for the Father is the most profound desire of the human heart. The vision of the Father alone can satisfy the human person's craving for validation, affirmation, and love. Jesus' mission was, and is, to become one with us that we may become one with the Father—and be satisfied.

Because of your baptism, Christ lives in you, and because Christ lives in you, you are capable of being like Christ—capable of imaging the eternal Father to your children. In addition to this, because the Son of the Father, Jesus, became the son of a human father, Joseph, fatherhood has been redeemed by Christ, and all fathers—including you—have been made capable of transmitting the Father's love to your children, in the manner that St. Joseph expressed his love for Jesus.

Pope St. John Paul II reminds us: "Efforts must be made to restore socially the conviction that the place and task of the father in and for the family is of unique and irreplaceable importance. As experience teaches, the absence of a father causes psychological and moral imbalance and notable difficulties in family relationships" (FC 25). You have a unique role; your fatherhood is irreplaceable. Philip's heartfelt desire is also the deepest longing of our children's hungry, if not starving, souls: Show us the Father and we will be satisfied. This is our noble duty, our divine purpose, our unique and unrepeatable mission: to show the Father to our children by means of our own fatherhood.

> **TAKE THE LEAD** Evaluate the last five conversations you have had with each of your children. Determine if you actually stopped, looked into your child's eyes, and intentionally listened. Now ask yourself, when was the last time I set out to choose to spend time with my child—to seek my child out? Make it your aim and purpose to choose your child above all those things you think cannot wait until tomorrow. Stop and gaze into your child's eyes and strive to see a heart that longs to be chosen, desired, and delighted in.*

* See Examen *Identify the Temple* on page 451

PILLAR 4: DISCOVER THE DISCIPLE [EMBRACE THE CHILD]

THE ESSENCE OF FATHERHOOD

162. BIOLOGICAL AND SPIRITUAL FATHERHOOD

What does it mean to be a father? Can being a father be reduced to the title given to a man who impregnates a woman? If a man impregnates a woman but abandons her and the child, is he a father truly?

Fatherhood is not as much biological as it is spiritual. Anyone can be a biological dad, but it takes a real man to be a spiritual father. But what does it mean to be a spiritual father?

Christ gives us the key to understanding spiritual fatherhood: "Whoever receives one such child in my name receives me" (Mt 18:5). By receiving our children as though they are Christ, our children are far more likely to receive Christ.

To be a spiritual father means that you and I become like St. Joseph who—though Jesus was not his biological son—spiritually adopted Jesus. Spiritual adoption simply means that we make the decision to move beyond the biological and temporal aspects of fatherhood (without neglecting to fulfill their duties) and intentionally provide for our child's spiritual needs—to find Christ in them and help them find Christ.

Jesus said, "What does it profit a man if he gains the whole world and yet loses his soul?" (Mk 8:36). Another way to say this is, "What good is it if you gain the world for your child, yet your child loses his soul?" When we spiritually adopt our children, we use common, ordinary occurrences of daily life—things of this world—and convert them into allegories that direct our children to what really matters—God. Yet if we are unaware of what really matters, we cannot relate to our children the greatest matter of God.

Joseph saw Christ, the Messiah, in his son, and because of this, he became a true spiritual father. By receiving your child as Christ, you will begin to find Christ in your child, and become a true spiritual father.

TAKE THE LEAD Do you know what your child really needs? If you could obtain from God one thing for your child, what would it be? Take that desire for your child to prayer and intercede on behalf of your child daily. Now, ask yourself, how badly do I desire this gift for my child? Am I willing to sacrifice for it? Make a commitment over the next several reflections to fast in some manner for your child. It could be refraining from using the radio, listening to podcast and news sites, watching movies, snacking between meals, or hot water in your showers. Regardless, unite the sacrifice to your petition and intercede for your child.*

---

* See Examen *Identify the Temple* on page 451

THE ESSENCE OF FATHERHOOD

163. RECEIVING YOUR CHILD IN DIFFICULT CIRCUMSTANCES

In ancient Roman societies, when a mother gave birth to her child, the infant would be placed on the ground for the father to inspect for any defects. The child's fate and future were determined by his or her father. If the father discovered that the child had a physical handicap, didn't like the sex of the child, or found unwanted physical blemishes on the child, the father could send the infant away to be devoured by wolves or to be drowned.

And though this custom is horrific and reprehensible, more often than not the pinnacle moment of the child's birth occurred when the father picked his child up, brought it to himself, and received the child as his own. The Latin word for this act of "receiving" the child is *susceptio*.

St. Albert the Great connected this ancient Roman custom of *susceptio* to St. Joseph, who though he was not the biological father of Jesus, nevertheless received (*susceptio*) Him as his own. St. Albert the Great said that by doing so, St. Joseph became a father in the truest sense.

How does this apply to us and our fatherhood? When our children spill the milk, draw on the newly painted walls with permanent marker, break a plate, become pregnant out of wedlock, arrive home inebriated, drop out of school, become addicted to drugs, question their gender, stop going to Mass, refuse to believe in God, do we reject them? Leave them in the dirt of their wrongdoing? Or do we lift them to ourselves?

The child's future, who the child becomes, to a great extent depends upon how we as fathers handle such precarious parenting moments.

Which raises the question, How are we as fathers to handle such situations? How do we *susceptio* our children when we don't feel like it? There are several essential factors to consider when approaching these delicate situations. First, we are to keep in mind that by receiving our child as Christ we will more likely find Christ in our child. In other words, we must look into the child, determined to find Jesus there.

Second, we must strive to err on the side of mercy rather than justice. It is better that a child breaks a glass than that we break the child's heart over what the child broke. The situation will indeed pass, but the relationship—good or bad—will endure.

Third, to be a father of mercy we must envision our children as ever-growing temples of the living God. In other words, when encountering disappointment in your child, look to the long-term goal: you desire that your child becomes a temple of God. Remember that how you embrace your child during such an episode could either encourage the child to press on with the project of becoming a temple of God or deter the child altogether from believing that God lives within him.

Much hinges on whether you reject or receive your child—even and especially with the child's imperfections and blemishes.

> **TAKE THE LEAD** Do you know what your child really needs? If you could obtain from God one thing for your child, what would it be? Take that desire for your child to prayer and intercede on behalf of your child daily. Now, ask yourself, how badly do I desire this gift for my child? Am I willing to sacrifice for it? Make a commitment over the next several reflections to fast in some manner for your child. It could be refraining from using the radio, listening to podcast and news sites, watching movies, snacking between meals, or hot water in your showers. Regardless, unite the sacrifice to your petition and intercede for your child.*

* See Examen *Identify the Temple* on page 451

THE ESSENCE OF FATHERHOOD

164. CHRIST'S GAME PLAN TO SAVE SOULS

Recall that our Lord's first public miracle occurred at a wedding, which is a certain sign of His desire to restore and redeem the sacrament of marriage. John in his Gospel mentions that Jesus' second miracle was the healing of the royal official's son. John tells us that the royal official, the father of the sick son, asked his servants when his son's health was restored. "And they told him, 'Yesterday, at the seventh hour, the fever left him.' The father knew then that it was at that very hour in which Jesus said to him, 'Thy son lives.' And he himself believed and his whole household" (John 4:46–53).

Remember that seven is a number that represents God's covenant with his people. If Jesus' first miracle, which occurred on the "seventh day," was a certain sign of his desire to heal and restore marriage, we can assume that Christ's second miracle, which occurred at the "seventh hour," is a certain sign of His intention and desire to restore and redeem the relationship between the human father and his child.

It is as if St. John is providing an outline for Christ's plan to save souls: first, as our Lord entered the silence of the womb of His Mother Mary and embraced the hidden, silent, domestic life in the humble confines of His home in Nazareth, so also we are to embrace silence. Second, as Jesus demonstrated His desire to heal marriage, a husband is to embrace his wife, remaining faithfully yoked to her. And third, as Christ restored the life of a father's son, so also we are to do all in our power to restore fatherhood by embracing our children.

Notice that when the son returned to health, the miracle inspired the father's entire family to believe. When we work with the Father to restore our children's faith in God, more often than not our family will come to believe. This is one of Christ's strategies to save souls, and you are at the center of His divine plan.

TAKE THE LEAD Do you know what your child really needs? If you could obtain from God one thing for your child, what would it be? Take that desire for your child to prayer and intercede on behalf of your child daily. Now, ask yourself, how badly do I desire this gift for my child? Am I willing to sacrifice for it? Make a commitment over the next several reflections to fast in some manner for your child. It could be refraining from using the radio, listening to podcast and news sites, watching movies, snacking between meals, or hot water in your showers. Regardless, unite the sacrifice to your petition and intercede for your child.*

* See Examen *Identify the Temple* on page 451

PILLAR 4: DISCOVER THE DISCIPLE [EMBRACE THE CHILD]

THE ESSENCE OF FATHERHOOD

165. LEARNING FROM THE ROYAL OFFICIAL: THREE STEPS TO BEGIN RESTORING YOUR RELATIONSHIP WITH YOUR CHILD

In the Gospel of John, Jesus performed His second recorded miracle of healing the royal official's son. What did the royal official "do" to obtain the favor of Jesus healing his son? From the royal official we learn that to restore our relationship with our children, and also restore their spiritual well-being in Christ, there exist three basic requisites.

The scriptural account tells us that, "There was a certain royal official whose son was lying sick in Capernaum. When he heard that Jesus had come from Judea to Galilea, he went to Him." The royal official with clear intent sought out Jesus, making the twenty-five-mile trek from Capernaum to Cana of Galilee. For a man who lived during a time without automobiles, trains, and bicycles, this was a great act of faith. He believed Christ would be there when he arrived, and he believed that Christ would heal his son. The first requisite is that you, as a father, seek out Jesus, go to Jesus—continually and consistently—believing Christ will be there for you.

God has given you the power of faith expressed by prayer, and prayer with faith can obtain great graces for your family.

Second, the official "besought [Jesus] to come down and heal his son, for he was at the point of death." He begged Jesus to heal his son. You have been given the ability to obtain from God Christ's healing mercy, peace, love, and salvation by means of your constant, heartfelt intercession. "Man is a beggar before God" (St. Augustine). And a father who begs on behalf of his child receives.

The scriptural account also discloses that after Jesus said to the official, "Unless you see signs and wonders, you do not believe." The royal official said to Him, "Sir, come down before my child dies." The third requisite is perseverance. When it appeared that Jesus may have been denying his request, the father persevered, incessantly interceding on behalf of his son.

This account expresses vividly how a father—so pained by and concerned for the loss of his child—is willing to do almost anything to ensure that his child lives.

Often, without knowing it, our children's souls "are at the point of death"—that is, eternal loss. You can imitate the persevering example of this father by seeking out Jesus, interceding on your child's behalf, and persevering in faith and trust that God will one day grant the graces you much desire.

> **TAKE THE LEAD** Do you know what your child really needs? If you could obtain from God one thing for your child, what would it be? Take that desire for your child to prayer and intercede on behalf of your child daily. Now, ask yourself, how badly do I desire this gift for my child? Am I willing to sacrifice for it? Make a commitment over the next several reflections to fast in some manner for your child. It could be refraining from using the radio, listening to podcast and news sites, watching movies, snacking between meals, or hot water in your showers. Regardless, unite the sacrifice to your petition and intercede for your child.*

* See Examen *Identify the Temple* on page 451

THE ESSENCE OF FATHERHOOD

166. WHEN GOD IS SILENT

How can we understand God, His motives and will, when He is apparently unresponsive to our prayers? What are we to do when after years of seeking Jesus, begging on behalf of our children, and persevering in our intercession for them, their situation worsens?

There is an account of a man whose child suffered permanent brain injury and nearly died. His child survived, but not without being severely impaired mentally and physically. The father sought Jesus, begged on behalf of his child, and persevered daily in his prayer for her healing. Yet, nothing seemed to change. In his desperation he cried out, "Lord, why won't you heal my daughter?" To which God responded, "It is not she who needs to be healed—you do. Your daughter is my gift to you that you may be healed by her wounds."

Like the royal official, this man was pained by and concerned for his child and was willing to do almost anything to ensure that his child not only survived but thrived. And yet, in the scriptural account, God initially appears to be silent. How can we understand this divine silence?

The act of a father interceding on behalf of his child deepens the faith of the father—because faith can only grow when it is tested. The persevering faith of a father, while peering into future's darkness, affords him the light of friendship with God, which actually heals him.

The act of interceding for another not only enlivens and deepens the faith of a father, but also the family of the father. Remember, it was not only the royal official who believed, but also "his whole household." Often, Sacred Scripture relates that after a father became a believer in Christ, his entire household believed.

So why is God often silent in response to our prayers? Because by means of the trial or test, God is accomplishing a greater miracle—namely our salvation.

TAKE THE LEAD Do you know what your child really needs? If you could obtain from God one thing for your child, what would it be? Take that desire for your child to prayer and intercede on behalf of your child daily. Now, ask yourself, how badly do I desire this gift for my child? Am I willing to sacrifice for it? Make a commitment over the next several reflections to fast in some manner for your child. It could be refraining from using the radio, listening to podcast and news sites, watching movies, snacking between meals, or hot water in your showers. Regardless, unite the sacrifice to your petition and intercede for your child.*

* See Examen *Identify the Temple* on page 451

THE GREATEST ATTRIBUTE

167. THE MOST IMPORTANT ATTRIBUTE OF A FATHER

What do you think is the most essential, useful, persuasive, magnetic, attractive attribute a father can have? If you and I are to be living, breathing, grace-transmitting signs of God's love to our children, our fatherhood should reflect God's fatherhood. But Who is the Father and how does He relate to us?

If we could simmer down God the Father's characteristics and attributes into one word, what would that word be?

Mercy.

The Father is mercy itself. St. Thomas Aquinas said that of all the virtues applied to our neighbor, mercy is the greatest above all. Pope St. John Paul II said that mercy is love's second name. "God is Love" (1 John), and love expresses itself by mercy. If God the Father's greatest expression of His love to us is mercy, then we must conclude that the greatest attribute of the human father is mercy. To be a father like God the Father is to be merciful like the Father.

So, what is mercy? The word mercy is derived from the Latin word *misericordia*—or *miserum cor*. *Miserum* means "compassion," and *cor* means "heart." In other words, when one is merciful, one has a compassionate heart. Notice that mercy is not disregarding a wrong or ignoring an infraction; rather it is entering into another's wrong and having compassion. Compassion literally means "to suffer with." Mercy, then, is the act of suffering with another.

In addition to this, the root word for mercy in Latin is *merces*, which means to "pay the price," a ransom for another. In other words, to be merciful is to have a compassionate heart, bearing another's suffering as your own, by paying the price of another's fault, errors, weaknesses, and sins for the purpose of liberating that person from their miseries.

For example, there is an account of a twenty-two-year-old man, Christopher, who was smoking marijuana with his roommate, his best friend, Donald. Christopher, while playing with a loaded gun, shot and killed his best friend. After he served several years in prison,

Donald's parents pleaded for their son's murderer to be paroled early. When Christopher was released, Donald's parents were the first to embrace him. Not only did they embrace him, but they gave him a job and a place to live. Donald's parents, particularly his father, by means of his mercy toward Christopher, is a living symbol of God the Father.

It was our offenses and sins that killed God the Father's Son, and yet, despite the just demands of sin, God the Father, through His Son pleads for us to return to the Father and embrace His mercy.

An essential aspect of mercy is being compassionate from the heart—to pay a price for another's failures, sins, and misfires for the purpose of liberating that person from their guilt and misery. This is what a father does for his child. This is the greatest attribute of a father.

> **TAKE THE LEAD** Is there anything that you have done, or been remiss in doing, that has caused damage to your relationship with your son or daughter? Does your child appear distant or resentful toward you? If so, it may be beneficial to assume that you do not understand the situation fully. Rather than assuming you know what's wrong, humble yourself and ask your child, "Where did I go wrong?" And listen. If your child has gone astray, ask yourself, "What can I do, even if I am only one percent wrong in this situation, to assure my child of the Father's love. Then make up your mind to be the link between God the Father and your child. Don't delay. As St. Augustine said, "Delayed obedience is disobedience."*

* See Examen *Identify the Temple* on page 451

THE GREATEST ATTRIBUTE

168. WHAT MERCY IS AND WHAT IT ISN'T

One of the scandals of modern Christianity and errors of contemporary preaching is the proclamation of "cheap mercy." In former ages, many a preacher used the pulpit to scare the hell out of people, and people out of hell. Sermons hyper focused on the wrath of God, death and judgment, the eternal pains of hell, and the like; while minimizing, if not neglecting altogether, God's mercy.

In response to this dynamic, contemporary Christian preaching often avoids the reality of sin, justice, loss of grace, and the reality of hell, while proclaiming God's unconditional love and mercy.

The consequence of this brand of preaching is that the message of God's love and mercy lacks any real value because there is nothing to which to compare such mercy. It is like telling a young, modern American boy that he is free. The boy cannot fully, or perhaps adequately, appreciate his freedom because he has never experienced slavery.

If we don't understand what sin is, the damage that it causes, the wounds it incurs, and the consequences and effect of not repenting from it, we will not be able to understand the mercy of God, who forgives the debt caused by such sin.

If we cannot comprehend the concept of justice and how it applies to our relationship with God and the body of Christ, we cannot begin to appreciate or receive the depth of God's mercy.

Justice without mercy is ruthless law enforcement that leads to domination. Mercy without justice is immoral chaos, which results in unbridled indulgence and permissiveness. To be a father of mercy is to understand both the justice and mercy of the Father.

One man, while meditating upon a depiction of the Crucifixion of Jesus, heard the words, "Come close and see what thy sins have caused; but draw even closer and see the mercy by which they are forgiven." To be a father of mercy, it is imperative that we understand the Father's mercy and how it applies to us.

After we consider and comprehend that without Christ's forgiveness we are destined for hell, but with Christ we are destined for heaven, then we will be capable of communicating the riches of divine mercy to our children.

> **TAKE THE LEAD** Is there anything that you have done, or been remiss in doing, that has caused damage to your relationship with your son or daughter? Does your child appear distant or resentful toward you? If so, it may be beneficial to assume that you do not understand the situation fully. Rather than assuming you know what's wrong, humble yourself and ask your child, "Where did I go wrong?" And listen. If your child has gone astray, ask yourself, "What can I do, even if I am only one percent wrong in this situation, to assure my child of the Father's love. Then make up your mind to be the link between God the Father and your child. Don't delay. As St. Augustine said, "Delayed obedience is disobedience."*

* See Examen *Identify the Temple* on page 451

THE GREATEST ATTRIBUTE

169. THE TARGET THAT WE ARE SHOOTING FOR

We have heard the word "sin" used often to describe an action that is immoral or evil. But what is sin fundamentally? "The [Greek] word for sin is *hamartia*, which . . . literally means *a missing of the target*" (William Barclay, Gospel of John, vol 2). When Greek archers missed the target, it was a sin. When we sin we miss the target. But what is the target that the Christian shoots for?

The target that you and I should be aiming at is the life of the Trinity, which is eternal, self-giving love, absent disordered selfishness. When we sin, we reject acting, living in, and receiving the self-giving love of God. When we miss the mark, we begin to use people as a means to obtain things. As one evangelist says, "People are to be loved and things are to be used. It should not be the other way around."

Sin kills the soul and hardens it against love. "The wages of sin is death" (Rom 6:23). Which means that according to divine justice, if we die in our sin (separation from God), we will not be able to partake in the eternal joy and ecstasy of God's love. Yet, "[a]ll men have sinned and are deprived of God's glory." Which indicates that we deserve hell, eternal isolation, a life of eternal darkness, and horror without hope.

In addition to this, we cannot understand the effects that our sinful actions have on ourselves and others. Throughout our life, we may have inadvertently led many others down the road to perdition. For this reason (and others), "the ransom for man's sin is beyond him, he cannot pay the price" (Ps 49:6).

If we comprehend the evil of sin, our participation in it, and the just demands of being guilty of it, we can begin to appreciate God's mercy, desire it, and receive it—particularly in the sacrament of confession.

God the Son agreed with God the Father to be compassionate, to have a heart of mercy, and literally to pay for the just demands of our sins in His body, so that we may be ransomed from the devil, hell, and eternal damnation, and be received (*susceptio*) by the Father.

Your child cannot appreciate mercy if you fail to communicate the consequences of sin and the justice of God. Yet, if you do convey the evil consequences of sin without condemning your child, and while also applying mercy, your child will embrace and trust you, and eventually trust in the Father of Mercy.

> **TAKE THE LEAD** Is there anything that you have done, or been remiss in doing, that has caused damage to your relationship with your son or daughter? Does your child appear distant or resentful toward you? If so, it may be beneficial to assume that you do not understand the situation fully. Rather than assuming you know what's wrong, humble yourself and ask your child, "Where did I go wrong?" And listen. If your child has gone astray, ask yourself, "What can I do, even if I am only one percent wrong in this situation, to assure my child of the Father's love. Then make up your mind to be the link between God the Father and your child. Don't delay. As St. Augustine said, "Delayed obedience is disobedience."*

* See Examen *Identify the Temple* on page 451

THE GREATEST ATTRIBUTE

170. THE TWO CONDITIONS OF MERCY

Besides understanding the just consequences of sin, mercy has only two conditions: first, that we receive it; and second, that we give it. Our Lord Jesus told St. Faustina, the apostle of mercy, "Tell all people, my daughter, that I am Love and Mercy itself." And again, "Before I come as a just judge, I first open wide the door of My mercy. He who refuses to pass through the door of My mercy must pass through the door of my justice." (*Diary*, 1146).

These words of our Lord are not a threat, but rather a plea for each of us to act now and receive God's endless mercy.

The second condition of mercy is that we give it. We fathers are to "[b]e merciful just as our Father is merciful (Lk 6:36). "For blessed are the merciful for they will receive mercy" (Mt 5:7).

Jesus told the parable of a steward of his master's house. A steward was like a property manager who hired subjects (subcontractors) to farm, raise crops, tend vineyards, and care for the estate. After some time, the master returned to his estate to settle accounts with his steward, who accumulated an incredible debt, owing ten thousand talents to his master.

A talent was equivalent to 19 years' worth of wages. The steward's debt is nearly unimaginable—190,000 years' worth of wages. If the average man works full time for 40 years of his life, this man owed 4,750 lives' worth of wages. Such a sum is difficult to comprehend.

"As he had no means of paying, his master ordered him to be sold, with his wife and children and all that he had and payment to be made" (see Mt 18:21–35). This is the justice demanded of sin. "But the servant fell down and besought him saying, 'Have patience with me and I will pay thee all!'" And moved with *compassion,* the master released him and forgave him the debt. Notice that the master—a symbol of God the Father—allows the steward—a symbol of a sinful father—feel the weight of the just punishment due to sin. And yet, the master bears his servant's burden as his own and pays the price for the steward's sin. This is mercy.

Yet, this servant went out immediately and found a man who owed him a hundred denarius, that is, one hundred days' wages, and threw him in prison until he would pay the debt in full. When the master discovered his servant's actions he handed him over to the torturers until the servant paid all.

What is the point?

In giving mercy, we will receive mercy, and receiving mercy, we become more capable of giving mercy. Why does this matter? Because to be like the Father in heaven is to be a merciful father on earth. Recall that you are a link between heaven and earth, you are the face of the Father that your children cannot see. If your children are to believe in God's mercy, it is vital that they see you being merciful.

Make mercy your measure and mercy will be measured out to you.

> **TAKE THE LEAD** Is there anything that you have done, or been remiss in doing, that has caused damage to your relationship with your son or daughter? Does your child appear distant or resentful toward you? If so, it may be beneficial to assume that you do not understand the situation fully. Rather than assuming you know what's wrong, humble yourself and ask your child, "Where did I go wrong?" And listen. If your child has gone astray, ask yourself, "What can I do, even if I am only one percent wrong in this situation, to assure my child of the Father's love. Then make up your mind to be the link between God the Father and your child. Don't delay. As St. Augustine said, "Delayed obedience is disobedience."*

* See Examen *Identify the Temple* on page 451

THE GREATEST ATTRIBUTE

171. MAGNETIC MERCY, PART I

Do you desire that your children would one day become like you? Most fathers would have great difficulty answering that question affirmatively. We know ourselves all too well. We understand how deep selfishness and the temptation toward disordered perversions run. We are very familiar with our weaknesses and tendency toward sin. Yet, even if we feel as though we would not desire our children to become like us, we can aspire to obtain one singular attribute that, if our children imitate, would make us most grateful. That attribute is mercy.

Our children are observant. They listen to half of what we say and all of what we do. They learn from our behaviors and habits—the good and the bad.

If our children are to live truly, it is vital that they learn from us how to forgive. To live one must forgive. This indicates that a father must embrace God the Father's forgiveness personally. And the condition to receiving God the Father's mercy is extending His mercy to those who have wounded us.

Ask yourself this question: Is there someone who sometime during your life has betrayed you, stolen from you, attempted to destroy your reputation, damaged your goods, maligned or marginalized you? Nearly all of us have experienced such trials; and yet so few forgive from the heart.

Holding on to resentment, failing to forgive, only hurts you and those who live in relationship with you. Unforgiveness is like drinking poison while expecting the other person to die. Unforgiveness allows another person to still retain power and control over you (Fr. John Joseph De Porres, original Fathers of St. Joseph chaplain).

A proven way to overcome forgiveness is to pray to God—not that the person who injured you will be destroyed, but rather, that they be blessed by God and drawn close to His Sacred Heart. By doing this, God will certainly set you free from the snare of bitterness, resentment, and unforgiveness. This freedom will be reflected in your fatherhood and in your children's ability to respond properly to those who injure them. Then your mercy will become magnetic.

> **TAKE THE LEAD** Is there anything that you have done, or been remiss in doing, that has caused damage to your relationship with your son or daughter? Does your child appear distant or resentful toward you? If so, it may be beneficial to assume that you do not understand the situation fully. Rather than assuming you know what's wrong, humble yourself and ask your child, "Where did I go wrong?" And listen. If your child has gone astray, ask yourself, "What can I do, even if I am only one percent wrong in this situation, to assure my child of the Father's love. Then make up your mind to be the link between God the Father and your child. Don't delay. As St. Augustine said, "Delayed obedience is disobedience."*

* See Examen *Identify the Temple* on page 451

PILLAR 4: DISCOVER THE DISCIPLE [EMBRACE THE CHILD]

THE GREATEST ATTRIBUTE

172. MAGNETIC MERCY, PART 2

A man recounted that his eldest son, during his teenage years, would consistently run away from home and disappear for months at a time, leading his parents to believe that he was dead. This dynamic continued for years, causing the father tremendous anguish, pain, and resentment toward his son.

Eventually, the father condemned himself for being a terrible father. It was in this moment of desperation that he surrendered his fatherhood—and his son—to God the Father, begging that God would come to his aid. During the following years, the situation did not change, and yet something did change—this man's heart became compassionate and merciful toward his dissident son.

After years of heartache, the son finally returned in earnest to his childhood home. His father embraced his son and welcomed him. The son proceeded to share with his father that his girlfriend was pregnant, and the child was his. The son also stated his intention to marry his girlfriend and raise the child properly. The father, dumbfounded, asked him, "How can you do this? Up to this point you have been irresponsible, and don't even have a consistent job." To which his son responded, "Because I've been watching you, dad." In other words, "Dad, your mercy is magnetic, and I want to be like you."

Mercy has the greatest power and potential to win our children to God and His Church. You and I have received mercy from God our Father and this mercy cost Him His Son. Yet, over two thousand years, billions of people have responded and received His mercy.

Wrath and anger may initially make children fearfully obedient, but it rarely wins hearts. Mercy wins hearts because those whose hearts are won know that the person who acted with mercy believed that he or she was worth the cost.

If we are to be among those fathers who win the hearts of our children, we will need to be convinced that our children are worth the cost of the sacrifice of being merciful.

TAKE THE LEAD Is there anything that you have done, or been remiss in doing, that has caused damage to your relationship with your son or daughter? Does your child appear distant or resentful toward you? If so, it may be beneficial to assume that you do not understand the situation fully. Rather than assuming you know what's wrong, humble yourself and ask your child, "Where did I go wrong?" And listen. If your child has gone astray, ask yourself, "What can I do, even if I am only one percent wrong in this situation, to assure my child of the Father's love. Then make up your mind to be the link between God the Father and your child. Don't delay. As St. Augustine said, "Delayed obedience is disobedience."*

* See Examen *Identify the Temple* on page 451

THE GREATEST ATTRIBUTE

173. STRETCHING US

To be a father who is filled with the Holy Spirit can be painful. A balloon without air is useless, but when air is pumped into its elastic shell, its skin stretches, allowing the balloon to achieve the purpose for which it has been designed. But notice that in order for the balloon to achieve its full potential, it has to endure the painful process of being stretched, until it becomes capable of soaring aloft.

Fathers are like balloons. Without the breath of the Holy Spirit, we are flat, lifeless, and fail to soar with God. Opening ourselves to "containing" more of the Holy Spirit demands that our souls be stretched, which involves suffering and sacrifice.

When the Spirit of God stretches us, He calls us to do things that seem painful, unattractive, and inconvenient. This stretching usually involves the sacrifice of our time, our wants, and the lowering of ourselves to serve those around us. Paradoxically, to soar with God is dependent upon lowering ourselves, particularly to serve our children. As Jesus taught, "He who is least among you all is the one who is greatest" (Lk 9:48).

The Holy Spirit enables us to soar by inspiring us to lower ourselves to the level of serving our children. The Holy Spirit will enable our children to soar if we lower ourselves to serve them.

It is probably safe to say that none of us want our children to merely survive this thing we call life; we want them to thrive and live truly. To ensure that our children live truly, it is imperative that we die to our selfishness so that we can truly live and pass on life to others.

Many fathers say that they would die for their children, but how many men use their talents, gifts, and efforts to ensure that their children truly live?

The father whose main attribute is mercy allows the Holy Spirit to stretch him. You will be stretched by serving your children, and your capacity to give more of yourself will increase. And in giving of yourself, you will receive more of the Holy Spirit. And being full of the Spirit, you will become a transmitter of eternal life to your children.

> **TAKE THE LEAD** Is there anything that you have done, or been remiss in doing, that has caused damage to your relationship with your son or daughter? Does your child appear distant or resentful toward you? If so, it may be beneficial to assume that you do not understand the situation fully. Rather than assuming you know what's wrong, humble yourself and ask your child, "Where did I go wrong?" And listen. If your child has gone astray, ask yourself, "What can I do, even if I am only one percent wrong in this situation, to assure my child of the Father's love. Then make up your mind to be the link between God the Father and your child. Don't delay. As St. Augustine said, "Delayed obedience is disobedience."*

* See Examen *Identify the Temple* on page 451

PILLAR 4: DISCOVER THE DISCIPLE [EMBRACE THE CHILD]

ICON OF THE HEAVENLY FATHER

174. BECOMING A FATHER ON EARTH LIKE THE FATHER IN HEAVEN

You and I are to be a link between God the Father and our children; but how do we become that connection between heaven and earth? How can our fatherhood transmit the presence of God the Father to our children? How do we spiritually adopt our own children?

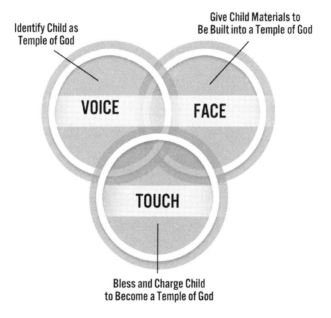

There are many ways that a father can reflect and transmit the love of God; however, if we could synthesize the many and various attributes and actions of the eternal Father, we would put them into two categories: first, how we are to "be" like the Father; and second, how we are to "act" like the Father.

First, we can "be" like the Father by becoming the voice of the Father that our children cannot hear; the face of the Father that our children cannot see; and the touch of the Father that our children cannot feel. Second, we "act" like the heavenly Father by 1) identifying our children as temples of the living God; 2) giving our child the materials needed for the child to become a holy temple of God; and 3) blessing your child to become a temple of God.

In other words, you are to be the voice of the Father when you verbally identify your child as a temple of God. You are the face of the Father when you give your child the "materials" with which the child builds the temple. You become the touch of the Father when you bless your children with God's favor and blessing.

This threefold manner of communicating God's love to our children is precisely the way that God the Father communicates His love to us. God the Father communicated His Word, His very life to us in Jesus' physical presence—in Jesus' voice, Jesus' face, and Jesus' very touch. "That which was from the beginning, which we have heard, which we have seen with our eyes, which we looked upon and touched with our hands, concerning the word of life... That which we have seen and heard we proclaim also to you, so that you too may have fellowship. . . . And indeed our fellowship is with the Father and his Son Jesus Christ" (1 John 1:1–3).

By becoming like Christ (by Christ living in us) we become the voice, the face, and the touch of the Father; we are spiritually adopting our children and becoming a link between God the Father and our children.

> **TAKE THE LEAD** Often our children will be more likely to receive Christ when we are striving to receive them as Christ. When a child experiences his father attempting to love him as though the child is Jesus, the child is more likely to love his father as God the Father. The key to helping your child find the Father in you, and you finding Christ in your child, is to make every effort to become the voice, face, and touch of the heavenly Father to your child. Make every effort over the next several reflections to discern whether you are striving to be the voice of the Father your child cannot hear; the face of the Father that your child cannot see; and the touch of the Father that your child cannot feel.*

---

* See Examen *Identify the Temple* on page 451

PILLAR 4: DISCOVER THE DISCIPLE [EMBRACE THE CHILD]

BECOMING THE VOICE OF THE FATHER

175. IDENTIFYING THE TEMPLE

Where do parenting disorders come from? Why do parents struggle between being too lenient and too severe; between being over attentive and neglectful? Although many parenting tendencies are a product of the many wounds we have received throughout our life, the answer—more fundamentally—exists in how we "see" our children.

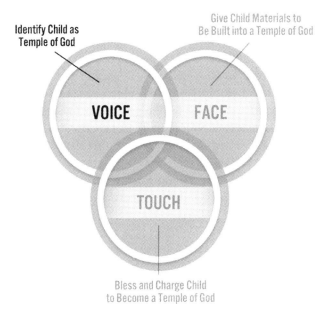

Our children, who appear to be common, fallen, inexperienced adolescents, are more than our eyes perceive. The human child is an outward sign that directs people, particularly fathers, to an interior mystery contained within them. Every baptized Christian is a temple of God, a temple of the Holy Spirit, a dwelling place of God in the making. Yet, how few realize this. This ignorance grieves and paralyzes the Holy Spirit, who lays dormant within the human person (see Eph 4:30).

By means of sharing with our children life's vital lessons, words of encouragement, words of correction, but most important, the knowledge that God dwells within them, we become the voice of the Father; the voice that transmits eternal, life-giving truths to our children. A father's words serve a singular goal: to help our children understand that they are temples of the living God, and that this is their very identity, dignity, and honor—not to mention their great potential.

Believing our visible children to be temples of the invisible God is perhaps one of the greatest challenges of fatherhood and demands great faith. How difficult it is for a father to see and believe that God lives in his child when his child is addicted to drugs, suffering from alcoholism or anorexia, or is stealing from the family to feed an addiction.

It is then, perhaps more than at any time, that our children need their fathers to intentionally look for and find God within them. Lack of faith in the reality that a child is a temple of God can lead to abuse or neglect—either by indulging and spoiling the child, failing to encourage or inspire him, or not making a real investment in the child.

Nearly every disordered parenting tendency is rooted in a lack of belief that the child is a sacred dwelling place of God.

> **TAKE THE LEAD** Over the course of the following mediations, identify the gifts, talents, and abilities in your children. Pray and ask God for the courage to verbally affirm those gifts, talents, and abilities. Most children question themselves and struggle with some level of insecurity. Make it a point to encourage your children in their endeavors. Thank them for a task accomplished. The more consistently you become the voice of the Father, the greater will be your children's ability to recognize the goodness of God the Father. Sometimes it is as simple as saying, "I realize that this is challenging, but I believe in you. God is in you—you can do this. And no matter what, I am with you."*

*   See Examen *Identify the Temple* on page 451

PILLAR 4: DISCOVER THE DISCIPLE [EMBRACE THE CHILD]

BECOMING THE VOICE OF THE FATHER

176. THE PROPHETIC POWER OF A FATHER'S WORDS

Have you ever witnessed a father call his child stupid, or tell his child that he is a "good for nothin'"? If a father consistently tells his child that the child will amount to nothing, there is a good chance that this curse will come to fruition. Why? Because children believe in their fathers, even when their fathers don't believe in their children.

A father's words, whether he realizes it or not, can have prophetic power. Why? Because at a deep subconscious level, a child believes that a father's word is a statement by God the Father on his life.

When a child is belittled and demeaned by his father, his inner person is cut, his heart bleeds, and in the deep and dark caverns of his soul exists a wound that few will ever encounter—because, most likely, the child will never trust anyone enough to expose it. To do so would require that the child become vulnerable, and the child intuits that such vulnerability is precisely what allowed his father to take advantage of him and wound him.

Why do the harsh words of a father hurt the child so intensely? Because the human father is the transmitter, the icon, the very symbol of the heavenly Father—at least this is what he is supposed to be. When the child is demeaned by his father, he cannot help but believe that the heavenly Father's sentiments are the same.

So, what prophetic word are we as fathers called to communicate to our children? You and I must be courageous enough to boldly proclaim to our children that they are temples of the Holy Spirit, and by doing so, our children will more readily strive to achieve this reality.

If you tell your child that he is good, he most likely will become good. When a father verbally communicates the goodness of his child to his child, he is instilling confidence in their filial relationship, which often results in building the child's trust in the heavenly Father.

By believing and expressing to your child that the Holy Spirit lives within him, you will awaken your child to his personal dignity and potential.

TAKE THE LEAD Over the course of the following mediations, identify the gifts, talents, and abilities in your children. Pray and ask God for the courage to verbally affirm those gifts, talents, and abilities. Most children question themselves and struggle with some level of insecurity. Make it a point to encourage your children in their endeavors. Thank them for a task accomplished. The more consistently you become the voice of the Father, the greater will be your children's ability to recognize the goodness of God the Father. Sometimes it is as simple as saying, "I realize that this is challenging, but I believe in you. God is in you—you can do this. And no matter what, I am with you."*

* See Examen *Identify the Temple* on page 451

PILLAR 4: DISCOVER THE DISCIPLE [EMBRACE THE CHILD]

BECOMING THE VOICE OF THE FATHER

177. ACTUALLY SEEING YOUR CHILD

Most fathers notice their child's existence. They know when they are present at home or are abroad. They see that their child is living, but do they see life in their child—do they actually see a person with dreams, hopes, fears, and a longing for completion and love?

If you were asked to name five unique gifts that your child has, would you be able to? Have you noticed the areas in which your child has attempted to be a gift? By noticing that our children are unique gifts who have their own personal gifts to share with the world, and by bringing their attention to their gifts, we assist them in becoming alive, truly.

Children practically come forth from the womb picking flowers for mom and drawing pictures for dad. Why do children do this? Because they are created by God to be a gift and to share themselves with the world around them.

Often, this giftedness is overlooked by a father, brushed aside as nothing unique or special, or worse, immediately discarded into the trash can. We tend to compare their gift to us with the manufactured, polished quality of products and resources that the world offers. We compare their drawing to a Monet, or their poem to a popular song. We remain on the surface of the gift rather than peering into it to see the love that inspired that gift into being. By giving a gift, your child is simply expressing love, affection, and admiration for you.

When our children attempt to be a gift to us we are to immediately acknowledge the gift, honor the gift, and receive the gift—for by doing so, we communicate to our children that we acknowledge, honor, and receive *them* as the *true gift*.

This is a crucial point. It is imperative that we congratulate and affirm our children when they attempt to be a gift—especially when it falls short—lest they refrain from being a gift because there is no one to receive the gift of themselves being presented in their gifts.

The act of verbally affirming our children in their giftedness is as simple as thanking your son for being kind to his sister or thanking your daughter for setting the dining table in preparation for dinner or congratulating your child for their *efforts* (not necessarily their grades) at school. It could be as simple as affirming your child for his witty sense of humor, or your daughter for her beauty, both interior and exterior, or for simply being who he or she truly is—unique and unrepeatable.

These types of verbal affirmations communicate the message not only that you do notice your children and that they are important to you, but that their heavenly Father notices and desires them.

Your children desire to be noticed, to be important, and if you don't provide this type of affirmation, they will struggle to believe that they are important to God, and they will try to obtain this affirmation elsewhere.

> **TAKE THE LEAD** Over the course of the following mediations, identify the gifts, talents, and abilities in your children. Pray and ask God for the courage to verbally affirm those gifts, talents, and abilities. Most children question themselves and struggle with some level of insecurity. Make it a point to encourage your children in their endeavors. Thank them for a task accomplished. The more consistently you become the voice of the Father, the greater will be your children's ability to recognize the goodness of God the Father. Sometimes it is as simple as saying, "I realize that this is challenging, but I believe in you. God is in you—you can do this. And no matter what, I am with you."*

* See Examen *Identify the Temple* on page 451

BECOMING THE VOICE OF THE FATHER

178. INSTILLING CONFIDENCE IN YOUR CHILD

Children are often insecure, shy, fearful of sharing themselves with others. One of the reasons for this is that they instinctively fear rejection. How often have we witnessed a young child desiring to share a story or sing a song, yet suffer from "stage fright," and hide his face in his parent's chest. Children want their entire self to be received entirely, but they sense that this may not occur. When they believe that they will not be received, they choose to avoid the risk of rejection.

It is true that when we fathers receive and affirm our children and their unique giftedness, they will desire to become more of a gift and will discover more of their true identity. Assisting you children in their giftedness frees them from the tendency to be selfish, and affords them the ability to live a life of self-giving love. There may not be anything as important in raising children as a father recognizing his child's unique, individual giftedness.

The reality, however, is that it is impossible for our children to avoid rejection. Rejection stings, cuts the heart of a child's selfless soul, and instills doubt about themselves. This is the devil's strategy: he uses rejection to instill doubt in children and to convince them to hide their unique giftedness and thus hide the very revelation of God's glory that they are to be.

How does a father instill the type of confidence in his child that helps them—despite the fear of rejection—continue to strike out and be a gift to others?

One of the most effective ways you can become the voice of the Father and instill resilient confidence in your child is by verbally expressing, in some manner, this truth: "Do you not know that your body is a temple of the Holy Spirit within you, which you have from God? (1 Cor 6:19).

If this truth is transmitted without manipulation or coercion, our children will be granted a confidence in and reverence for themselves—a respect for the power of God living within them.

When you communicate this truth to your child—the truth that God lives within him—that child has an instinctive desire to live up to that reality. The human father is the voice of the Father that our children cannot hear.

> **TAKE THE LEAD** Over the course of the following mediations, identify the gifts, talents, and abilities in your children. Pray and ask God for the courage to verbally affirm those gifts, talents, and abilities. Most children question themselves and struggle with some level of insecurity. Make it a point to encourage your children in their endeavors. Thank them for a task accomplished. The more consistently you become the voice of the Father, the greater will be your children's ability to recognize the goodness of God the Father. Sometimes it is as simple as saying, "I realize that this is challenging, but I believe in you. God is in you—you can do this. And no matter what, I am with you."*

* See Examen *Identify the Temple* on page 451

BECOMING THE FACE OF THE FATHER

179. GIVING YOUR CHILD THE MATERIALS TO BECOME A TEMPLE

After we have identified our children as temples of the Holy Spirit, it is vital that we supply them the materials to continue to build that temple.

The time of providing "materials" is a season of preparation, a period of training, in which a father builds the child's trust and confidence in God the Father by building trust between his child and himself.

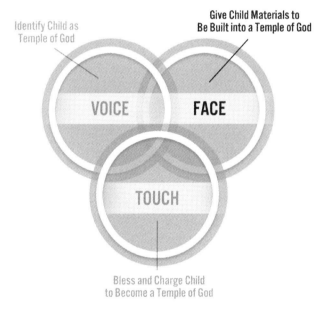

A father accomplishes this by being the face of the Father to his child, that is, he makes himself present to his child. When we make ourselves present to our children, we become a "present," a gift, that transmits the presence of the Father to our children.

By being present to your children, they begin to believe that they are worthy of your time. By being present, you give your children, by means of your example—over and above your words—the much-needed materials to be built into a temple of God.

Indeed, a father's example is more powerful than words, and his time spent with his child is more effective than lectures.

This is one reason why breaking promises that we have made to our children can undermine years of formation. If a child cannot trust his father to keep his promises, how can He trust that God will keep His promise? A father who keeps his promise is one who instills the Father's promise in his child.

> **TAKE THE LEAD** When was the last time you spent individual time, with each of your children? Set out today to establish ways to spend time with each of your children simply to assure them that you choose them over yourself. By doing this, your children will come to believe that they are chosen by God.*

* See Examen *Give Materials to Build Temple* on page 451

BECOMING THE FACE OF THE FATHER

180. THREE WAYS TO BE THE LIVING FACE OF GOD

Now that we understand that a father's main purpose is to supply his child with the materials to help the child be built into a temple of God—by the power of the Holy Spirit, it will be of great benefit to us to understand two fundamental errors that we fathers can make.

The first error is to burden the child by placing expectations upon him beyond what he is capable of fulfilling. This type of parenting disorder is usually the result of a father attempting to live vicariously through his child. A father who is striving for holiness makes the fatal mistake of "making" his child holy and making him holy "now." What takes a lifetime for us to achieve cannot be accomplished in our children within a year, two years, or the formative years that occur under our patronage. We must be patient. A tree doesn't grow in a day it demands a lifetime of growth; and so it is with the raising of saints.

Never expect your child to evangelize at school when you struggle at sharing the Gospel with your co-workers, friends, and relatives. When a father tries to "make" his child holy "now," the premature pressure can cause "spiritual burnout," resentment for the faith, or worse, rejection of the person and love of Jesus Christ.

If you want to change your child, change yourself. If you want your child to be a saint, strive for sainthood. If you desire that your children be holy for God the Father, become a holy father.

The other extreme is allowing the years of training, preparation, and formation to slip by unused, until one day the child sets out on his own without any real sense of mission, and without comprehending the key to happiness is in self-giving love.

The golden mean between these two extremes is easy to know but challenging to live. You become the face of the Father by spending time with and gazing upon your child with love. This gaze of delight and approval imparts to the child a confidence in the truth that God the Father loves him. This confidence animates the child, inspiring him to turn his gaze trustingly toward God the Father.

You and I become the iconic presence of the Father and are afforded ongoing opportunities to offer the gaze of the Father by working, praying, and playing with our children.

> **TAKE THE LEAD** When was the last time you spent individual time, with each of your children? Set out today to establish ways to spend time with each of your children simply to assure them that you choose them over yourself. By doing this, your child will come to believe that he is chosen by God.*

* See Examen *Give Materials to Build Temple* on page 451

PILLAR 4: DISCOVER THE DISCIPLE [EMBRACE THE CHILD]

BECOMING THE FACE OF THE FATHER

181. STOP, LOOK, AND LISTEN

Our lives are busy. Perhaps that is an understatement. Some say that B.U.S.Y. is an acronym that stands for "Burdened Under Satan's Yoke." As men we sense the daily pressure to perform, to be "on call," to come through, be the man, and continually be responsive. As men, we tend to compartmentalize and prioritize our life according to significance. In other words, those things that appear to be more significant, noteworthy, or deserving of recognition and honor, or that are more demanding, take priority; while often those elements of our lives that appear to be most consistent and stable are often overlooked.

This may be one of the reasons why a father is surprised when he realizes that his daughter is suffering from anorexia, or his son attempted to commit suicide; or his wife has "suddenly" decided to leave him. Satan buries a father under the burden of busyness for the purpose of blinding him to his true purpose, to what is most significant: his children, his wife, his vocation.

The first step is discovering significance in what is seemingly insignificant, the supernatural in the natural, the divine in our common humanity, is to simply stop the train of busyness. This is perhaps one of the most challenging things that a driven, hardworking, dutiful father can do.

Children, when they are young, literally chase their father down, longing for his attention. We sense their intense need for us, and yet we often neglect to stop, look, and listen.

We wonder why our teenage child no longer desires to spend time with us, let alone talk with us.

After you have stopped and broken away from your mental or physical busyness, look into your child's eyes often, peering *into* his or her soul. By stopping what you are doing and engaging your child face-to-face, you are transmitting your presence to your child, your attention, and the message that he or she is more important than the task at hand.

Realistically, this cannot happen all the time. But this ideal should be present in our minds, so that we strive to make every effort to do this as often as we can.

The second step is to listen. A father doesn't only hear—he actively listens. It is important to listen to what *isn't* being said as much as to what is being said. A daughter may say that things are going well, but if her father does not stop, look into her eyes, and listen for her heart, he may miss the hidden message: *Dad, I'm struggling at school. Dad I feel like a failure. Dad, I have no real friends. Dad, is there something wrong with me?*

The more we stop, look into our children's eyes, and actively listen, the more our children will entrust us with their hearts and eventually learn to trust God with their entire heart.

> **TAKE THE LEAD** When was the last time you spent individual time, with each of your children? Set out today to establish ways to spend time with each of your children simply to assure them that you choose them over yourself. By doing this, your child will come to believe that he is chosen by God.*

* See Examen *Give Materials to Build Temple* on page 451

WORKING TO RAISE A CHILD

182. TRAINING YOUR CHILD WITH SELF-GIVING LOVE

Recall that it is a father's mission to teach his child how to love, how to become a sincere gift to others. The primary method of teaching a child to love is to work side by side with the child, teaching the child to work within the context of the family, for the sake of the family.

The modern American family has been blessed with temporal riches, technological benefits, and comforts and luxuries unknown to previous generations. Often, because of these benefits, we forget the glory, and even the necessity, of work as a means of educating our children to grow in self-giving love.

Work has been redeemed and transformed into a way of making us holy by Christ, the carpenter (Mk 6:3), the son of the carpenter (Mt 13:55), who faithfully worked at Joseph's side, learning the value and meaning of work. This indicates that Christ's own participation in family work has given familial work the power to perfect us.

Familial work offers a way for our children to participate in family life by using their abilities, gifts, and talents, and by doing so, our children discover more of their particular identity.

As the Church proclaims, "[Man] cannot fully find himself except through a sincere gift of himself" (GS 24). Within the context of familial work, a child can discover how to work selflessly for the sake of others, rather than for selfish gain.

> **TAKE THE LEAD** We men have an endless list of projects that need completing. The temptation is to use our children as forced labor to lighten the load. The other temptation is to neglect to allow the child to participate in the project for fear that something will go wrong, or that the job could take twice as long. Look at your list of to-do's and determine which projects you and your child could work on together. Teaching your child how to work is not simply saying, "Go do this." Rather, when a child is granted entrance into his father's world, he is more apt to grant the Father entrance into his world.*

* See Examen *Give Materials to Build Temple* on page 451

WORKING TO RAISE A CHILD

183. WORKING WITH YOUR CHILD

One of the most important things a father can do is assist his children in cultivating their gifts for the sake of others. The primary context in which a father accomplishes this is familial work as an expression of love.

A child will likely follow the example of a father who sacrifices himself in little ways by working on the house, framing walls, landscaping, and even cleaning without receiving a wage—all for the sake of the family.

A father who serves his children will naturally teach his children to serve. When children learn this lesson of self-donation, the burdens of life are shared, love is exchanged, persons are given to one another, talents are discovered, and the child learns to give himself to those around him.

In case any clarification is needed, a father cannot be the only servant, but is obligated as leader of his family to teach his children how to participate in sharing the work. In a similar way, a child cannot be a slave, but should learn to work side by side with his father. It is vital that our children not only see us work, but work with us.

Sharing ideas, participating in small talk, discussing strategies to complete the project, all will eventually open a child to deeper dialogue that allows the father to share his faith by means of examples, stories, and personal witness. Training your child to participate in familial work is indispensable to raising saints, and demands patience in bearing with your child's inexperience. Yet, if such inexperience is endured patiently, a child will eventually learn to willingly offer himself for the purpose of assisting others.

> **TAKE THE LEAD** We men have an endless list of projects that need completing. The temptation is to use our children as forced labor to lighten the load. The other temptation is to neglect to allow the child to participate in the project for fear that something

will go wrong, or that the job could take twice as long. Look at your list of to-do's and determine which projects you and your child could work on together. Teaching your child how to work is not simply saying, "Go do this." Rather, when a child is granted entrance into his father's world, he is more apt to grant the Father entrance into his world.*

* See Examen *Give Materials to Build Temple* on page 451

WORKING TO RAISE A CHILD

184. CRAFTING THE CROSS OF SELF-GIVING LOVE

According to Pope St. John Paul II, "Work was the daily expression of love in the life of the Family of Nazareth." Joseph blessed Jesus with an environment for the perfect Son of God to perfect human nature through mutual self-giving—within Joseph the carpenter's workshop.

Joseph worked with Jesus and for Jesus, who worked with Joseph and for Joseph. By means of work, Joseph trained Jesus in the art of self-donation, and in doing so, Joseph was trained in that same art. Indeed, raising a child raises a man.

Working, sweating, conversing, sharing ideas and burdens, Joseph trained his son, by means of self-sacrificial love, for His project of building the temple of sacrifice in His person. Within the humble carpenter's workshop, Joseph and Jesus crafted the cross of self-giving love by means of sharing themselves in the work they shared.

You and I, as fathers, are to be like Joseph and work with Jesus—who lives in our own children—side by side, offering all our work to Jesus so that by means of our self-giving love, you and I will assist our children in becoming temples of the Holy Spirit.

> **TAKE THE LEAD** We men have an endless list of projects that need completing. The temptation is to use our children as forced labor to lighten the load. The other temptation is to neglect to allow the child to participate in the project for fear that something will go wrong, or that the job could take twice as long. Look at your list of to-do's and determine which projects you and your child could work on together. Teaching your child how to work is not simply saying, "Go do this." Rather, when a child is granted entrance into his father's world, he is more apt to grant the Father entrance into his world.*

* See Examen *Give Materials to Build Temple* on page 451

PILLAR 4: DISCOVER THE DISCIPLE [EMBRACE THE CHILD]

WORKING TO RAISE A CHILD

185. CRAFTING AND CONFLICT

As we work side by side with our children, there will be times when we attempt to craft the cross of self-giving love and the crafting ends in conflict.

When we attempt to be a gift to our children by means of work, we may experience tension and may become impatient, particularly with their lack of experience. Indeed, the very experience of this work, which was intended to unite us, can become an occasion for disagreements, frustrations, and arguments.

There will be times when working side by side actually drives a wedge between a father and his child.

We all fail. We all make mistakes. But it is essential that we persevere and try again. Sacred Tradition recounts that Jesus fell three times on His way to Calvary, and we can learn from this that we are also called to begin again, again, and again. The biggest man in your child's life is you. You will never appear bigger than when you ask your child for forgiveness when you do fail. On the other hand, a father will never appear smaller and weaker than when he buries the wrong he has committed and pretends that it never occurred.

Our children can cause us to become impatient. Impatience is a sure sign of a deep-seated pride. Why? Because when we become impatient we are essentially expressing the fact that we believe that everything should go our way, and now. Our children are God's means to perfect a man in patience.

While it is true that our children will learn much as they work alongside us, it is also true that we will learn much from them—particularly how to be patient and understanding of their limitations, and our own.

Jesus, while serving Joseph, learned from Joseph, and Joseph, while serving Jesus, learned much from Jesus. Our children, while we serve them, will teach us some of the most valuable lessons that there are to learn.

Resilience, perseverance, and patience are necessary characteristics of a father who desires to see his children become holy temples of the living God. We all fail and make mistakes, but the father who succeeds is the man who learns from his failures, and by God's grace, rises, and will eventually become a father worthy of following.

> **TAKE THE LEAD** We men have an endless list of projects that need completing. The temptation is to use our children as forced labor to lighten the load. The other temptation is to neglect to allow the child to participate in the project for fear that something will go wrong, or that the job could take twice as long. Look at your list of to-do's and determine which projects you and your child could work on together. Teaching your child how to work is not simply saying, "Go do this." Rather, when a child is granted entrance into his father's world, he is more apt to grant the Father entrance into his world.*

* See Examen *Give Materials to Build Temple* on page 451

THE FACE OF THE FATHER—PRAYING

186. THE BIGGEST MAN

As one evangelist asks: "Do you want to be the biggest influence in your child's life? You already are" (Jason Evert). You already are the biggest man in your child's life. The question is how do you, the biggest man, lead your child to the One who is bigger?

You and I, as fathers, should not be concerned that our children are not always listening, but instead be more concerned that they are always watching.

Karol Wojtyla recounted that after his mother and older brother died, he and his father slept in the same room. Often Karol would awake in the middle of the night to see his father kneeling on the floor praying, just as he did in church. Karol said, "We never spoke about a vocation to the priesthood, but his example was in a way my first seminary, a kind of domestic seminary." Karol eventually became Pope St. John Paul II.

When our children see that God is our top priority, they will be more likely to make God their top priority. It is essential that our children see us attending and participating in Holy Mass, receiving Holy Communion and the sacrament of confession. In order to see us do these things, we need to take our children with us while we do these things.

It is vital that our children see us leading prayer before meals, praying the Rosary (not just saying it), sharing Sacred Scripture with our family. Our example demonstrates that religion and rules are at the service of a relationship with Jesus.

A man recounted that as a child he opened the door to his parent's bedroom and saw the biggest man in his life—his father—kneeling before someone bigger—the Father. From that point on, the child wanted to know who this "bigger person" was.

Your example is far more powerful than lectures. As the saying goes, your life may be the only Bible your child will ever read.

TAKE THE LEAD By now, you are abiding by a daily prayer schedule and some form of daily prayer routine. Identify one devotion, whether it is attending daily Mass, going to monthly confession, praying the Rosary, praying from Scripture, and invite your family into that devotion. Invite your children to know the God you are encountering in your own prayer life. As Fr. Peyton said, "The family that prays together, stays together."*

* See Examen *Give Materials to Build Temple* on page 451

PILLAR 4: DISCOVER THE DISCIPLE [EMBRACE THE CHILD]

THE FACE OF THE FATHER—PLAYING

187. ONE OF THE MOST DIFFICULT THINGS TO DO

You not only become the face of the Father and provide the "materials" necessary for your child to become a temple of God by working and praying, but also by playing.

Though we are to become true men, and to become a true man is to master the boy within, such mastery does not mean killing the child within. The child within imagines, has dreams, and even at a subconscious level still desires to play. This desire explains why so many men who are beyond their "glory days" watch televised sports. The child who wants to play never really dies—he simply believes the lie that playing is not mature, or that he doesn't have the time to play, and would be irresponsible.

Jesus said that to enter the kingdom of God we must become like little children. He could have said, "For a father to inherit the kingdom of God he must become like a child by playing with his child." However, the actual intention of Jesus' words is that to be a child is to repent of our self-sufficiency, our determination to find security in things like money, prestige, popularity, and human respect, and rather turn to God and find our security in Him alone. And this is one of the reasons God gave fathers children.

Children, and their desire to play with us, cause us to refrain from the many responsibilities that mentally drain us. By playing with our children, we break away from those false idols that we subconsciously believe will grant us security, and momentarily turn our gaze toward what matters most.

But for many men, playing with our children can be far more difficult than working and praying with them. Yet, we become the face of the Father, in a very intimate way, by playing with our children.

Playing can consist of focused relaxation, athletic activities, horsing around, wrestling, games, or outdoor adventures such as hiking, camping, hunting or fishing. It can consist of other forms of entertainment or conversation. Hunting trips, daughter dates, going to an art exhibit, a symphony, or a professional sports game are all forms of "playing" that simply involve a father being involved with, and present to, his child in a fun, relaxed setting.

Regardless, it is vital that you and I stop, listen, and look into the eyes of our children, and actually see a child that longs to be loved, known, and worthy of our time.

> **TAKE THE LEAD** Take a moment and reflect on the greatest moment of your childhood. For most of us, those precious moments involved some form of playing, adventure, fun; and often there was an adult fostering the event. Identify ways that you can make your relationship with your child memorable. It could be as simple as taking them on a picnic by the river or taking the family to an amusement park. For many, the memory revolves around food and fun. But those memories will not simply happen. You have to make those happenings memorable.*

* See Examen *Give Materials to Build Temple* on page 451

PILLAR 4: DISCOVER THE DISCIPLE [EMBRACE THE CHILD]

BECOMING THE TOUCH OF THE FATHER

188. BLESSING YOUR CHILD TO BECOME A CHILD OF GOD

Often the world's strife, rebellion, and pride streams from ruptured relationships between fathers and their children. Division between a child and his father can often instill resentment and deep-seated anger in a child, causing a child to deny the blessing that he inherits from his father and to become preoccupied with making a name for himself—that is, building himself into a god.

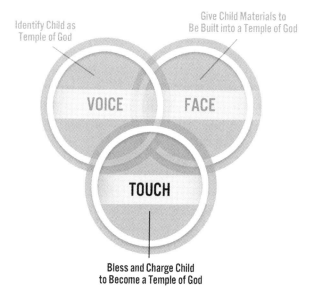

This dynamic has been prevalent since the beginning of human history. Recall the motive of the people who built the Tower of Babel: "Come, let us build ourselves a city, and a tower with its top in the heavens, and let us make a name for ourselves, lest we be scattered abroad upon the face of the whole earth" (Gen 11:4).

The plan on the surface sounds innocent enough; they wanted a strong, fortified city, with an awe-inspiring view. We, however, know the rest of the story: "[T]he Lord scattered them abroad from there over the face of all the earth, and they discontinued building the city. Therefore, its name was called Babel, because the Lord confused the language of all the earth" (Gen 11:8–9).

To understand why God scattered the people of Shinar we need to understand the backstory.

Noah had three sons, Ham, Shem, and Japheth. Ham was the son who found Noah, his father, drunk and naked in his tent, and exposed his father's shame to his brothers. Shem and Japheth obtained a cover, walked backward into the tent, and laid the cover over their father's nakedness. Noah, upon awakening, discovered "what Ham had done unto him," and consequently cursed Ham's son Canaan and his bloodline. In the same breath, Shem, whose name means "name" or "fame," received Noah's fatherly blessing.

The ruler of the kingdom of Babel was Ham's great-grandson, Nimrod, who inherited Noah's curse. Nimrod and the descendants of Canaan attempted to build a "Shem"—a name—for themselves in order to prove that they could build a kingdom that would rival Shem's—a kingdom that would reach heaven without heaven's God, that would reach the Fatherland without the Father's blessing.

The lesson is that children who do not receive a blessing from their fathers in some form can become resentful and rebellious and attempt to build a temple of self-absorption—self-worship—rather than allowing themselves to be formed into a temple of God.

This type of building project ends in tragedy. Just as strife and discord between Noah the father and Ham the son led to the eventual demise of Babel, so also such tension between fathers and their children can cause confusion, disharmony, and resentment in their relationships—and consequently cause a child to resent God the Father.

> **TAKE THE LEAD** Make it a priority to bless your child each day. Determine a time, a rough outline of the prayer, and be committed to doing it daily. Initially, you may feel awkward granting your child a blessing. But over time, the fruits of this divine gift of God's grace and favor to your child will be evident (see reflection 192 to learn how to bless your child).*

---

* See Examen *Charge the Child to Build Temple (Blessing)* on page 452

PILLAR 4: DISCOVER THE DISCIPLE [EMBRACE THE CHILD]

BECOMING THE TOUCH OF THE FATHER

189. GIVING YOUR CHILD THE ABILITY TO THRIVE

Do you want your child to merely survive, or thrive? Can you ensure that your child will thrive?

Noah's curse upon Ham dramatically impacted his life and the life of his descendants. From that point on Ham was simply trying to survive. This survival was expressed in the form of selfishness, and this selfish disposition was transmitted to his son, grandson, and great-grandson.

The third way that we discover the disciple, and spiritually adopt our children is by blessing the child and charging him to be built into a temple of God. By means of hugs, kisses, pats on the back, and perhaps most important, the daily blessing, the human father becomes the touch of the Father that his children cannot feel.

One of the most important ways in which a father communicates the Father's love is by touching his child. So often, particularly in our American culture, men are somewhat apprehensive, if not fearful, of touching their child. If our children do not physically experience their father's love, they will attempt to obtain that physical touch in disordered ways.

It is a fact that some of the most confident, secure, and stable young adults have received physical affection and affirmation from their fathers throughout their lives. This fatherly affirmation grants the child a subconscious belief that he or she is worthy of love and is capable of loving; and has a dignity that should be upheld, and not sold or squandered.

Do you want your child not only to survive, but to thrive? To have confidence that is rooted in knowing that he or she is loved? Be the touch of the Father that your child longs to feel.

> **TAKE THE LEAD** Make it a priority to bless your child each day. Determine a time, a rough outline of the prayer, and be committed to doing it daily. Initially, you may feel awkward granting your child a blessing. But over time, the fruits of this divine gift of God's grace and favor to your child will be evident (see reflection 192 to learn how to bless your child).*

---

* See Examen *Charge the Child to Build Temple (Blessing)* on page 452

BECOMING THE TOUCH OF THE FATHER

190. HAVING FAITH IN THE POWER OF THE BLESSING

"Without faith it is impossible to please God" (Heb 11:4). Faith in God opens our souls to His blessing and favor. Have you considered that not only your future and your salvation are dependent upon your faith, but also your children's future, hope, salvation, and relationship with God could be, to a significant level, dependent (at least initially) on your faith? A father who is trustworthy must first become a son who trusts God the Father; and a trusting son of the Father becomes a father who raises trusting sons.

One of the most important expressions of trust in the Father and of the Father's love is the fatherly blessing. It is one of the greatest powers in that it can assist a child in his efforts to become giving and loving.

You, as a father, have been granted that authority to transmit God the Father's blessing. To be clear, God is the source of every blessing—not man. Yet, each father should trust that he has a vital role as transmitter of grace. This demands that even though we are fathers, we become trusting sons of the Father by believing in and transmitting this blessing.

Often fathers neglect to bless their children, or worse, do not believe that they have been divinely ordained with the power to do so. From Abraham to Isaac, Isaac to Jacob, Jacob to Joseph—and down to St. Joseph son of Jacob, who transmitted the divine blessing to Jesus—God the Father has given the human father the power to transmit His blessing to his children.

Recall that as a father you are to communicate the Father's love by means of looking, listening, and touching. When you bless your child, you communicate God the Father's love by looking at your child with the Father's love, speaking the Father's favor with His voice, and touching your child with the heavenly Father's blessing. In a single moment you become the voice, the face, and the touch of the heavenly Father.

PILLAR 4: DISCOVER THE DISCIPLE [EMBRACE THE CHILD]

TAKE THE LEAD Make it a priority to bless your child each day. Determine a time, a rough outline of the prayer, and be committed to doing it daily. Initially, you may feel awkward granting your child a blessing. But over time, the fruits of this divine gift of God's grace and favor to your child will be evident (see reflection 192 to learn how to bless your child).*

* See Examen *Charge the Child to Build Temple (Blessing)* on page 452

LEAD | THE FOUR MARKS OF FATHERLY GREATNESS

BECOMING THE TOUCH OF THE FATHER

191. ARE YOU WORTHY ENOUGH TO BLESS YOUR CHILD?

According to Jewish tradition, on the eve preceding the Sabbath, the father of a Jewish family summons his children and invokes upon them, in the name of the Lord, a special blessing.

Joseph, being a "just man" who fulfilled the law and followed his ancestral customs, certainly participated in this tradition by summoning Jesus to himself, placing his hands on the head of his beloved Son, and invoking God's blessing upon Him.

As Jesus allowed Himself to be baptized by John the Baptist, so also Christ allowed Himself to be blessed by Joseph to indicate that every father should bless his child. By blessing your child, you become a vital link between your child and the heavenly Father.

Joseph's example is fitting testimony to fathers who sense their own unworthiness to confer the divine blessing upon their children. Regardless of how great your child is, or how unworthy you as a father are, you are ordained by God to bestow the fatherly blessing.

If it was fitting for God the Son to be blessed by a human father, how much more fitting is it that we human fathers are to bless our children?

Remember: God does not call the qualified, but qualifies the called. You are called to be a father on earth, like the Father in Heaven—and one of the most powerful ways to do this is by blessing your child regularly.

> **TAKE THE LEAD** Make it a priority to bless your child each day. Determine a time, a rough outline of the prayer, and be committed to doing it daily. Initially, you may feel awkward granting your child a blessing. But over time, the fruits of this divine gift of God's grace and favor to your child will be evident (see reflection 192 to learn how to bless your child).*

* See Examen *Charge the Child to Build Temple (Blessing)* on page 452

BECOMING THE TOUCH OF THE FATHER

192. HOW TO BLESS YOUR CHILD

For many of us praying is challenging—but to pray in front of our children and bless our children can be daunting, awkward, and intimidating.

The fact that we sense the tremendous challenge indicates how vital the act of blessing your child is. The devil will assail you and convince you that you, a sinner, are a hypocrite in your desire to bless your child.

Keep in mind that this act of blessing your child is of divine importance. God desires and wills it, and the devil hates it. It is our duty to claim our children for Christ, for if we don't claim them, the devil will.

So, how does a father bless his child?

A father blesses his child by summoning the child to himself, placing his hands upon his child's head, tracing the sign of the cross upon the child's forehead, and calling upon God to bless the child.

We don't need to complicate the matter by making the blessing an intricate, time-consuming, formulaic ritual. The act of blessing is quite simple and yet has profound effects. First, choose a time to bless your children—perhaps before bedtime, or before their school day. Regardless, it is important to schedule a time of day in which you bless your children and to be committed to granting the blessing every day.

Second, keep the prayer simple. The main elements for the invocation are: First, bless the child in the name of the Father, the Son, and the Holy Spirit. Second, ask God to bless your child with His peace, mercy, and favor, that he may become a temple of God's glory. Perhaps you can memorize a biblical blessing, such as "The Lord make His face to shine upon you, be gracious to you: The Lord lift up his countenance upon you and give you peace" (Num 6:24–26).

Third, be consistent and have faith that God the Father will bestow tremendous blessings upon your child through you, His transmitter of fatherly love.

Though you may not be able to quantitatively assess the effects that your blessing has on your child, nevertheless you should not doubt that it has supernatural power and can have a profound, lasting, positive impact on your child.

> **TAKE THE LEAD** Make it a priority to bless your child each day. Determine a time, a rough outline of the prayer, and be committed to doing it daily. Initially, you may feel awkward granting your child a blessing. But over time, the fruits of this divine gift of God's grace and favor to your child will be evident (see reflection 192 to learn how to bless your child).*

* See Examen *Charge the Child to Build Temple (Blessing)* on page 452

RECONCILING WITH YOUR CHILD

193. THE PRODIGAL FATHER

In our Lord's Parable of the Prodigal Son, the younger son demands that his father give him the inheritance that is to come to him. This son failed to appreciate his father's protection and provision, and therefore turned to the world and the flesh, to such an intense degree that he rebelled.

In fact, to demand that his share of the inheritance came to him indicates that the son desired his father's death. In other words, the son's love for his father had died.

Upon receipt of his inheritance, the son trekked to a foreign land, where he squandered his father's provisions on loose living. Living in a foreign land is indicative of the son being in exile, in slavery, away from his true land of freedom—the Father's land. Indeed, the son was enslaved by his own passions, which drove him from his father.

After a severe famine swept the land, the son acquired a job feeding swine—a grave insult to a Jew, to whom Mosaic Law dictated that hoofed animals were unclean. As he worked, the son realized his sinfulness, that he'd lost sight of the ultimate ideal—his father's house, a symbol of the heavenly Father's house. He mustered the courage to return home.

Day and night the father gazed intently upon the horizon, aching for his son's return. Then, one day, the father saw a frail, weary soul who resembled his son. Without hesitation, he dashed in frantic hope to his son, and upon meeting him kissed him, fell on his neck, weeping with joy.

To comprehend the radical nature of the father's actions we must consider that a grown Middle Eastern man in that time period and culture would avoid running so as not to appear immature and foolish. Yet this father breaks all cultural norms with great abandon, hurrying to embrace his rebellious son.

The father in the parable symbolizes God our Father, Who relentlessly pursues us, desiring us to come home to Him. And yet, the father also symbolizes you and me, the human father who constantly looks for opportunities to love his children, to share with them the radical, self-giving, relentless love of the Father.

Often, we fathers envision our children as the culprit, the one at fault, who has rebelled against our authority; and yet, we neglect to see that we may be the one who has faulted by not desiring our children. A child's rebellion is often the result of a child not believing that he or she is desired and chosen. Let us pray for the desire to desire our children, and run out to embrace them, convincing them that they are chosen, desired, and delighted in.

> **TAKE THE LEAD** There are children who are no longer living at home. Other children are living at home but have little connection with their father. And still others have given up altogether on having a relationship with their dad. Regardless of your situation, to be like God the Father is to do everything in your power to reconcile with your child. This may mean that you have to seek out your child, apologize for being a neglectful father, or simply send a text saying, "I'm proud of you." It is never too late to reconcile with your child. You know what you need to do. Don't delay. Run out to embrace your child.*

* See Examen *Charge the Child to Build Temple (Blessing)* on page 452

PILLAR 4: DISCOVER THE DISCIPLE [EMBRACE THE CHILD]

RECONCILING WITH YOUR CHILD

194. SAVING A CHILD, SAVES A FATHER

When our Lord Jesus was twelve years of age, Mary and Joseph, according to tradition, trekked with the boy to Jerusalem for the purpose of celebrating the annual feast of the Passover (see Lk 2:42). This, the first of Jesus' journeys to Jerusalem, marked the official inauguration of His masculine adulthood.

After fulfilling the demands of the Law and completing their act of worship, the couple began journeying home to Nazareth. But Jesus had remained behind, though Mary and Joseph were unaware of his absence.

As discussed previously, Joseph lost sight of Jesus and from the moment he realized it, Joseph was focused on only one hope, one desire—to find Jesus, to reunite with his Son.

In his anxious search and longing for Jesus, Joseph realized that Jesus did not need Joseph to save Him as much as Joseph needed Jesus to save him.

You and I, at the core of our souls, have this inherent, God-given desire and need to be united with our children. You need your child because Christ is in your child, and you need Christ. By working to save your child for Christ, Christ in your child will help to save you.

> **TAKE THE LEAD** There are children who are no longer living at home. Other children are living at home but have little connection with their father. And still others have given up altogether on having a relationship with their dad. Regardless of your situation, to be like God the Father is to do everything in your power to reconcile with your child. This may mean that you have to seek out your child, apologize for being a neglectful father, or simply send a text saying, "I'm proud of you." It is never too late to reconcile with your child. You know what you need to do. Don't delay. Run out to embrace your child.*

* See Examen *Charge the Child to Build Temple (Blessing)* on page 452

CONCLUSION: A NEW BEGINNING

You have received the call to be a true man. Authentic manhood finds its fulfillment in fatherhood, the pinnacle of true masculinity—to beget spiritual life to another.

By now, you have become aware of your divine purpose: To be a father on earth like the Father in heaven; to be a link between heaven and earth, between God and your child; to be the face, the voice, the touch of the heavenly Father.

You have been given the plan: Assume your location and fulfill your vocation. Your location in God's plan is the role of *Custos,* guardian, protector of woman and the child. Your vocation is to L|E|A|D: *L*isten to discover your identity and mission (embrace silence); *E*mbrace your essence (embrace woman); *A*ssume your authority (embrace your charitable authority); and *D*iscover the disciple (embrace the child).

Now it is up to you to participate in the plan which is comprised of these four pillars of St. Joseph's spirituality. The more you intentionally participate, the more your passion for God, heaven, your wife, and your children will increase. This passion is magnetic and cannot help but be transmitted to your own family, but also to people throughout the generations.

Recall that God through the prophet Malachi disclosed His heart's intention and the divine strategy for saving the world: fathers turn your hearts toward your children and your children will turn their hearts not only to you, but ultimately to God the Father. This is God's plan; this is your plan.

During the last apparition at Fatima, God reiterated his plan to save the world through fatherhood. As the sun appeared to descend and destroy the earth, the three young visionaries witnessed St. Joseph and the Child Jesus simultaneously blessing the world. It was during this blessing that the sun returned to its original location in the sky and disaster was averted.

Our Lady's message at Fatima was, "In the end my Immaculate Heart will triumph." How will her heart triumph? When we fathers turn our gaze upon St. Joseph and his fatherly relationship to Jesus and learn from his timeless wisdom and ageless example how to be fathers of glory who raise other Christs.

By turning our gaze and attention on Joseph's example, we will again be inspired to turn our gaze upon our children; and our children, by receiving our gaze, will trust that they have the gaze of our Father and will surrender their hearts trustingly to Him.

St. Isidore of St. Joseph prophesied, "The victory bell will sound in the Church when the faithful recognize the sanctity of St. Joseph." How will the faithful recognize the sanctity of St. Joseph? When they witness you and me embodying St. Joseph's spirituality. Then will the victory bell ring among the faithful.

Let us "Go to Joseph" (Gen 41:55) and return to our post—to our location as *Custos,* and live our vocation as fathers who embark upon the path to greatness by doing what Joseph did.

Society goes by way of the family, and the family goes by way of the father. Go home and be Joseph—a father on earth like the Father in heaven.

A FATHER'S EXAMEN

> Without analyzing whether he has fulfilled or neglected his vocational responsibilities, the father becomes a bystander who idly watches his life pass, a man who has lost, or never has discovered, a "vision for charity."

LEAD
THE FOUR MARKS OF FATHERLY GREATNESS

THE REASON FOR THIS EXAMEN

It is not uncommon for a person who is desirous of maintaining physical health to undergo annual clinical examinations to determine his or her well-being. Consider also that those who visit a dentist regularly maintain dental health, while those who neglect such evaluations tend to compromise the good of the gums and teeth. A vehicle owner routinely has his automobile inspected in order to identify potential maintenance needs rather than waiting to act when problems arise. Corporate analysts and leadership teams convene quarterly, if not more frequently, to determine factors that will contribute to their company's financial growth. In each of these cases, analyzing and evaluating past and current behaviors, while identifying obstacles, encumbrances, needed changes, and solutions that have the potential to encourage future growth, are essential to maintaining stability and achieving success.

So also is the human father's growth in holiness dependent upon proper evaluation of his actions, his words, his commissions and omissions, all of which constitute the full expression of his lived or unlived vocation of fatherhood. Without analyzing whether he has fulfilled or neglected his vocational responsibilities, the father—having no moral compass or manner in which to gauge or measure his actions—becomes a wayfarer who aimlessly wanders through his fatherhood, a bystander who idly watches his life pass, a man who has lost, or never has discovered, a "vision for charity." Such a father becomes the blind leader of blind followers who simply accept the monotony and banality of a life overshadowed by spiritual darkness. The father who measures himself against a rule, however, more easily determines the factors that extinguish or enflame within him the vibrancy of the Spirit of the Father.

The father's examen is not intended to be an exhaustive list of rules, laws, and commandments particular to the vocation of fatherhood, but rather an outline that highlights a father's most fundamental and essential responsibilities to God, his marriage, and his family. This examen is founded upon the four pillars of St. Joseph's fatherhood, and begins by evaluating the interior motivations that lead to exterior behaviors. By examining his vocation is this manner, the human father is better equipped not only to comprehend the profound connection between the interior and exterior life, but also to identify solutions that, if acted upon, will shape his own life as well as the lives of the members of his family.

LISTEN TO DISCERN YOUR MISSION

EXAMEN FOR REFLECTIONS 26–43
SILENCE WITHIN HIMSELF
The interior life gives form to the exterior life.

- Do I purposefully place myself in a position to receive divine direction by setting aside time and space in which I am more capable of conversing with God?
- How many times a day do I present myself in silence and stillness before God?
- To what voices do I consistently listen? When alone, do I avoid entering silence by means of listening to music; watching television or movies; using the radio, computer, or cell phone? Can I shut these devices off and enter into silence?
- Do I heed and follow the so-called gospel of the world more than I read and follow the Gospel of Christ? To which voices do I listen more? In which voices do I place my trust?
- Do I trust and have faith that when I set aside specific times to listen to God, God will infuse His divine presence and life into me?
- Have I set aside a "tent of meeting," that is, a specific place or places dedicated to prayer alone?
- Do I begin prayer by speaking to God briefly, and afterward listen to Him? Or do I fill my prayer time with vocal prayer?

EXAMEN FOR REFLECTIONS 44–47
SILENCE BEFORE MEN
Strive to be known by God rather than noticed by men.

- Do I trust that God the Father loves me, desires me, has chosen me, and has destined me for some specific purpose that will bring Him glory? Do I believe that I am a son of the Father, and that the Father has a specific mission for me?
- Do I seek disordered affirmation, accolades, lauds, honors, and attention from human beings?

- Do I have a prevalence to talk about myself or center my conversations with others on myself? When another is speaking, do I listen attentively, desiring to enter into his life, or do I use his words as a means to discuss myself?
- Do I seek to be noticed in public only to neglect my family and the attention they need? Do I tend to assist in building the Church at the expense of building my domestic church?
- Do I ask God for the desire to be little, silent, and hidden? Do I desire to desire this desire?
- When discerning the possibility of serving the Church or working in the public sphere, do I ask God to help me discern my motives? Do I truly examine whether I am attempting to glorify myself or authentically desiring to glorify God?
- Do any of my endeavors, initiatives, or activities conflict with my primary vocation of building the domestic church and raising my family to be holy and living saints?

EXAMEN FOR REFLECTIONS 48–51
SILENCE BEFORE GOD

The human father is an icon of the heavenly Father Who is in secret.

- Do I understand that one of the heavenly Father's divine attributes is hiddenness (see Matthew 6), and do I imitate this divine characteristic of hiddenness?
- Do I boast of my work, offerings, penances, successes, self-offerings, and talents?
- Do I complain about my vocation, work, offerings, penances, failures, self-offerings, and apparent shortcomings and limitations?
- Do I specifically offer my sacrifices secretly to the Father by means of the secret father, St. Joseph, in union with the most august Queen, Mary, and ultimately through, with, and in Christ Himself? Have I missed opportunities to do so?
- Do I trust that God has requested of me certain works? Do I believe that these duties are too insignificant for me, or too great for me, are beyond me?
- Do I believe that God is requiring me to collaborate with Him, that He will aid me in this collaboration of fulfilling works of secret sacrifice?
- Do I believe that Jesus Christ will transform my secret works, my water, into grace, into wine?

EMBRACE YOUR ESSENCE

EXAMEN FOR REFLECTIONS 52–65
EMBRACE WOMAN
EMBRACE THE DIGNITY AND GENIUS OF ALL WOMEN
See the woman as a symbol of the Church and uphold her dignity.

- Do I understand and believe that my essence as a man is to set the pace of self-giving love, in imitation of Christ the Bridegroom, Who sacrificed Himself for the Church?
- Do I strive to uphold the beauty of all women by refraining to reduce them to objects for my own gratification?
- When I encounter an attractive woman, how do I respond? Do I imagine her fulfilling my disordered desires, or ask God to bless her and save her from the lusts of men?
- Do I speak of women and their physical attributes in demeaning ways?
- Do I strive to see the mystery of a woman's person being expressed by means of her body? When looking at a woman, where do my eyes initially rest? Do I look into her eyes with the purpose of seeing her person? Or do I simply see a body attached to a person?
- Do I shun pornography in all its forms? Do I avoid videos, movies, and printed material that do not uphold the God-given dignity and beauty of woman?
- When tempted to objectify a woman and reduce her to fulfilling my lusts, do I call on Christ to provide the redemptive grace necessary to liberate me from lust and grant me the freedom to love as Christ loves His bride?

EXAMEN FOR REFLECTIONS 66–106
EMBRACE MY WIFE
Husbands, love your wives as Christ loves the Church.

- Do I honor my wife as an image and symbol of Christ's Church, encouraging and edifying her, or do I tear her down, discouraging, degrading, and demeaning her? Do I compliment or demean my wife in my children's presence?
- Do I become resentful, defensive, or bitter when my wife gives advice, expresses disappointment in me, or requests me to provide some act of service? Am I attentive to her concerns as though they are my own?
- In order to unite myself to my wife fully, do I strive to sacrifice my ego, pride, selfish ambitions, and lusts with the purpose of helping to save her soul?

- Do I neglect to have intercourse with my wife because I believe her not to be as attractive as I desire her to be? Do I use my wife as though she is another woman?
- Am I involved in a physical or emotional affair? Am I addicted to lust and pornography?
- Do I use contraceptives in order to objectify my wife and indulge my lusts or do I sacrifice my disordered sexual desires in order to protect her from the shame of lust?
- Do I become resentful, grumble, or complain when my wife does not engage in intercourse? Do I ask Christ for His redemptive grace to offer myself in sacrifice on her behalf as Christ offers Himself for His Bride, the Church?

EXAMEN FOR REFLECTIONS 107–109
EMBRACE THE WOMAN, MARY
The Woman crushes the serpent, enabling every father to become a true man.

- Do I have an aversion to Marian devotion?
- Do I believe that Mary is an obstacle or encumbrance to my relationship with Christ? Or do I believe that Mary is necessary for my salvation?
- Do I ask Mary to be my Mother as she is the Mother of Christ?
- Do I actually refer to Mary affectionately as my Mother?
- Do I invoke Mary daily, asking her for guidance? Do I converse with Mary as a child talks to his mother? Do I have daily devotions to Mary, the Mother of God?
- Have I consecrated my life, my soul, my family, my vocation as a father to Mary and Joseph in order to be fully possessed by Jesus Christ?
- Do I believe that submitting to Mary is a sign of weakness or makes me less of a man, or do I believe that she obtains the strength needed for me to become a true man in the image of the True Man, Jesus Christ?

ASSUME YOUR AUTHORITY

EXAMEN FOR REFLECTIONS 110–123
EMBRACE CHARITABLE AUTHORITY
LEAD BY LOVING. LOVE BY LEADING
Understanding, believing in, and exercising charitable authority in order to protect, provide for, and teach my family.

- Do I understand, believe in, and exercise my charitable authority in order to protect, provide for, and teach my family? Do I lead with love, and love by leading?
- Do I initiate a spirit of joy in my home?
- Do I initiate a spirit of self-sacrifice in my home?

EXAMEN FOR REFLECTIONS 124–142
THE AUTHORITY TO PROTECT
The human father protects his child from the perversion of sexuality, peer pressure, the pursuit of prestige, pervasive media, pursuit of pleasure, and poor parenting.

- Do I explain to my child why God created sexual complementarity and the one-flesh union? Do I uphold the dignity, honor, and beauty of human sexuality? Do I protect my children from the satanic distortion of the true meaning of sexual intercourse? These questions beg another question: Do I understand God's meaning and intention for sexual union? Have I learned these truths and can I explain them to my children?
- Do I protect my children from slavishly looking to their peers for value by valuing my children at home? Do I explain that peers do not determine our value, but that only God determines our value?
- Do I protect my children by avoiding all tendencies to live vicariously through their lives?
- Do I protect my children from being enslaved to activities? Are activities at the service of my family or is my family sacrificed for the sake of activities? Do I need to sacrifice some activities for the sake of my family?
- Do I protect my children from the desire to be noticed by men rather than being known by God?

- Do I protect my children from the pervasive media as encountered through television, computers, social media, and mobile device technology? Have I established balanced and proper boundaries that establish moral standards for content, time allocated, and valid use of these resources? Do I and my family master our media resources, or do these resources master us?

- Do I teach my child how to discover the fundamental, authentic good in everything, while also teaching my child how to identify demonic counterfeits?

EXAMEN FOR REFLECTIONS 143–154
THE AUTHORITY TO PROVIDE

The human father's occupation is at the service of his vocation. Material goods are at the service of leading our children to the ultimate Good.

- Do I place my occupation at the service of my vocation? Is my identity founded on those for whom I am living rather than on what I do for a living?

- Do I use my goods as a means to provide a path for my family to the ultimate good—God? Do I provide for my child's spirit by using the goods of the flesh or rather do I provide for the flesh at the expense of my child's spirit?

- Do I make the family home a refuge, not only from the elements, but also from the evil one? In other words, have I built my home to be a domestic church, a place that fosters the fulfillment of the project of the child being built into a temple—a house of God?

- Is my home adorned, in prominent places, with images of Our Lord, His Mother, and the saints?

- Am I committed to dining consistently together as a family? Do I lead thanksgiving prayer to the Almighty Father before and after each meal? Do I foster and generate enriching, encouraging, and edifying conversation during family meals?

- Have I made material goods and carnal ideals idols? Have I allowed my fleshly appetites for food, money, and material goods drive my decisions and thus affect my fatherly leadership?

- Do I provide clothing to ensure that my child is protected from physical exposure, and more importantly to enable my child to comprehend God the Father's desire to protect my child from the shame of lust? Do I encourage my child to dress modestly, or encourage the child to submit to fads, trends, and clothing that draws inordinate attention to him or her?

EXAMEN FOR REFLECTIONS 155–158
THE AUTHORITY TO TEACH

The human father teaches by example and words. His word must be informed by God's Word.

- Do I teach my children—by means of my example and word—the law of God and the precepts of the Church, particularly the two greatest commandments: "To love the Lord your God with all of your heart, soul, strength, and mind . . . and to love your neighbor as yourself"?
- Are my words informed by the Father's Word? Does my life reflect the life and love of the Word? In other words, do I know God and His Word, and is His example and teaching reflected in my actions?
- Have I embraced my role as the priest of my domestic church, offering the silent sacrifice of self on behalf of my family?
- Do I offer my acts of service without complaining, grumbling, becoming bitter or resentful, or boasting about them?
- Do I teach by means of my word? Do I use analogies, examples from life, stories, and words of encouragement in order to teach my child life's most important lessons? Do I seriously engage my children's frustrations, dilemmas, and questions? If I don't know the answer, do I search for the answer in order to communicate the truth to my child? Or do I ignore my child's plight, believing that he or she will "get over it"?
- Do I share Christ's Gospel with my family at least once a week? Do I trust the Holy Spirit will grant insights that will encourage my family's love for God?
- Do I pray with my family each day? Is family prayer time a priority or an afterthought? Do I frequent the sacraments, especially the sacrament of reconciliation, with my children?

DISCOVER THE DISCIPLE

EXAMEN FOR REFLECTIONS 159–178
IDENTIFY THE CHILD AS A TEMPLE OF GOD
The human father is the voice of the Father that our children cannot hear.

- Do I believe that my child is a living, breathing temple of God?
- Do I believe that by receiving a child in Christ's name I am receiving Christ in my child?
- Am I deliberate in identifying my child's gifts and talents? Do I encourage my child and congratulate my child for using these gifts?
- Do I nag, condemn, demean, belittle, or criticize my child, or do I comment, correct, guide, and discipline in an affirming, encouraging manner? Do I overcorrect and attempt to control my child, or do I neglect to correct my child?
- When I discipline my child, do I focus excessively on the evil that the child has committed? Or do I strive to explain, from a divine perspective, why certain actions are good or evil?
- Do I audibly express to my child that God lives within him or her? Do I specifically convey to my child the fact that the Holy Spirit lives within him or her?
- Do I express to my child his or her potential for greatness, that he or she is called to be a manifestation of God's glory?

EXAMEN FOR REFLECTIONS 179–187
GIVING THE CHILD THE MATERIALS TO BECOME THE TEMPLE OF GOD
The human father is the face of the Father that our children cannot see.

- Do I meditate upon the reality that my presence transmits God the Father's presence to my child? Do I understand that my spiritual, moral, physical, and emotional absence can be misinterpreted by my child as God the Father not loving my child?
- Do I teach my child to become an authentic and sincere gift of self for the sake of others and ultimately for God's sake? Do I encourage the cultivation of my child's gifts and talents with the purpose of serving others and ultimately God?
- Do I involve my children in familial work as an expression of love? Do I work side by side with my children to teach them the importance of serving without selfish gain?
- Do I spend weekly or biweekly, individual time with each of my children? Do I take my daughter on dates and spend quality time with my son?

- Do I stop what I am involved in, avoid being preoccupied, and look into my child's eyes when he or she is speaking to me?
- Do I become impatient and perturbed by the incessant conversations of my children, or do I persevere in engaging them by engaging myself in the conversation?
- Do my children trust me with their thoughts? If so, this is a certain sign that I have been spending quality time with them.

EXAMEN FOR REFLECTIONS 188–194
CHARGING THE CHILD WITH AND
BLESSING THE CHILD FOR THE BUILDING OF THE TEMPLE
The human father is the touch of the Father that our children cannot feel.

- Do I hug or kiss my child daily?
- Do I give my child natural, consistent, physical signs of affirmation?
- Do I meditate upon the reality that my physical affection, or lack thereof, can be interpreted by my child as an expression of God the Father's love or lack thereof for my child?
- Do I bless my child daily?
- Have I developed a blessing based on the three invocations: first, asking for God's presence to dwell in the child more fully that he/she may become a temple of the living God; Second, asking for God's mercy to rest upon the child, forgiving the child his or her sins; third, asking God to grant my child the peace that is derived from doing His will in order that the child may enjoy eternal communion with God forever?
- Have I designated a specific time each day to bless my children? Have I remained steadfast in fulfilling this commitment?
- When I bless my child, do I trace the sign of the cross on my child's forehead, invoking the Father and the Son and the Holy Spirit?

L|E|A|D
THE FOUR MARKS OF FATHERLY GREATNESS

THE FATHER'S WAY.

Often after we encounter a taste of something that begins to change our lives we want more. That's why we designed **L|E|A|D: The Four Marks of Fatherly Greatness**. More than a one-and-done program, L|E|A|D is a father's way of life. By means of videos, books, podcasts and more, L|E|A|D is designed to offer continual, life-changing, content for you, your fellow brothers, and your parish.

Continue your journey to become the husband, father, and leader God has called and destined you to be.

BEGIN YOUR LIFE-CHANGING JOURNEY NOW

CHOOSE YOUR PATH.

INDIVIDUAL TRACK

From manhood to fatherhood, A-Z, move at your own pace to become the leader that God has called and destined you to be.

MEN'S GROUP TRACK

The pinnacle of authentic manhood is spiritual fatherhood. Journey with your band of brothers toward fatherly greatness with L|E|A|D'S ongoing, transformational experience.

FATHERSOFSTJOSEPH.ORG/LEAD